Interpretation

Writer

Reader

Audience

Wilma H. Grimes

The University of Washington

Alethea Smith Mattingly

The University of Arizona

INTERPRETATION

Writer

Reader

Audience

Wadsworth Publishing Company, Inc.
San Francisco

Interpretation: Writer-Reader-Audience
Wilma H. Grimes and Alethea Smith Mattingly

L. C. Catalog Card No.: 61-9890
Printed in the United States of America.

COPYRIGHTS AND ACKNOWLEDGMENTS

John Betjeman: "In Westminster Abbey" from *Collected Poems*, 1959, by John Betjeman. By permission of the author.

Brandt & Brandt: Quotation from George Orwell's *Such, Such Were the Joys*, 1953. By permission of Brandt & Brandt.

Jonathan Cape Ltd: Quotation from *Literary Taste* by Arnold Bennett. By permission of Jonathan Cape Ltd.

Copeland & Lamm, Inc.: "Dunkirk" by Winston Churchill, from *The World's Great Speeches*, edited by Lewis Copeland and Lawrence W. Lamm, and published by Dover Publications, New York 14, New York. By permission of Copeland & Lamm, Inc.

Crown Publishers, Inc.: Quotation from "On Dramatic Poetry" by Denis Diderot in *European Theories of the Drama* by Barrett H. Clark, Revised Edition, 1947. By permission of Crown Publishers, Inc.

J. M. Dent & Sons Ltd: "And Death Shall Have No Dominion" by Dylan Thomas. By permission of J. M. Dent & Sons Ltd.

Mrs. Bernard DeVoto: "Homily for a Troubled Time" by Bernard DeVoto. By permission of Mrs. Bernard DeVoto.

Doubleday & Company, Inc.: Quotation from Arnold Bennett, *Literary Taste*. By permission of Doubleday & Company, Inc.

The Expression Company: Quotation from *The Province of Expression* by Samuel S. Curry. Reprinted by courtesy of the publisher.

Faber and Faber Ltd: "Musée des Beaux Arts" by W. H. Auden from *Collected Poems*. "Macavity: The Mystery Cat" by T. S. Eliot from *Old Possum's Book of Practical Cats*. Both these poems by permission of Faber and Faber, Ltd.

Farrar, Straus and Cudahy, Inc.: "Definition of 'A Nice Person'" from *The Selected Writings of Sidney Smith*, edited by W. H. Auden. "Poetry" from *Selected Writings* by Juan Ramon Jimenez, tr. H. R. Hays, ed. Eugenio Florit, copyright 1957 by Juan Ramon Jimenez. Both selections reprinted by permission of the publishers, Farrar, Straus, and Cudahy, Inc.

Harcourt, Brace & World, Inc.: Quotation from I. A. Richards, *Practical Criticism*, 1929. Quotations from "The Love Song of J. Alfred Prufrock" and from "Choruses from 'The Rock'" (IX) from *Collected Poems 1909-1935* by T. S. Eliot, copyright, 1936, by Harcourt, Brace & World, Inc. "Macavity: The Mystery Cat" from *Old Possum's Book of Practical Cats*, copyright, 1939, by T. S. Eliot. Quotation from George Orwell's "Poetry and the Microphone" from *Such, Such Were the Joys*, copyright, 1953. Quotation from *The Common Reader* by Virginia Woolf, copyright, 1925, by Harcourt, Brace & World, Inc., renewed, 1953 by Leonard Woolf. "Jazz Fantasia" from *Smoke and Steel* by Carl Sandburg, copyright, 1920, by Harcourt, Brace & World, Inc.; renewed, 1948, by Carl Sandburg. All these selections reprinted by permission of Harcourt, Brace & World, Inc.

Harper & Brothers: Quotation from Stephen Spender, "On Teaching Modern Poetry," in *Essays in Teaching*, ed. Harold Taylor, 1950. Reprinted by permission of Harper & Brothers.

Harvard University Press: Quotation from Stephen C. Pepper's *The Basis of Criticism in the Arts*. Reprinted by permission of Harvard University Press.

A. M. Heath & Company, Limited: "The First Death of Her Life" by Elizabeth Taylor from *Hester Lilly and 12 Short Stories*. By permission of A. M. Heath & Company, Limited.

Hermes Publications, Los Altos, Calif., and Mr. Kenneth Burke: Quotation from *Counter-Statement*, 2nd ed., revised, 1953. By permission of the publisher and the author.

The Hogarth Press Ltd: Quotation from *The Common Reader* by Virginia Woolf. By permission of The Hogarth Press Ltd.

Holt, Rinehart and Winston, Inc.: "Acquainted with the Night" from *You Come Too* by Robert Frost. Copyright © 1959, 1928, by Henry Holt and Company, Inc. Copyright 1956 by Robert Frost. "To An Athlete Dying Young" from *Complete Poems* by A. E. Housman, copyright, 1940, by Henry Holt and Company, Inc., copyright © 1959 by Holt, Rinehart and Winston, Inc. "The Lament" by Anton Chekhov. Reprinted by permission from *Masters and Masterpieces of the Short Story*, ed. Joshua McClennon, copyright, 1957, Holt, Rinehart and Winston, Inc. "The Fear" by Robert Frost from *Complete Poems of Robert Frost*. Copyright, 1930, 1949, by Henry Holt and Company, Inc. These selections by permission of Holt, Rinehart and Winston, Inc.

Houghton Mifflin Company: Quotation from *Dramatic Technique* by George Pierce Baker, 1919. Reprinted by permission of Houghton Mifflin Company.

Indiana University Press: "Dirge" from *New and Selected Poems* by Kenneth Fearing, published by Indiana University Press. Reprinted by permission of Indiana University Press.

Little, Brown & Co.: "My Life Closed Twice Before Its Close" from *Poems by Emily Dickinson*. "Young Love" from *As I Remember Him* by Hans Zinsser, Copyright 1939, 1940, by Hans Zinsser. These selections reprinted by permission of Little, Brown & Co.

The Macmillan Company: "Ah, Are You Digging On My Grave" from *Collected Poems* by Thomas Hardy. "Poetry" from *Collected Poems* by Marianne Moore; Copyright 1935 by Marianne Moore. "The Ballad of Moll Magee" by William Butler Yeats from *The Collected Poems of W. B. Yeats*. These selections reprinted by permission of The Macmillan Company.

The Macmillan Company of Canada Limited: "Ah, Are You Digging On My Grave" reprinted from *Collected Poems of Thomas Hardy* by permission of The Trustees of the Hardy Estate, Macmillan & Co. Ltd., and The Macmillan Company of Canada Limited. "The Ballad of Moll Magee" from *The Collected Poems of W. B. Yeats* by permission of Mrs. W. B. Yeats and The Macmillan Company of Canada Limited.

Preface

Interpretation: Writer-Reader-Audience is a book with a threefold purpose. It is meant to serve as an aid and guide to the full understanding of literature, to aesthetic appreciation of the arts of literature and interpretation, and to the attainment of bodily and vocal skill for the communication of meanings in literature.

With literature kept firmly in the center, this book sets forth a rationale for the study of interpretation; suggests the influences of psychological, educational, and literary developments upon the art of interpretation; formulates techniques for analyzing literature as a whole; provides examples of how these techniques may be applied to specific literary selections from traditional categories; indicates the direction that interpretative techniques must take if they are to serve the cause of literature; and furnishes standards for judging the interpreter's art.

We have sought to strengthen relationships among aesthetic and communication theory, literary study, and linguistic study. The framework of the book (writer, reader, audience) is rhetorical, and we have drawn upon rhetorical theory for our concept of liberal education, guides to levels of usage and to categories of style, and standards of criticism.

The twelve chapters of *Interpretation* fall into four divisions. Part One presents the rhetorical, humanistic, and literary bases of interpretation, the latter basis being developed in detail.

Part Two makes an application of the techniques of literary analysis to each of four literary modes and includes an anthology of selections under appropriate headings. No study guides or comments accompany these selections, for the analyses within chapters are sufficiently detailed to serve as examples for the serious student who would prefer to make his own application to new material. The brief anthology, meant only to serve as a suggestion of the literature available to the interpreter, is sufficiently varied to appeal to different interests and to provide the student with training in adapting his techniques to a wide range of material. The bibliography at the end of the book includes indices which may be helpful in stimulating the student to search unceasingly for worthwhile material.

Part Three presents a discussion of bodily and vocal skills, with selections for practice.

Part Four includes an examination of the role of the audience, standards for evaluation of interpretation, and principles of programing, with a unique section on the contemporary form known as Readers' Theater. The chapter on programing is applicable to classroom and public situations alike. Especially toward the end of a given term, the class hour can be used advantageously for the presentation of planned programs.

We recognize that the good teacher brings to the classroom things never found in books and that the organization of the book, while reasonable to us, may not be what an individual teacher will wish to follow. Varying sequences can be set up to fit the particular demands of those who prefer not to follow the given order of chapters. Some may wish to move from Part One to Part Three, and there may be those who do just the opposite.

Since its inception, *Interpretation* has been a joint endeavor in the truest sense. Dr. Grimes is primarily responsible for Chapters 1, 2, 4, 5, 6, 7, and 9, and Dr. Mattingly for Chapters 3, 8, 10, 11, and 12.

We would like to enumerate all the teachers past and present who have influenced us, but to do so is an impossible task. Yet we would begin with a grateful acknowledgment to Gertrude E. Johnson, professor emeritus of the University of Wisconsin, and end with warm thanks to those who have directly aided us by careful perusal of the manuscript: Wallace A. Bacon, Northwestern University; Eugene Bahn, Wayne State University; Donald C. Bryant, State University of Iowa; Francine Merritt, Louisiana State University; and Daniel E. Vandraegen, University of California at Los Angeles.

W.H.G.
A.S.M.

Contents

Part One

Part One

I

The Art of Interpretation

Language and science are abbreviations of reality; art is an intensification of reality. ∽ ERNST CASSIRER

Art is a translation, and every translation is a compromise (although be it noted, a compromise which may have new virtues of its own, virtues not part of the original). ∽ KENNETH BURKE

There must be a goal beyond the goal of social improvement—to give significance to better conditions of living when they have been achieved. ∽ STEPHEN SPENDER

INTERPRETATION HAS ANCIENT FORBEARS. It was originally associated with tribal religious ceremonies and dances, and the interpreter was a poet and priest, influential in the councils of his tribe. In medieval times the interpreter appeared as minstrel or roving reporter, but with the invention of printing his authority as prophet and ethical counselor dwindled, and his place as artist became clearer. Today the art of interpretation is flourishing and many-sided. Sometimes it serves utilitarian purposes: minutes and reports, instructions and classroom lectures, and sometimes public documents are heard. On record, radio, and film, trained readers provide information on many subjects. More often the art of interpretation enters the service of literature. Among the professionals, Charles Laughton, Agnes Moorhead, Raymond

3

Massey, Charles Boyer, John Gielgud, Kurt Kazner, Vincent Price, and Emlyn Williams have toured the United States to entertain audiences with interpretations of the masterpieces of literature, and the spoken word on records and tapes is a phenomenon of our culture.[1]

Interpretation and Education

A well-rounded education includes vocational training and self-development. The art of interpretation makes a sizable contribution to both these facets of education. The ability to communicate affects every human activity, and the individual who learns the art of interpretation is perfecting his communicative abilities. It is difficult to separate the uses of language, but ordinarily we teach them as reading, speaking, listening, and writing. In interpretation all four skills are at work. The oral basis of language, often overlooked in the teaching of reading, becomes clear as the interpreter translates to listeners the written symbols for thought, feeling, and action. Awareness of the vocal origins of language awakens interest in the voice behind the page and brings vigorous life to literature. The combination of seeing, voicing, and hearing words reinforces and stimulates mental activity—comprehension, memory, and enjoyment.

Because the movements of the vocal mechanism take more time than the movements of the eye back and forth along the page, the interpreter has a chance to pay attention to verbal structures, as well as to the words themselves. Most of his training in reading has been geared to high-speed travel toward the passing of examinations. Perhaps before coming to the study of interpretation, he has had little opportunity to enjoy his reading along the way. Very likely he has never taken time to see how an idea is developed, but has picked it out full-blown as a topic sentence. The connections between parts of a sentence or paragraph, the weighing of words, the infinite number of possibilities for meaning in figures of speech and allusions may never have received adequate attention before. The interpreter must find meaning in order to communicate it. Resembling as it does the processes of the literary artist, the interpreter's search for meaning adds much more than silent reading to the improvement of writing skills.

[1] See *Spoken Poetry on Records and Tapes: An Index of Currently Available Recordings* (ACRL). Prepared by the Association of College and Research Libraries, Monograph No. 18 compiled by Henry C. Hastings (Chicago: American Library Association, 1957).

Sources of Knowledge

Literature makes a distinctive contribution to knowledge, and interpretation is a way of discovering this contribution. Because it demands activity and leads to a social (audience) situation, interpretation often seems more inviting than other literary study. Events today indicate that man is no closer to self-knowledge than he was centuries ago and suggest that the wisdom of past ages may never have been put to full use. As a record of man's ethical standards, aspirations, and emotional life, literature is an almost inexhaustible source of self-knowledge. Just as we understand current events better by comparing them with events in history, so we sometimes understand ourselves better through the characters in literature. Is it conceivable that guides to living set down in the old records of literature have never been completely utilized? Tucked away in libraries and lusterless classrooms, too often literature has seemed a dusty relic unrelated to the challenges of living. Interpretation is a means of making literature accessible and attractive to large numbers of persons.

Aesthetic Fulfillment

Individuals and society suffer when the need to communicate on a level beyond the utilitarian is suppressed. Alfred North Whitehead, scientist, mathematician, and philosopher, pointed out that although the expression of the human spirit is not *confined* to literature, it and other arts make a contribution to the life of the spirit which cannot be overlooked without grave consequences to the vitality of workmen and statesmen alike.[2] Dr. Karl Menninger, from the field of psychiatric medicine, approved the following statement of the role of art in education: "To provide children with aesthetic experiences and training in aesthetic expression that will develop patterns useful to them for maintaining morale, for relieving tensions, for identifying themselves with a cultural group and, in general, for sensitizing them to beauty."[3] Is it possible that a program in education giving the arts a position of importance might have therapeutic values unrealized in our present

---

[2] Alfred North Whitehead, *The Aims of Education* (New York: New American Library, 1953), pp. 57–68.

[3] From a report to the American Council of Education, by Daniel A. Prescott of the Committee on Relations of the Emotions to the Educative Processes. Quoted in *Love Against Hate* (New York: Harcourt, Brace and Company, Inc., 1942), p. 252.

policy of teaching everything else first and then, if there is time, attending to poetry, drama, music, and the visual arts?

Art and literature, stemming as they do from the primal needs which they also nourish, affect the main energies of life. They offer a vital balance between knowing and doing. Again, in the words of Whitehead, ". . . education should turn out the pupil with something he knows well and something he can do well. This intimate union of practice and theory aids both. The intellect does not work best in a vacuum. The stimulation of the creative impulse requires, especially in the case of a child, the quick transition to practice." [4] *Interpretation* is a doing that rests on a foundation of knowing. Its practice requires intimate knowledge of literature; active participation with the literary artist in the creation of patterns of language; and cultural identification leading to improved personal and group morale. It can unify educational practices and yield a balanced perspective to the subjects closely allied to it: language, psychology, philosophy, aesthetics, and history.

Interpretation as Communication

Alfred North Whitehead stressed the importance of "doing" to achieve the aims of education, and Dr. Karl Menninger stressed the need for identification with a cultural group. Interpretation combines "doing" with social stimulation. As a rule, the silent reader is solitary and often has lost his original enthusiasm for what he has read before he has a chance to talk about it with friends. The interpreter, with book in hand, can deepen his own appreciation simultaneously with the act of communication. The response he evokes from his audience provides an enlargement or enhancement of all the values in the situation. Mutual enjoyment thus gives the interpreter a degree of cultural identification, affirms the meaning of literature, and sheds a favorable light upon the twin arts of literature and interpretation.

Responding to the events and objects in his world, John Steinbeck created a short story and entitled it "Flight." Browsing in the library, you discover "Flight" (Created Object I) and by your deep involvement with its plot and characters have an aesthetic response. The story sticks in your mind, and some time later, when asked to provide a program for a discussion club, you decide to become interpreter and

---

[4] Whitehead, p. 58.

CREATED OBJECT

I

LITERARY ARTIST

Artistic response to
materials

SILENT READER

Aesthetic response to
CREATED OBJECT I

Community of Experience
Pleasure

CREATED OBJECT

II

SILENT READER as

INTERPRETATIVE ARTIST

Artistic response to

CREATED OBJECT II

AUDIENCE

Aesthetic response to
CREATED OBJECT II

Community of Experience
Pleasure

to present "Flight" as your program (Created Object II). When, after thoughtful preparation, you face the group and present the story, it has taken on added dimension through your understanding, enjoyment, and skill. The audience may not respond to "Flight" exactly as you have, but if you have preserved the original plot, characterizations, and mood, enough endures so that writer, audience, and you, the interpreter, have had overlapping (if not identical) experiences.

Interpretation as Art

All art is an organization of experience. The interpreter is concerned with the organization of experience as he finds it in literature. The diagram above indicates that the author's relationship with the external "world" contains the seeds of his creativity, and the literature produced from this relationship becomes the "world" to which the interpreter reacts. In his turn, the interpreter takes on the task of communicating his responses. When he does so, he illuminates literature as the author has illuminated life.

All art implies form. The form of interpretative art in the main is the form with which the author has endowed his materials. Any given subject may be molded by an artist into what seems to him appropriate form, and no two artists will create identical forms. Using words to express their reactions to the element of beauty, John Keats, John Masefield, Wallace Stevens, and Willa Cather achieved strikingly different results: "Endymion" and "Ode on a Grecian Urn," a series of sonnets, "Peter Quince at the Clavier" and other lyrics, a volume of short stories entitled *Youth and the Bright Medusa*. The interpreter choosing any of these will retain their identifying characteristics: the concreteness of the lyrics, the compression of the sonnets, the plot lines and character rhythms of the narratives.

The interpreter's stance, vocal quality, rate, and imaginative power and range will lend themselves to the creation of interpretative form, in keeping with the formal characteristics of the literary work being interpreted. Often we speak of the interpreter's "style" instead of his "form," but no matter which term we use, we are referring to the formal quality of the achievement. We may say that something was too dramatic, meaning that the interpreter went beyond the writer's intention, changed the form. Or we may say that an interpretation of a lyric missed the point by being didactic or oratorical or argumentative. Interpretative form cannot exist apart from the work of the literary artist.

All art has originality. The originality of an interpretation arises out of the total effect of a personality in combination with a given work of art. Individual rhythm, vocal quality, and physical appearance give infinite variety to interpretations of the same poem, story, or play by different interpreters (or actors). Nevertheless, an interpreter is obliged to discover and to express accurately and fully the meaning of the work under consideration. He cannot react as he *wishes* the author had reacted or in any way exceed the limits of his material.

All art arouses a pleasurable response. The pleasure ensuing from interpretation is somewhat dependent upon the situation and theme of the selections: serious or tragic selections arouse a pleasure different from that called forth by humorous selections. But the pleasure of the interpretation depends even more upon the interpreter's treatment of all the factors: his understanding and sensitive response to his material, his relationship with his listeners, and his skill in using his body and voice to convey meaning. When the listener fails to grasp meaning, is uneasy about the interpreter's control, or is disturbed by personal mannerisms or awkwardness of the interpreter, the experience fails to yield aesthetic response, or pleasure. When the listener can label the event, can look back to it and say, as John Dewey suggests, "That *was* an experience,"[5] there has been aesthetic pleasure.

To be truly artistic, the act of interpretation must possess recognizable and memorable form and originality within designated limits, and it must yield pleasure to the observer or listener. Thus, interpretation may be defined as *the full revelation of whatever experience is inherent in the literature.*

Many persons who never think of themselves as artists get and give pleasure from the simple act of communicating from the printed page. A father reads to his children at bedtime, a professor introduces his lecture by reading selected passages from Shakespeare, an aroused citizen reads an editorial to his associates on a civic committee. In each case, if the interpreter is successful, his listeners will participate in the experience contained in the material under consideration. There are, of course, many degrees of expertness in the art of interpretation as in other arts.

Perhaps no art can ever be taught directly. During the Renaissance, young painters served apprenticeships in the studios of established older painters, and learned by watching, listening, practicing, and receiving criticism of their own efforts. Today we likewise observe a tendency for painters, writers, musicians, actors to find each other, to live in colonies or neighborhoods, and to absorb from each other certain matters of technique and form. It is difficult for the practitioner of any art to develop outside the mainstream of that art. With or without organized classes, the would-be artist puts himself in touch with other artists.

So an interpreter must listen and watch other interpreters and actors, and become acquainted with many types and moods in literature, and in short, immerse himself in the art. He will learn the best current theories, and he will avail himself of the help of a competent teacher. A textbook like this one is best used in conjunction with the evaluation and encouragement of a teacher and fellow students of the art. The teacher is a firm bridge between understanding and performance, for no existing textbook can supply the magic formula for transferring acquired understanding to the audience situation.

Understanding is the starting-point of our study of interpretation, and it consists first of all of understanding what one reads. Secondly, it involves understanding of interpretation as an art form. Understand-

_____
[5] *Art As Experience* (New York: Minton, Balch and Company, Inc., 1934), p. 37.

ing includes knowledge of ideal standards as well, and in the setting of standards, the teacher is invaluable. By himself, a student may set a standard that is much too high, or even one that is false. The teacher is at first the one reliable judge of whether or not the standard has been attained. Eventually, the interpreter will be able to judge his own performance with considerable discernment. Chapter 11 suggests criteria for judging interpretation.

Another important step in the study of interpretation is achieving the management of the body and the voice, the physical means of expression. We have come to look upon behavior in any situation as a link in a chain of experience, and we know that habits and attitudes invariably control physical manifestations such as posture and rate of utterance. For this reason, there is frequently an indirect approach to improving bodily and vocal skills. Interpretation itself, through its literary material, may induce forgetfulness of self and thereby disclose power, flexibility, and freedom totally unexpected in an individual pattern of behavior. Yet we cannot rely upon this therapeutic accompaniment to literary or interpretative study, and at times the approach to technical skill needs to be exceedingly direct. Certain mannerisms and difficulties, for example, must be acknowledged before they can be overcome. A direct attack along with awakened interest in one's material will be helpful in overcoming the following distractions: shuffling feet and uneasy stance, shifting eyes, limp muscles, lowered head, nervous hands, shortness of breath (unrelated to physical health), inaudibility, an overfast rate, monotonous pitch or loudness level. The teacher's role is vital in recognizing distracting behavior and suggesting remedial practice. Student and teacher together must find a few significant points for concentrated effort and avoid the error of a broadside atttack on trivialities.

The hazards of the audience situation often affect the interpreter and modify his interpretation, no matter how thorough his preparation has been. There is no way of calculating to a certainty beforehand how a collection of individuals in any gathering will behave, nor is there any way of foretelling one's own reaction. Practice periods in advance of performance will give the interpretation fluency and firmness; frequent experiences before varied audiences will give the interpreter sureness and ease. Chapter 10 specifically sets forth the variables in the audience situation and, along with Chapter 12, which discusses and illustrates programing for an audience, attempts to give the interpreter understanding, confidence, and skill in the audience situation. Chapters 8 and 9 contain backgrounds for studying techniques of voice and body for interpretation, but, in addition, these two chapters offer practical exercises for developing these requisite skills.

But interpretation rests upon literature, drawing its techniques from the techniques of the literature being presented. For this reason, Chapter 2 sets forth materials, classifying the well-known types and suggesting selections for study and presentation. Likewise, Chapter 3 is devoted to literature, but to its analysis for the purpose of comprehending, assimilating, and presenting it to an audience. Chapters 4 through 7 approach comprehension in another way, through applying the techniques of analysis to selections suitable for presentation. Since each work of art is unique, each analysis must likewise be unique, but, as we shall see, the traditional forms of literature give us guidelines to follow; and the analysis of a selection typifying each of the main forms suggests the method to be used for other selections.

Each chapter is designed to add its weight to the interpreter's power to communicate meaning so that, in the end, his interpretative efforts will arouse pleasurable feeling in his audience. The interpreter himself must find the opportunities for practice in the light of the theory contained in the textbook and with the assistance of his teacher.

Summary

The modern art of interpretation contributes to education by its wholesome effect upon the skills of writing and silent reading. It is a key to literature and a means for finding aesthetic fulfillment, as well as an important kind of communication. Like other arts, it is an organization of experience with identifiable form and a measure of originality. Interpretation is a source of pleasure in informal and formal situations.

The interpretative artist acquires proficiency through hearing trained artists, learning current theory, and availing himself of the help of competent teachers. An understanding of literature and an awareness of attainable goals are as important to the student of interpretation as the technical skills of expression.

The Literary Object

Even now most uneducated people think that poetical language makes the finest discourse. That is not true: the language of prose is distinct from that of poetry. ∾ ARISTOTLE

It is not merely useless, it is harmful, for you to map out literature into divisions and branches, with different laws, rules, or canons. The first thing is to obtain some possession of literature. ∾ ARNOLD BENNETT

WE SHALL SEE IN ENSUING CHAPTERS that the interpreter's success in preserving the author's original work depends upon his willingness to accept the following four responsibilities:

1. To become acquainted with a large body of literature.
2. To perfect his understanding of the literary selection (or selections) chosen for the experience.
3. To perfect his technical skills in order to meet the requirements of selection and situation.
4. To determine his point of contact with a given audience and try to understand the motivations and interests of its members.

In this chapter the literature available and suitable for interpretation is our chief concern.

Ideally, an interpreter would be thoroughly acquainted with the literary masterpieces of all time and steeped in tradition; able to discern the relations between literature and life; skillful in the use of his voice and body for the communication of meaning; and poised before any and all audiences. In reality, most of us who study and practice interpretation are using it as a means of self-development.

Backgrounds of Interpretation

Traditionally the arts of language have treated the forms known as *rhetoric* and *poetic*. When Aristotle surveyed these arts in Athens in the fourth century B.C., he concluded that *rhetoric* was the useful art of persuasion, concerned with the practical affairs of men and designed to influence action; and that *poetic* was the art of delighting or pleasing, concerned with the emotional life of man and designed to cause an emotional release. As they were integrated into the daily lives of the Athenian citizens, these two categories helped to describe existing verbal behavior, but failed even in that ancient time to describe exactly what went on. Fact and feeling in language as in life cannot be fitted conveniently into pigeonholes and neatly labeled, for they are mixed in continuously shifting proportions. If we remember that the two categories of *rhetoric* and *poetic* are not mutually and finally exclusive, they will be extremely useful to us in our study of literature for interpretation. Both rhetoric and poetic employ language embodying ideas and feelings, language selected and arranged to create an effect upon the listener or beholder. Ordinarily reflecting the artist's awareness of an audience, both arts may include the voicing and full expression of the created object. We call the full expression of rhetorical materials *public speaking* or *public address*, and the full expression of poetical materials *interpretation* or *acting*.

The greatest difference between *rhetoric* and *poetic* (and between public speaking and interpretation) lies in the planned effect. The art of rhetoric involves material (ideas and feelings) organized to influence practical action; the art of poetic involves material (ideas and feelings) organized to give pleasure to the listeners or readers.

The Modes of Literature

As you proceed in the study of literature and its interpretation, you will observe interesting differences in classifications of materials in anthologies and literature textbooks. With *rhetoric* and *poetic* as major headings, we have prepared a chart (see the next page) for the five sub-headings: speech and essay under rhetoric; and lyric, narrative, and drama under poetic.

Much as we should like to avoid rigidity in making distinctions, we find it convenient to keep the traditional names of these modes, names carrying associations not unlike those clustering around musical classifications, such as *symphony* and *opera*. Most listeners can detect changes in forms and sub-forms of music and can hear the very measure in which a waltz tempo is altered; but the normally alert listener, concentrating upon meaning, may not easily distinguish the shifting tones and effects within a literary composition. In literature as in music, departure from an established motif is likely to be temporary, and the dominant tone will reappear at or before the close. We must learn to find the clues which guide the reader as the musical signature guides the musician.

The interpreter's study of any literary work is simplified if he recognizes its formal characteristics, for authors work with existing patterns, although a highly original author will bend a traditional pattern to his own intention. Thus, in an effort to identify an author's response to the external world, we may speak of the lyric or lyrical tone, of exposition or an expository tone. The dominant tone of a composition is closely allied with its form, and yet subject to modification, so that we find all forms exceedingly flexible and versatile. Exposition may include narrative, argument may approach lyric, and drama may involve argument. Such modifications may be found in works of any length, in particular, the speeches of Patrick Henry and Daniel Webster and the writings of William Beebe and George Bernard Shaw.

Later we shall see that not only literary study, but also the interpreter's own style, is benefited by an awareness of literary form.

Choosing Among the Available Modes

The classification of literature into modes is useful in our study of meaning, but insufficient as a guide to the selection of materials for an interpretative event. The interpreter cannot follow his own taste entirely, but must examine selections for their *appropriateness* to a given occasion. Good judgment of appropriateness requires knowledge of literature and of the prospective audience. The interpreter will be meticulous about fitting into allotted time limits, sensible of the mood of

		TIME	SUBJECT	ELEMENT	RELATION OF MATERIAL TO CREATIVE ARTIST	SELECTED EXAMPLES
Rhetoric	Speech	Current	Politics, national and international affairs; public policy and welfare; events; ethics.	Facts, ideas, reasoning from facts; incidental narration. Prose structure (sentence and paragraph).	Speaker expects his own personality to influence his hearers directly.	Jesus: "The Beatitudes" Edmund Burke: "On Conciliation with America" George Washington: "Farewell Address"
	Essay	Current	Similar to the speech; may be concerned with human nature and character; manners; with places and things.	As above.	Writer influences only through verbal printed structure; style of paramount importance.	Ralph Waldo Emerson: "On Friendship" Aaron Copland: "How We Listen" E. B. White: "The Distant Music of the Hounds"
Poetic	Lyric	Timeless	Unlimited, dependent upon author's vision.	Feeling and emotion; ideas; poetic structure and form (verse).	Speaks through heightened sense of self, or may take on fictitious identity.	Thomas Gray: "Elegy" Robert Burns: "To a Mouse" Sidney Lanier: "Song of the Chattahoochee"
	Narrative	Past	Incidents, problems, conflicts of human life.	Plot; author creates characters as agents of plot action; may be verse or prose structure.	Speaks from selected point of view; may vary within a given work. Setting specifically provided.	Folk Ballad: "Sir Patrick Spens" Henry Fielding: *The History of Tom Jones* Mark Twain: *The Adventures of Tom Sawyer*
	Drama	Present (in sense of happening before your eyes)	As above.	Any and all of above but in form of *dialogue*; may be verse or prose structure.	Point of view is omniscient; dramatist speaks through his characters. Setting specifically provided and vivified.	Shakespeare: *Macbeth* Lillian Hellman: *The Little Foxes* Tennessee Williams: *The Glass Menagerie*

an occasion, and considerate of the traditions and habits of his audience. The college girl who tried to fit *Western Star* into a twenty-minute spot, the teacher who read a stark bit from *Grapes of Wrath* at a gay spring luncheon, the young woman who chose "The King's Breakfast" for a convention of insurance executives could all have selected more wisely. Yet before other groups or on different occasions, these identical selections might have been suitable. *Western Star* is a stirring evening's reading, *Grapes of Wrath* could fit into a serious session on social change, and "The King's Breakfast," despite its appeal for the child-audience, might fit very well into a convention program for restaurant owners or managers! Limits imposed by time, purpose, and outlook must be realistically faced in connection with all groups, even though audiences will usually go a long way toward accepting and enjoying anything an interpreter obviously understands and relishes.

AUDIENCE LIMITATIONS. Even among selections suitable for a given occasion, there may be those which "read well out loud" and those which do not. Abstract philosophical essays by Schopenhauer, Santayana, or Bertrand Russell may qualify as literature and still not be readily accessible to the ear. Two facts which cannot be overlooked operate in the reader-audience situation; *one* is the fact that words following each other in a span of time are not recoverable. The silent reader can turn back the page and cast his eye over the preceding sentence when he realizes he has lost the thread of the discourse. The listener cannot courteously interrupt or ask for repetition. The *second* fact is that the audience offers distractions not faced by the solitary reader. These distractions can be held to a minimum by the interpreter who reinforces meanings through vocal stress, extended pauses, or illustrative movement. Yet he is committed to his text, and there are definite limits to the emphasis and exaggeration he may resort to. With these two limitations of the audience situation in mind, the interpreter will be wise to choose material which is concrete and well ordered, written by an author with an ear attuned to the sound of word-combinations.

INTERPRETER LIMITATIONS. We are all tempted to turn to the forms and materials we know best and can prepare with confidence. Some of us prefer essays and speeches and are fearful of dramatic forms; others of us find light verse or humorous comment preferable to reflective lyrics or exalted expression. If we are to gain the personal development that literary study and interpretation offer us, we shall need to widen our interests. Human values, catholic taste, and versatility in interpretation come only with reading and presenting many attitudes and styles.

It is unrealistic to suppose that everyone who wants to become an effective interpreter has previously read enough that he has authors' names and titles on quick recall. Yet the first place to start is to make a survey of your own resources, enlivening this introspective activity by any notes you may have and by talking with friends. The next step is a survey of your personal library, to be followed by a browsing session in a city or college library. To make such browsing effective, some notion of where to begin is essential. To help in the organization of your browsing time, we have placed a few headings and lists at the end of this chapter.

The Modes of Literature and the Interpreter's Style

As we proceed we shall examine the modes of literature in detail, studying them with full awareness of the psychological implications of the writer-interpreter-audience event and adding immeasurably to our knowledge of the bases for choosing literature for the enjoyment of our listeners. We will look for revelations of meaning in the forms themselves in an attempt to discover all that makes the literary composition a living entity. Most of all, we will search in the work for the qualities of style determining the style of the interpretation. As in the search for materials, there must be a starting-point, and we have selected the situational aspects of the work for this first step.

Open and Closed Situations

Every utterance occurs in time and place and requires a speaker and a listener and some motivation. These we call the essentials of the situation. As interpreters we become acquainted with the situation in a literary work and then present it to an audience, thereby giving the literary situation another setting and in effect creating a *second* situation, in which we function as speakers. When the situational aspects of a work are so tightly organized that they constitute an environment of their own, one which we as readers observe but do not partake of, the situation is *closed*. In the presentation of such a work to an audience, we must make sure that the audience stands in the position of observer throughout. When, on the other hand, some of the situational aspects are missing or suggested rather than explicitly stated, the situation is said to be *open*. In presenting such a work to an audience, we try to obtain its participation in the situation.

The motivation in a situation is often strongly emotional. When, for example, a poet imbues his materials with intense feeling or the characters of a narrative are in conflict, ordinary communication will not suffice to express the dominant tone. Such emotional coloring leads us away from direct communication and the open situation toward indirectness and the closed situation.

A clear-cut example of the *closed* situation is the traditional drama, meant to be played behind the proscenium. The author presents his characters without comment (except in stage directions), and the characters, by means of dialogue and indicated action, represent *life*. When the drama is played, the audience peeps at the unfolding action as though a fourth wall had been removed from a house; we see the characters make responses to other characters, but make no direct statement or appeal to the audience. Even in our more intimate arena-style theater, the players are outwardly unaffected by the audience. Occasionally a play is written with a situation that opens out and includes the audience. Among these are Thornton Wilder's *Our Town* and *The Skin of Our Teeth*, and Tennessee Williams' *The Glass Menagerie*. Also you will remember that there was exchange at close quarters between actor and audience in the Elizabethan theater. Nevertheless, in the main, drama exemplifies the utmost closure.

The *open* situation exists when the speaker stands alone to inform, convince, appeal to, entertain, or impress an audience. While the speaker reveals himself, the audience remains silent. There is direct exchange between the two environments as the speaker seeks to affect the listening audience. Similar openness exists in the essay. We think of it as the uninterrupted utterance of one individual hoping to affect his reader much as the speaker hopes to affect his audience, although the essayist writes to a more nebulous audience, one that cannot be characterized except by the adjective "willing." When an essay is interpreted, there is direct response from the audience to the ideas of the essay.

The lyric is not so readily placed along the continuum from closed to open. It may be as open as the essay, addressed to all willing readers and listeners, or it may move along the continuum slightly and be addressed to specified listeners: to the Creator, to real or imaginary individuals, or to personified natural objects. Occasionally the outline of an incident in a lyric such as Robert Frost's "Wild Grapes," or E. A. Robinson's "Luke Havergal," draws us even farther away from openness. The so-called dramatic lyrics of Robert Browning are further examples of semi-closed and closed situations, presenting clearly drawn characters as speakers and suggesting listeners within the work.

The narrative, too, has many variants, but can always be considered less open than the essay and less closed than the play. Traditionally written in verse, narrative today includes novel, novelette, and short story, as well as the epic and metrical tale. When the narrative is a series of word pictures or contains symbolic import, it tends toward openness.

Our classifications are not iron-clad, for within each mode there are gradations in openness, and even within a given work, there may be variations. As the relationships between speaker and listener shift, they affect and are affected by the other elements of the situation—the time, place, and motivation. Ordinarily, rhetorical modes give us open situations and poetic forms give us closed situations.

OPEN SITUATION		CLOSED SITUATION
Rhetoric: Speech, Essay (Argument, Exposition, Satire, Criticism, Description)	The Lyric	*Poetic:* Short Story, Novel, Ballad, Metrical Tale, and Epic Drama

We ought to be able to appraise a situation as *open* or *closed* after asking the following questions:

1. To what degree is there exchange between a single speaker and an external audience to which he addresses himself?
2. To what degree is there specific presentation of speakers and listeners within a given work?
3. To what degree do the speakers and listeners within the work affect each other?
4. To what degree is the idea touched with imaginative power and intense feeling?

The interpreter always meets his audience in his own person, his body and voice reacting to the audience and the occasion as well as to the situation in the literature. When his material contains an *open* situation, there will be lively, direct communication between him and his audience. Because material with an open situation is likely to be dominantly factual and low in emotional content, the *open* situation ordinarily calls for directness, vigor, and clarity of utterance. When the material contains a *closed* situation, however, the interpreter must compromise between the external communication with his audience and the internal communication of the work. Often the interaction of characters is so lively that the interpreter can have little or no eye contact with his audience. We can illustrate the effects of the situation upon style of interpretation very briefly by pointing out possible adaptations to each of the modes.

SPEECH AND ESSAY

For the most part, except in impassioned appeals or denunciations, direct eye contact and conversational liveliness prevail.

Under the influence of strong emotion there is some tendency to withdraw from immediate contact, just as there is in personal conversation which takes an emotional turn.

LYRIC

Contact between interpreter and audience is modified by strength of feeling.

Whether the speaker in the literary situation addresses an external audience or a specified listener within the work, the interpreter is only a symbol of the total meaning: if he insists upon maintaining unvarying face-to-face communication, he may mislead his audience into accepting him as the sole source of idea and feeling.

NARRATIVE AND DRAMA

Internal exchange in the work is constant and central.

In narration there is alternation of directness with indirectness, as the author has alternated between summary and scene.

In drama the only direct communication occurs when the interpreter sets the scene or bridges gaps left by the omission of certain speeches or scenes.

In the next chapter, you will again meet the open and closed situations intended to clarify the relationships within literary selections and to assist you in establishing the proper relationship with your audience. The continuum from *open* to *closed* situation also affects the order in which the analysis chapters are arranged. We move from the open situation of speech and essay (Chapter 4), through lyric (Chapter 5) and narrative (Chapter 6), to the closed situation of drama (Chapter 7).

Summary

In meeting his responsibility to become acquainted with a large body of literature, the interpreter finds knowledge of traditional labels extremely useful. Distinctions between *rhetoric* and *poetic*, the ancient categories, help him to understand the characteristics of the five subheadings: speech, essay, lyric, narrative, and drama. Although understanding the different modes helps him to understand content, the interpreter's choice of material for various occasions will depend upon his awareness of two elements: the nature of his audience and his own temperament and ability.

There are situational aspects which affect the interpreter. There is the situation in which he reads, involving time, place, material, audience, occasion, and interpreter. There is in addition for the poetic materials an imaginative or created situation, involving events and characters in time and place. When the situation within the literary work is clearly different from that which the interpreter and his audience compose, the situation is considered "closed." When the dominant situation is that existing between the interpreter and his audience, the situation is considered "open." The use of the open and closed situations helps the interpreter to see the relations within a literary work and to communicate them to his audience.

Selected Bibliography

GENERAL

Beardsley, Monroe, and others, eds. *Theme and Form.* Englewood Cliffs, N. J.: Prentice-Hall, Inc., 1956.

Brooks, Cleanth, and others, eds. *An Approach to Literature,* 3rd ed. New York: Appleton-Century-Crofts, Inc., 1952.

Burnett, Whit, ed. *The World's Best.* New York: The Dial Press, Inc., 1950.

Shrodes, Caroline, and Justine Van Gundy, eds. *Approaches to Prose*. New York: The Macmillan Company, 1959.

Stallman, R. W., and R. E. Watters. *The Creative Reader*. New York: The Ronald Press Company, 1954.

Woollcott, Alexander, comp. *The Woollcott Reader*. New York: The Viking Press, Inc., 1935.

SPEECHES

Baird, Albert Craig. *American Public Addresses, 1740–1952*. New York: McGraw-Hill Book Company, 1956.

Brigance, William Norwood, comp. *Classified Speech Models*. New York: F. S. Crofts & Company, 1928.

Lindgren, Homer, comp. *Modern Speeches*. New York: F. S. Crofts & Company, 1926.

O'Neill, James M. *Classified Models of Speech Composition*. New York: The Century Company, 1921.

Parrish, Wayland M., and Marie Hochmuth, comps. *American Speeches*. New York: Longmans, Green & Company, Inc., 1954.

Sarett, Lew R., and William T. Foster, eds. *Modern Speeches on Basic Issues*. Boston: Houghton Mifflin Company, 1939.

Wrage, Ernest J., and Barnet Baskerville, eds. *American Forum: Speeches on Historic Issues (1788–1900)*. New York: Harper & Brothers, 1960.

ESSAYS

Edman, Irwin. *Under Whatever Sky*. New York: The Viking Press, Inc., 1951.

Edwards, Oliver. *Talking of Books*. London: Heinemann, Ltd., 1957.

Nye, Russel, ed. *Modern Essays*, rev. ed. Chicago: Scott, Foresman and Company, 1957.

Orwell, George. *Such, Such Were the Joys*. New York: Harcourt, Brace and Company, Inc., 1953.

Taylor, Deems. *Music to My Ears*. New York: Simon & Schuster, 1949.

Thurber, James. *Alarms and Diversions*. New York: Harper & Brothers, 1957.

LYRICS

Engle, Paul, and Warren Carrier, eds. *Reading Modern Poetry*. Chicago: Scott, Foresman and Company, 1955.

The Literary Object 23

Friar, Kimon, and John Malcolm Brinnin, eds. *Modern Poetry; American and British*. New York: Appleton-Century-Crofts, Inc., 1951.

Hill, Caroline Miles, ed. *The World's Great Religious Poetry*. New York: The Macmillan Company, 1938.

Rosenthal, M. L., and A. J. M. Smith. *Exploring Poetry*. New York: The Macmillan Company, 1955.

Thomas, Wright, and S. G. Brown, eds. *Reading Poems*. New York: Oxford University Press, 1941.

NARRATIVES

Gummere, Francis B. *Old English Ballads*. New York: Ginn and Company, 1894.

Hall, James B., and Joseph Langland, eds. *The Short Story*. New York: The Macmillan Company, 1956.

Leach, MacEdward, ed. *The Ballad Book*. New York: Harper & Brothers, 1955.

Ludwig, Jack Barry, and W. Richard Poirier, eds. *Stories, British and American*. Boston: Houghton Mifflin Company, 1953.

DRAMAS

Ashton, John, ed. *Types of English Drama*. New York: The Macmillan Company, 1940.

Bentley, Eric. *The Play: A Critical Anthology*. Englewood Cliffs, N. J.: Prentice-Hall, Inc., 1951.

Bierman, Judah, and others, eds. *The Dramatic Experience*. Englewood Cliffs, N. J.: Prentice-Hall, Inc., 1958.

Cooper, Charles W. *Preface to Drama*. New York: The Ronald Press Company, 1955.

Gassner, John, ed. *Treasury of the Theatre*, rev. ed. New York: Simon & Schuster, 1951.

Kreymborg, Alfred, ed. *Poetic Drama*. New York: Tudor Publishing Company, 1941.

Millett, Fred Benjamin. *Reading Drama*. New York: Harper & Brothers, 1950.

Tucker, Samuel Marion, ed. *Twenty-Five Modern Plays*. New York: Harper & Brothers, 1948.

 *3*

Understanding the Literary Object

Whatever else we may do by the light of nature it would be folly to maintain that we should read by it. ∾ I. A. RICHARDS

INTERPRETATION, WE HAVE SAID, is a writer-reader-audience event, and we are now ready to look more closely at the part the writer plays in this three-part activity. As an interpreter you perhaps will share with your audience, though not on a single occasion, an essay by Charles Lamb, a sonnet by William Wordsworth, some nonsense verses by Ogden Nash, a story by Joseph Conrad, and a scene from *Death of a Salesman* by Arthur Miller. Different as these selections are in content and structure, there are aspects they share in common with all literature, and there are means of analysis that will further our understanding of them or of any other piece of literature.

Be it lyric or story or drama, as silent readers we respond, of course, to the total effect of the composition, but for greater understanding—which precedes full appreciation—it is necessary to perceive the elements of the work of art. Perception can be broken down into thinking and feeling with the object. In other words, there are both *cognitive* and *affective* elements in any piece of writing, and we seek to become aware of as many as possible. The finest writers give us such complexity that we are challenged to read and reread in our search for understanding and enjoyment. Children enjoy the rhyme about

Humpty Dumpty time and again but not until years later do they consider its possible symbolism;[1] adults may go back many times to read, for example, "The Open Boat" by Stephen Crane, pondering all the implications of the story, or college students perhaps will heatedly discuss the reasons for Hedda's suicide, seeking the appropriate way to voice certain lines in *Hedda Gabler*.

Provided we have a minimum command of the language the writer uses, a hurried reading may furnish a degree of understanding, but for enjoyment of literature rather than for mere grasp of fact, a more leisurely and complete reading must take place. As a part of the preparation for interpretation, thorough, discriminating reading is an essential. Full meaning, with its multiple aspects—variously referred to as depth, thematic, and symbolic meanings or as levels of meaning—hides itself for most people until training develops skill in reading. A serious reader keeps improving this skill throughout his life. As he reads more and more, as he travels to far lands, and as he extends all his life experiences—falls in love, marries and has children, widens his range of acquaintance and circle of friends, pursues hobbies, accepts responsibility in profession or business, faces sorrow, and so on—he gains familiarity with verbal and textual traditions upon which writers draw. Knowledge of religions, manners and customs of people, and economic and social conditions of civilizations, gives insight, making the writer's point more readily available to the reader.

Thus, in the study of interpretation, the richer your present background in history, art, philosophy, and languages, the better equipped you are, but it is also true that the study itself will offer opportunities to enrich your cultural background as you become acquainted with literature providing a wide range of vicarious experience. Moreover, the close reading demanded on the part of the interpreter leads him to the full richness of the experience inherent in the literature.

The Literary Object: Its Situational Components

In analysis of the literary object, our starting point, as was stated in the last chapter, concerns the situational components of the work. Any human utterance is a composite of these. It is spoken by someone (*Who?*), to another (to *Whom?*), in a place (*Where?*), at a time

---

[1] See Bernard M. Knieger, "Humpty Dumpty and Symbolism," *College English*, XX (February, 1959), 244–245.

(*When?*), for a reason (*Why?*), to communicate something (*What*), and in a certain manner (*How?*). This framework gives us a basic approach to any piece of writing. (It is a general guide taught to all young journalists who learn to include each component in reporting news or in writing a story). For our purposes let us say that the *cognitive* elements are speaker (Who?), subject (What?), place (Where?), time (When?), and listener (to Whom?) and that the *affective* ones are attitude and pervasive feeling (Why? and How?). In a given piece of writing these factors may or may not be equally obvious or clear; some may be subservient to others. Generally a reader will look for the cognitive aspects first, since it seems safe to say that for the most part there is no feeling without comprehension of cognitive elements. Or, put it this way, misunderstanding of them distorts a reader's perception of the others.

Let us consider the situational components in several examples. First, in a sonnet:

SHALL I COMPARE THEE

William Shakespeare (1564–1616)

Shall I compare thee to a summer's day?
Thou art more lovely and more temperate:
Rough winds do shake the darling buds of May,
And summer's lease hath all too short a date;
Sometimes too hot the eye of heaven shines,
And often is his gold complexion dimm'd;
And every fair from fair sometimes declines,
By chance or nature's changing course untrimm'd:
But thy eternal summer shall not fade
Nor lose possession of that fair thou ow'st;
Nor shall Death brag thou wand'rest in his shade,
When in eternal lines to time thou grow'st;
    So long as men can breathe or eyes can see,
    So long lives this, and this gives life to thee.

True, Shakespeare is the writer of this sonnet, but the speaker of a poem is not to be confused with the actual author, who may or may not present himself as the speaker. Some writers present the same speaker in all they write; others—Shakespeare in his plays, for example

—present many speakers. Frequently there is great similarity between the speaker of the poem and the author himself, as is the case in this sonnet, where the speaker is a young poet addressing his loved one (Who? to Whom?). As sometimes happens, the time and place (When? Where?) of the situation are not specified in this poem, except that the figurative language, a subject later to be discussed, and total form of the poem may place it in time for many readers. What is the attitude, or what are the feelings evoked by the words? What is the effect of the lines? Reading the poem to yourself, can you hear, in imagination, the voice of the speaker of the lines? Does the voice combine loving admiration, half-teasing in its unexpected refusal to liken the loved one to nature's beauties as less imaginative lovers do, with a hint of allowable pride in the speaker's skill as a poet?

In this sonnet of Shakespeare's we may say, then, that there is a single speaker, defined only as one who pens the lines, addressing a listener defined only as "lovely," and that there is no precise definition of time or place. It is possible to have even less definition than that. For example, let us take a poem by Drayton and one by Dickinson. From the lines themselves it may not be apparent whether the "I" of the poem is man or woman, old or young, although we tend to assume that the poet speaks in each case:

THE PARTING

Michael Drayton (1563–1631)

Since there's no help, come let us kiss and part—
Nay, I have done, you get no more of me;
And I am glad, yea, glad with all my heart,
That thus so cleanly I myself can free;
Shake hands for ever, cancel all our vows,
And when we meet at any time again,
Be it not seen in either of our brows
That we one jot of former love retain.
Now at the last gasp of Love's latest breath,
When, his pulse failing, Passion speechless lies,
When Faith is kneeling by his bed of death,
And Innocence is closing up his eyes,
    —Now if thou wouldst, when all have given him over,
    From death to life thou might'st him yet recover.

MY LIFE CLOSED TWICE BEFORE ITS CLOSE

Emily Dickinson (1830–1886)

My life closed twice before its close;
It yet remains to see
If Immortality unveil
A third event to me,

So huge, so hopeless to conceive,
As these that twice befell.
Parting is all we know of heaven,
And all we need of hell.

Where, as in the second of these poems, the speaker is scarcely defined and the listener even less so, we shall call the situation *open.*[2] Most essays are of this kind, and many narratives. Lyrics tend to be addressed to all who hear, although, as we have seen in Shakespeare's sonnet and in Drayton's, the listener may be specified, in which case the lines are in direct address and the situation comparatively *closed.* Also, the personal and highly emotional quality of many lyrics makes them more closed than open; some seem so private that we feel the writer is speaking only to himself.

Some stories, like the three poems we have read in this chapter, make use of the pronouns *I* and *my.* "The Apostate," at the end of Chapter 6, does this, but in it the writer and the well-defined speaker of the story are not one and the same person. In stories like "Amy Foster" by Joseph Conrad or "La Mère Sauvage" by Guy de Maupassant, however, the "I" of the story seems to be the author himself.

Often the writer lets a third person tell the story or make the comment of the poem, and this third person may be well defined or defined not at all. (The term *point of view* is frequently used in reference to the teller of the story.) In "Sir Patrick Spens," an old Scotch ballad, the speaker of the story does not intrude in any personal way and remains undefined, but he seems omniscient—that is, he knows all that is necessary in the telling of the story:

---

[2] See p. 18 f.

Anonymous

The King sits in Dumferling toune,
   Drinking the blude-reid wine:
"O whar will I get guid sailor,
   To sail this schip of mine?"

Up and spak an eldern knicht,
   Sat at the kings richt kne:
"Sir Patrick Spens is the best sailor,
   That sails upon the se."

The king has written a braid letter,
   And signd it wi his hand,
And sent it to Sir Patrick Spens,
   Was walking on the sand.

The first line that Sir Patrick red,
   A loud lauch lauchéd he;
The next line that Sir Patrick red,
   The tear blinded his ee.

"O wha is this has don this deid,
   This ill deid don to me,
To send me out this time o' the yeir,
   To sail upon the se!

"Mak hast, mak hast my mirry men all,
   Our guid schip sails the morne:"
"O say na sae, my master deir,
   For I feir a deadlie storme.

"Late, late yestreen I saw the new moone,
   Wi the auld moone in hir arme,
And I feir, I feir, my deir master,
   That we will cum to harme."

O our Scots nobles were richt laith
   To weet their cork-heild schoone;
Bot lang owre a' the play wer playd,
   Thair hats they swam aboone.

O lang, lang may their ladies sit,
  Wi thair fans into ther hand;
Or eir they se Sir Patrick Spens
  Cum sailing to the land.

O lang, lang may the ladies stand,
  Wi thair gold kems in their hair,
Waiting for thair ain deir lords,
  For they'll see thame na mair.

Haf owre, haf owre to Aberdour,
  It's fiftie fadom deip,
And thair lies guid Sir Patrick Spens,
  Wi the Scot lords at his feit.

Similar to the storyteller of this ballad, the narrator of Stephen Crane's "The Open Boat" seems to be all-knowing and unobtrusive:

> None of them knew the color of the sky. Their eyes glanced level, and were fastened upon the waves that swept toward them. These waves were of the hue of slate, save for the tops, which were of foaming white, and all of the men knew the colors of the sea. The horizon narrowed and widened, and dipped and rose, and at all times its edge was jagged with waves that seemed thrust up in points like rocks.
>
> Many a man ought to have a bath-tub larger than the boat which here rode upon the sea. These waves were most wrongfully and barbarously abrupt and tall, and each froth-top was a problem in small-boat navigation.
>
> The cook squatted in the bottom and looked with both eyes at the six inches of gunwale which separated him from the ocean. His sleeves were rolled over his fat forearms, and the two flaps of his unbuttoned vest dangled as he bent to bail out the boat. Often he said: "Gawd! That was a narrow clip." As he remarked it he invariably gazed eastward over the broken sea.[3]

---

[3] Stephen Crane, "The Open Boat." Reprinted from *Stephen Crane: An Omnibus,* ed. Robert Wooster Stallman, by permission of Alfred A. Knopf, Inc.; copyright 1952 by Alfred A. Knopf, Inc.

A variation of the omniscient point of view seen in this excerpt is found in stories where one character, either a major or a minor one, is the teller of the story, and everything reported is seen, heard, or thought by that one person. A good example of this is "The First Death of Her Life" by Elizabeth Taylor, which is to be found at the end of Chapter 6.

From the *predominantly open* situation seen in "Sir Patrick Spens" we can move to its opposite, the *closed* situation seen in drama, where there is more than one speaker and the dialogue is an interplay between characters more or less fully drawn. These two situations are not absolutes, of course, and, as we move from an utterance like the ballad, much of which seems to be addressed to all who hear, to a dramatic monologue or a drama, we find the handling of the situational aspects (speaker, listener, and so on) leading from the open to the closed situation moves along a continuum of gradual changes.

So far we have looked at utterances with slight characterization of speaker or listener. Here is a poem in which the single speaker is well characterized and the listener specified, though not fully defined:

THE LABORATORY

Robert Browning (1812–1889)

Now that I, tying thy glass mask tightly,
May gaze through these faint smokes curling whitely,
As thou pliest thy trade in this devil's-smithy—
Which is the poison to poison her, prithee?

He is with her, and they know that I know
Where they are, what they do: they believe my tears flow
While they laugh, laugh at me, at me fled to the drear
Empty church, to pray God in, for them!—I am here.

Grind away, moisten and mash up thy paste,
Pound at thy powder,—I am not in haste!
Better sit thus, and observe thy strange things,
Than go where men wait me and dance at the King's.

That in the mortar—you call it a gum?
Ah, the brave tree whence such gold oozings come!
And yonder soft phial, the exquisite blue,
Sure to taste sweetly,—is that poison too?

Had I but all of them, thee and thy treasures,
What a wild crowd of invisible pleasures!
To carry pure death in an earring, a casket,
A signet, a fan-mount, a filigree basket!

Soon, at the King's, a mere lozenge to give,
And Pauline should have just thirty minutes to live!
But to light a pastile, and Elise, with her head
And her breast and her arms and her hands, should **drop dead!**

Quick—is it finished? The color's too grim!
Why not soft like the phial's, enticing and dim?
Let it brighten her drink, let her turn it and stir,
And try it and taste, ere she fix and prefer!

What a drop! She's not little, no minion like me!
That's why she ensnared him: this never will free
The soul from those masculine eyes,—say, "no!"
To that pulse's magnificent come-and-go.

For only last night, as they whispered, I brought
My own eyes to bear on her so, that I thought
Could I keep them one half minute fixed, she would fall
Shrivelled; she fell not; yet this does it all!

Not that I bid you spare her the pain;
Let death be felt and the proof remain:
Brand, burn up, bite into its grace—
He is sure to remember her dying face!

Is it done? Take my mask off! Nay, be not morose;
It kills her, and this prevents seeing it close:
The delicate droplet, my whole fortune's fee!
If it hurts her, beside, can it ever hurt me?

Now, take all my jewels, gorge gold to your fill,
You may kiss me, old man, on my mouth if you will!
But brush this dust off me, lest horror it brings
Ere I know it—next moment I dance at the King's!

If we accept the word *personality* as referring to the combination of traits distinguishing one person from another, or as "an individual's potential meaning for those who come into contact with him," how clearly can you say Browning depicts the personality of the speaker of this poem? Is the speaker man or woman? Young or old? From what social class? What does "minion" mean in this context? What motivates the speaker? Are there any hints as to the speaker's bearing and appearance? What is the implication when the speaker invites the kiss "on the mouth"? Do you admire the speaker? Why?

The listener in this poem is called "old man" and is described as busy concocting poisons; he is thus specified but not defined in any detail. Although his presence is sensed several times by the speaker and his actions are observed, he does not seem to furnish the speaker the chief motivation for the words spoken. Not many details of the setting are given, but, with the title and with phrases like "faint smokes curling whitely" and "brush this dust off me, lest horror it brings," the author creates a definite atmosphere contributing to the pervasive feeling of the entire poem. What words would you use to denote this feeling? What is the total effect the poem seems to produce?

As we have said, the *closed* situation sometimes gives us more than one speaker and reveals the interplay of characters. This form is typical of drama, but it is found also in this ballad, where mother and son speak alternately, without any author comment:

LORD RANDAL

Anonymous

"O where hae ye been, Lord Randal, my son?
O where hae ye been, my handsome young man?"
"I hae been to the wild wood; mother, make my bed soon,
For I'm weary wi' hunting, and fain wald lie down."

"Where gat ye your dinner, Lord Randal, my son?
Where gat ye your dinner, my handsome young man?"
"I dined wi' my true-love; mother make my bed soon,
For I'm weary wi' hunting, and fain wald lie down."

"What gat ye to your dinner, Lord Randal, my son?
What gat ye to your dinner, my handsome young man?"
"I gat eels boil'd in broo; mother, make my bed soon,
For I'm weary wi' hunting, and fain wald lie down."

"What became of your bloodhounds, Lord Randal, my son?
What became of your bloodhounds, my handsome young
    man?"
"O they swell'd and they died; mother, make my bed soon,
For I'm weary wi' hunting, and fain wald lie down."

"O I fear ye are poison'd, Lord Randal, my son!
O I fear ye are poison'd, my handsome young man!"
"O yes! I am poison'd; mother, make my bed soon,
For I'm sick at the heart, and I fain wald lie down."

Many hints are here furnished us, but much is left for the imagination to fill in. The immediate situation is clear: a young man presumably has been hunting; he returns home and reports to his mother that he dined with his true-love, eating eels in broth, and that his dogs died; he has been poisoned. But there is more to the story than that: Is the mother unduly suspicious, does she jump to conclusions? Has she connived with the "true-love"? What kind of mother is she? Does Lord Randal know from the beginning of the conversation that he is poisoned? If not, where does his realization come and why? Does he say "true-love" affectionately, bitterly, or ironically? Why did the dogs die? How do you account for the variation of the refrain in the last line? Who is the central character in this story?

Thus far we have been largely concerned with the *cognitive* elements of the selection, examining particularly the speaker and the listener aspects of the situation. Let us look now at the *affective* elements, the *Why?* and *How?*—or the attitude and pervasive feeling of the selection. The attitude of the speaker includes both his position toward the *What?* of the composition and toward the listener. It is a composite of subject and style, coloring an entire work. In a short poem the dominant attitude tends to be single, but in longer works it is heightened by the use of variety and contrasts, shadings and nuances. In general, attitudes are of three kinds: the speaker invites a favorable, approving response, or an unfavorable, disapproving one, or an undecided one. There are innumerable degrees and variations of these three. A little introspection over a day's time will reveal that our feelings do indeed run a range, conditioned not only by the subject of our conversation, but also by our listeners, the time and place, and our intention. And as feeling and attitude change, there are changes in language, and vice versa, though the *subject* of the utterance remains the same. Thus Wordsworth, in the early nineteenth century, and Kenneth Fearing, in the twentieth, both deplore materialism, but they do not write the same way. Compare the attitudes of these poems:

THE WORLD IS TOO MUCH WITH US

William Wordsworth (1770–1850)

The world is too much with us; late and soon,
Getting and spending, we lay waste our powers:
Little we see in Nature that is ours;
We have given our hearts away, a sordid boon!
This sea that bares her bosom to the moon;
The winds that will be howling at all hours,
And are up-gather'd now like sleeping flowers;
For this, for everything, we are out of tune;
It moves us not.—Great God! I'd rather be
A Pagan suckled in a creed outworn;
So might I, standing on this pleasant lea,
Have glimpses that would make me less forlorn;
Have sight of Proteus rising from the sea;
Or hear old Triton blow his wreathèd horn.

DIRGE

Kenneth Fearing (1902–   )

1-2-3 was the number he played but today the number
    came 3-2-1;
    bought his Carbide at 30 and it went to 29; had the
    favorite at Bowie but the track was slow—

O, executive type, would you like to drive a floating
    power, knee-action, silk-upholstered six? Wed a
    Hollywood star? Shoot the course in 58? Draw to
    the ace, king, jack?
O, fellow with a will who won't take no, watch out
    for three cigarettes on the same, single match; O
    democratic voter born in August under Mars, be-
    ware of liquidated rails—

Dénouement to dénouement, he took a personal pride in
    the certain, certain way he lived his own, private
    life,
  but nevertheless, they shut off his gas; nevertheless,
    the bank foreclosed; nevertheless, the landlord
    called; nevertheless, the radio broke,

And twelve o'clock arrived just once too often,
    just the same he wore one grey tweed suit, bought one
    straw hat, drank one straight Scotch, walked one
    short step, took one long look, drew one deep
    breath,
  just one too many,

And wow he died as wow he lived,
    going whop to the office and blooie home to sleep and
    biff got married and bam had children and oof got
    fired,
  zowie did he live and zowie did he die,

With who the hell are you at the corner of his casket,
    and where the hell we going on the right hand
    silver knob, and who the hell cares walking second
    from the end with an American Beauty wreath
    from why the hell not.

Very much missed by the circulation staff of the New
    York Evening Post; deeply, deeply mourned by the
    B.M.T.,

Wham, Mr. Roosevelt; pow, Sears Roebuck; awk, big
    dipper; bop, summer rain;
  bong, Mr., bong, Mr., bong, Mr., bong.

We are not yet ready to point to all the differences between these
poems, but even a preliminary reading will reveal that Wordsworth
speaks seriously and formally and that Fearing speaks satirically, almost sneeringly, and in a familiar, colloquial fashion. The vocabulary
of the sonnet seems a step removed from that of our daily conversation, whereas Fearing to serve his purpose employs slang and cliché.
On the whole, Wordsworth asks us to accept what he says; he speaks

persuasively in his indictment of man's concentration upon earning money and spending it and gives us a view of Nature to which ideally we would respond. We might say that the attitude is chiefly rational. Fearing's attitude seems chiefly that of comedy, and he intends that, with him, we reject the picture of man which he gives us. He mocks both the advertiser and the purchaser, pointing ironically to the conformity which characterizes modern man, to his superstitions, and to his inconsequentiality. These two poems, then, treating the same subject, show sharp contrast in attitude, or in the affective elements which we have called the *Why?* and *How?* of the literary object.

In this preliminary view of the literary whole we have scrutinized the cognitive elements of a selection, asking by whom the words are spoken, to whom, when and where, and what is said. The attitude of the speaker and the pervasive feeling of the selection or the tone of voice in which the words seem to be spoken constitute the affective elements. The situation may be *open*, with little definition of listener or time and place and with speaker more or less defined, or it may be *closed* as we find it in dramatic dialogue. Between these two extremes there is a changing scale of varieties in definition and specification of the situational aspects. In any literary object, however, something is being said, and we are now ready to turn our attention to the theme or the comment of the literary object.

Emergence of Theme

The framework of cognitive and affective elements we have just viewed may be likened to a man's skeleton, the details we are about to discuss to his flesh and blood. Without the padding of muscles, connective tissue, and blood vessels and nerves there is no life, and it is the total relation of skeleton and the rest of man's body that individualizes him. In literature *theme* is the compound of thinking and feeling, simple or complex, arising from the interrelationships of all the elements of the writing, but particularly from the *What? How?* and *Why?* It is the total comment made by the writer. It may or may not be a positive belief, but it is indicative of a set of values and a view of life. Just as people differ in finding the point of a joke, so do readers differ in their perception of theme. Less sophisticated readers accept "pat" morals or tags like that in Longfellow's "Psalm of Life," while others prefer hidden gold as did Bassanio when he chose the leaden casket. The latter readers are alert to the many kinds of clues a writer uses, and enjoy the writer's ability to furnish such guides in a subtle, complex fashion. The skillful writer organizes and controls the experience he evokes, at the same time leaving room for the reader's imagination and creativity.

The title of a work is the first clue furnished us. Why "My Last Duchess" instead of "My Late Duchess"? Why "A Downward Path to Wisdom" when we all know wisdom leads upward? Why "The Killers" when the story is not about them, but about Nick, a young boy growing up? Why "Two Blue Birds" for a story of coldness between man and wife? Or "A Bottle of Milk for Mother" for a story of murder? Or "Neutral Tones" for a poem about love's disillusionment? Sometimes the title points simply to the subject or the situation, and sometimes it is ironic, signaling the tensions developed in the story, poem, or drama. Look for ways in which the title connects with the work itself, leading the reader to both cognitive and affective elements. A good example of an ironic title is found in Fearing's poem "Dirge," quoted in the preceding section. The dictionary defines a dirge as the "Office for the Dead" and as a composition "expressive of grief," accompanying funeral rites. The title prepares us, then, for words of bereavement, but the poem itself contradicts this expectation, and the tension thus created gives rise to bitter amusement. Fearing asks not for grief but for laughing scorn.

A second clue may be in the author's life and in statements made by and about him. The intellectual climate surrounding a writer affects both what he says and how he says it. So too do his own experiences—his economic and social environment, his education, and all cultural and personal influences. Information beyond his birth and death dates often illuminates his words for us, helping us to look beneath the surface of the lines. In "Mr. Flood's Party," for example, are these lines: "He set the jug down slowly at his feet/With trembling care, knowing that most things break." [4] A reader who knows anything about Edwin Arlington Robinson's broken familial and social relations finds in the words a poignancy otherwise unperceived, and the lines point to the theme, which is *not*, as a student recently called it, drunkenness! Some writers aid us by their own statements about their

---

[4] Edwin Arlington Robinson, "Mr. Flood's Party," from *Collected Poems* by Edwin Arlington Robinson, copyright 1921 by E. A. Robinson, copyright renewed, 1949, and used by permission of The Macmillan Company.

works—T. S. Eliot, Henry James, or George Bernard Shaw, among others. Such statements may be both expressions of general philosophy and notes on specific works. What others say by way of criticism of an author is also helpful, but criticism should be read after one has done careful study himself; it can never be a substitute for first-hand acquaintance with the literature.

Key lines, like those quoted from Robinson's poem, are third clues to meanings. When an author interrupts the action of a story to make comments applicable to all men, not just to the John or Jane of the story, when he moves from the particular to the general, he is giving us a signal. In Frost's "Home Burial," a dialogue between a man and a woman who have buried their child, the woman says: "The nearest friends can go/With anyone to death, comes so far short/They might as well not go at all." [5] That sentence clarifies her view toward death, a view not shared by her husband. In Sophocles' *Antigone*, at the close of the play, the leader of the chorus speaks these key lines: "There is no happiness where there is no wisdom;/No wisdom but in submission to the gods./Big words are always punished,/And proud men in old age learn to be wise." [6] Here, a general statement points to theme and helps us to know what, within the play, to emphasize, what to subordinate.

The key line may introduce the work as it does in W. H. Auden's poem "Musée des Beaux Arts": "About suffering they were never wrong,/The Old Masters: how well they understood/Its human position . . ." [7] The rest of the poem enumerates illustrations of this observation, and without attention to the words just quoted the reader might well miss the statement which the author makes.

Sometimes a key line is repeated, setting up a rhythm and serving as an echo which helps organize the experience of the entire work. This is evident in "The Lament." [8] Occasionally key lines and titles are connected, as in Marjorie Kinnan Rawlings' story entitled "Cocks Must Crow." When the teller of the story sees her husband, whom she has tried to boss, enter a winning cock in a cock fight, when, unseen by him, she observes the pride in his face as he lifts up the cock

---

[5] Robert Frost, "Home Burial," from *Complete Poems of Robert Frost*. Copyright, 1930, 1949, by Henry Holt and Company, Inc. By permission of Holt, Rinehart and Winston, Inc.

[6] From *The Antigone of Sophocles*, an English version by Dudley Fitts and Robert Fitzgerald (New York: Harcourt, Brace and Company, Inc., 1939).

[7] See p. 137.

[8] See p. 180.

with its broken wing, she says, "And I knew cocks must crow," a remark which is both figurative and literal and points to the theme of the whole story. Such repetitions are often called *motifs*.

Examples given so far relate to the cognitive elements of the selection. Theme, as has been said, relates also to the affective elements. The author asks us to go along with him, adopting a certain attitude toward the subject matter: to laugh, to deplore, to pity, to question, sneer, wonder, and so on. He establishes a dominant mood, with or without contrast and variety, and he promotes a certain effect. He speaks in a certain way and for a reason. Our awareness of the whole literary object will be a blend of thinking and feeling, and words purposely arranged produce the totality or whole, which combines form with feeling.

Style

Style is an all-inclusive term pertaining to the choice and arrangement of words, the selection and arrangement of content, rhythm, and structure. In a narrower sense let us use *diction*, to refer to the correctness, clarity, appropriateness, and vividness of the words chosen by the writer.

Diction

IMAGERY AND CONCRETE LANGUAGE. A single word may carry meaning as idea, as sound, and as symbol. We shall look now at word meaning as idea. In literature there is much use of concrete language, of specific references, and of appeals to sensory response, all of which contribute to clarity and vividness. *Hunter* is a more specific word than *sportsman*; *African Bushman hunter* brings clearer meaning—to an anthropologist, at least—than the single word *hunter*. *The long-legged African Bushman hunter, clad in breech-cloth, his skin black and his hair kinky, his bow slung over his shoulder* brings into focus a visual image. *Music was heard* is less meaningful than *The gramophone blared out a jazz tune of the twenties*. In the second sentence the auditory image is vivid and exact, the author directing the reader's experience with concrete, specific words.

Besides appeals to the visual and auditory senses, the writer may use words calling forth memories of taste, smell, touch, movement, and of general muscle tonus or degree of muscle tension and relaxation. These senses are the individual's avenues to life—the means by which he becomes aware of the world around him. Although it is true that modern psychology speaks of more kinds of senses than those we have just named, a limited list will be sufficient for our purposes. The writer usually directs attention more to one sense impression than to another, but he may wish to evoke several that are subordinate to the primary sense appeal. A single image—*stagnant pool, icy wind,* or *stale coffee*—can evoke a prism of sensory responses. What dominates for one reader may not do so for another, but we need always to consider what the primary image seems to be. If the line is, A *nauseous, acrid odor filled the room,* attention obviously is first directed to the sense of smell, although the interpreter speaking the lines might at the same time sense a stinging in the eyes such as could be caused by foul air, and he might also sense a general increase in body tension, which accompanies discomfort.

Here is a paragraph by Somerset Maugham loaded with concrete words and appeals to the senses:

> He scratched his mosquito bites. He felt very short-tempered. When the rain stopped and the sun shone, it was like a hot-house, seething, humid, sultry, breathless, and you had a strange feeling that everything was growing with savage violence. The natives, blithe and childlike by reputation, seemed then, with their tattooing and their dyed hair, to have something sinister in their appearance; and when they pattered along at your heels with their naked feet you looked back instinctively. You felt they might at any moment come behind you swiftly and thrust a long knife between your shoulder blades. You could not tell what dark thoughts lurked behind their wide-set eyes. They had a little the look of ancient Egyptians painted on a temple wall, and there was about them the terror of what is immeasurably old.[9]

No doubt we would agree that the paragraph as a whole stirs up feelings of uneasiness and apprehension and increases over-all body tension. In other words, the primary sensory appeal is kinesthetic.

---

[9] Somerset Maugham, "Miss Thompson," *The Trembling of a Leaf* (New York: Doubleday & Company, Inc., 1921). Permission by Doubleday & Company, Inc., Mr. W. Somerset Maugham, and Messrs. William Heinemann Ltd.

There are also specific movements imaged, as in the words *scratched, looked back,* and *thrust.* The sentence about the rain may evoke, secondarily, memories of the smell of rain, the look of it, and the feeling of heat and humidity against the skin. (Memory of heat and cold seems to combine the kinesthetic and the tactile sense.) We will tend to see, in our minds, the natives with *tattooing and their dyed hair* and to hear them as they *patter along* (which is also a certain way of moving) on *naked feet.* The idea of a knife between shoulder blades, though primarily kinesthetic, can bring visual response and perhaps auditory (the sound of a knife driven into flesh). There is visualization again in the last two sentences, and an increase in tension. Thus, in one short paragraph, by an author's use of concrete, specific words, we find appeals to the sense of sight, hearing, touch, muscle tone, and muscular movement.

CONNOTATION. Sometimes language is used less for what it denotes than for what it suggests or connotes. We rely on the dictionary for denotative meanings; we find connotative ones in our experience or background. The latter are associated or implied meanings—fringes of meaning and extra-literal meanings, often leading directly to the affective elements of a selection. Note how different feelings arise from these words: *boy, urchin, lad, youth, a male of ten.* Feeling differs because connotation differs. Take a common noun like *tree,* which the dictionary tells us is a "woody, perennial plant having a single main axis or stem commonly exceeding ten feet in height." Is that all that *tree* means to you? Or does it mean the apple tree you climbed as a child, a coconut palm bending in the trade winds, or the welcome shade of an elm on a hot day? Or does it symbolize the tree of life? According to our own knowledge and experiences, and depending upon the context in which the word is found, connotations vary. By his choice and arrangement of words a writer controls the associations or connotations of the words in any passage, and the reader too must control them. When Amy Lowell describes a garden and speaks of "night-scented stock," she is not appealing to one's memory of the barnyard. When the speaker in Browning's poem, "Count Gismond," says, wiping away a tear, "how vain," she is not admitting that she is arrogant! Proper denotation precedes connotation.

FIGURES OF SPEECH. Figurative language, in particular, contributes to connotation and the suggestive power of words. Poetry is full of such use of language. There are several possible classifications; we shall use five terms: personification, hyperbole, irony, metaphor, and simile.

Personification is a device that lends vividness to the writing, as may be seen in the Drayton poem (quoted earlier in this chapter) in which Love, Passion, Faith, and Innocence all are given human attributes— Love has breath and pulse; Passion, speech; Faith kneels; and Innocence apparently has hands and fingers. *Hyperbole*, or gross exaggeration, is often heard in daily conversation (*I nearly died laughing!*) and is used by writers also, as when, in "Dirge," Fearing says, "deeply, deeply mourned by the B.M.T." (There is personification here also.) B.M.T., of course, is the Brooklyn-Manhattan Transit system, hereafter to be deprived of one commuter who will scarcely be missed. In this instance, hyperbole gives both emphasis and irony. *Irony* itself is a rhetorical device or use of figurative language in which the intended implication of the words is the opposite of the literal sense of them. Sometimes it is found in the disparity between expectation and realization, as in the title of Fearing's poem. In drama, irony is often found between what the character seems to be and what he really is, or between what the character believes to be true and what we in the audience know to be true.

Probably the most frequently used figures are *metaphor* and *simile*, both of which use comparison as a basis. *Like* and *as* are signs of the simile; dozens of our clichés are of this sort—*blue as indigo, mad as a hatter, sweet as honey*, and *grew like a weed*. These expressions are devoid of life, because, when we use them, we no longer think of indigo or, perhaps, even know what a hatter is. When poets, however, show originality and imagination in the comparisons to which they point, we feel that the comparison arrests attention and gives vivid meaning, as in Sandburg's line, "Pocahontas' body, lovely as a poplar, sweet as a red haw in November or a pawpaw in May." [10] The similes richly connote grace, slenderness, fragrance, and the freshness of youth. They influence our feelings, arousing our admiration for Pocahontas; the effect is swift, direct, and economical.

A *metaphor*, sometimes called an implied simile, functions in much the same way, but it omits the words *like* and *as*. It might be designated the art of name-calling; we use it in daily conversation when we say, "She's a doll," or "He's a shrimp." (These examples of metaphor are also epithet.) The hero of Eliot's poem, "The Love Song of J. Alfred Prufrock," says, ". . . I have measured out my life in coffee

---

[10] Carl Sandburg, "Cool Tombs," from *Cornhuskers* (New York: Henry Holt and Company, Inc., 1918).

spoons . . ." and asks, ". . . Then how should I begin/To spit out all the butt-ends of my days and ways? . . ." [11] Clearly life, literally, cannot be measured by coffee spoons, nor do days have butt-ends, but the poet's relating hitherto unrelated objects suddenly illuminates our vision of a life that has not known fulfillment. Comparison gives the entire frame to these lines:

MY LOVE IS LIKE TO ICE

Edmund Spenser (1552–1599)

My love is like to ice, and I to fire:
How comes it then that this her cold so great
Is not dissolved through my so hot desire,
But harder grows the more I her entreat?
Or how comes it that my exceeding heat
Is not allayed by her heart-frozen cold,
But that I burn much more in boiling sweat,
And feel my flames augmented manifold?
What more miraculous things may be told,
That fire, which all things melts, should harden ice,
And ice, which is congeal'd with senseless cold,
Should kindle fire by wonderful device?
    Such is the power of love in gentle mind,
    That it can alter all the course of kind.

The first line of the poem gives us a simile, but in the rest of the poem the simile is extended and the meaning expressed metaphorically.

It has been said that words themselves are fossil poetry. This is to say that all language has a figurative basis. Ample evidence of this lies in any unabridged dictionary and makes a dictionary truly illuminating reading! Look up the story behind these words: *caprice, scapegoat, scuttlebutt, filibuster, tarantella*—or find out what it means *to tap the admiral.*

With use through the decades words change meaning and lose meaning. In a comment about the poet E. E. Cummings, R. P. Blackmur explains some of this loss of word meanings:

[11] T. S. Eliot, "The Love Song of J. Alfred Prufrock," from *Collected Poems 1909–1934* by T. S. Eliot, copyright, 1936, by Harcourt, Brace and Company, Inc., and reprinted with their permission.

Since people are occupied mostly with communication and argument and conversation, with the erection of discursive relationships, words are commonly spoken and written with the *least* possible meanings preserved, instead of the most. History is taken for granted, ignored, or denied. Only the outsides of words, so to speak, are used; and doubtless the outsides of words are all the discursive intellect needs. But when a word is used in a poem it should be the sum of all its appropriate history made concrete and particular in the individual context; and in poetry all words act *as if* they were so used, because the only kind of meaning poetry can have requires that all its words resume their full life; the full life being modified and made unique by the *qualifications* the words perform one upon the other in the poem.[12]

ALLUSIONS. The full life of the word rests often upon what are called *allusions.* Having both denotative and connotative value, these references to familiar historical and literary items contribute to the suggestive power of words, and, unless we recognize the basic frame of reference, they are meaningless in the context. Allusions may be in the form of proper names or of phrases which call to mind certain events or literary works. Some writers, especially those of centuries prior to ours, assume that their readers will quickly recognize and have knowledge of allusions to the Bible and to classical mythology. Topical allusions of our own time may be immediately intelligible to us, but future generations of readers may find "a day that will live in infamy" as perplexing as "the faith that moveth mountains" is to one who has never read the Bible. In our daily conversation many allusions appear, some of which are trite and hackneyed: *according to Hoyle; the land of the free and the home of the brave; a rose by any other name; a pound of flesh; the bard of Avon; the Midas touch; a Don Juan; the patience of Job; grew like Topsy;* and many more. Allusions are "dead" unless we know the connotations and connections with their sources. When we know the story behind proper names, the fabric of the writing is enriched by our recognition of what Blackmur calls the "full life" of words.

The poem "Dirge" which appears earlier in this chapter has many topical allusions, some of which you may not have understood. "Hollywood star" and "Shoot the course in 58" are easy, but what about the first stanza of the poem, which gives three separate, topical allusions—can you identify them?

Here is a list of words, phrases, and proper names upon which to

---

[12] R. P. Blackmur, *Language and Gesture* (New York: Harcourt, Brace and Company, Inc., 1952), p. 323.

test yourself; understanding of any of them rests upon recognition of an allusion:

a bed of Procrustes
a veritable Cassandra
a doubting Thomas
a quisling
Charon's boat
a coat of many colors
the Gibson girl
a modern Croesus
"Sophocles long ago/Heard it on the Aegean"
"Leda and the Swan"
Brueghel's *Icarus*
the skull of Pharaoh
a Montague-Capulet romance
the tortoise and the hare
the day Persephone returns to earth
"On Looking into Chapman's Homer"

bust of Pallas
Carrara marble
a World War II Madame Butterfly
the face that launched a thousand ships
money-changers at the temple
no room at the inn
tilting at windmills
thirty pieces of silver
Phoebus's chariot
a Hydra-headed problem
Hymeneal bonds
the peace that passeth understanding
Janus-faced
"a Daniel come to judgment"
the seven Deadly sins

Recently a writer remarked that "Even the average college student yearns vaguely for a life that will provide him with the wealth of a Texas oil man, the social position of a Lodge in Boston or at least a Swift in Lake Forest, the general intelligence of Walter Lippmann, the experience of Ernest Hemingway, and the mobility of Eleanor Roosevelt." [13] You probably recognize these allusions. And it is hoped you would laugh if anyone told you he was "as loyal to you as Jezebel was to Ahab!"

LEVELS OF USAGE. Further considering diction as an element of style, we turn attention to levels of usage or appropriateness of language. For many centuries strict rules obtained for what were called *high, middle,* and *plain* styles of writing. Generally speaking, epic and tragedy were couched in language of the high style; comedy used the middle style; familiar letters and conversation employed the plain style. Differences in the styles were evident in choice of vocabulary and in word arrangement, both of which were dictated supposedly by appropriateness to subject matter. Poetry was the form of the high style and

---

[13] Martin J. Svaglic, "On Teaching the Appreciation of Literature," *AAUP Bulletin,* Vol. 39, No. 3 (Autumn 1953), 491.

of some of the middle, and even today there are occasionally those who maintain that poetry is the proper vehicle for drama, particularly for tragic drama. Ever since the eighteenth century, however, prose has been more and more the usual form of drama, and the theory of the "genres" no longer dictates to writers of any form of literature. Poets write about any subject whatsoever and do not restrict themselves to a "poetic" vocabulary, and prose writers show similar freedom. (A poet's freedom in these respects in illustrated in "The Ballad of Billy Potts" by Robert Penn Warren.)

This freedom does not mean, on the other hand, that appropriateness is no longer a guide or that vocabulary does not set a tone. Even an elementary book on composition will include discussion of what is called *levels of usage*. Language forms and words appropriate to a doctoral dissertation are not those the same writer would use in an article on the same subject for the *Saturday Evening Post* or in a dinner-table conversation with friends from other professions. Instead of the words *high, middle,* and *plain* regarding language, contemporary scholars substitute the words *formal, informal,* and *vulgate*.[14] The vocabulary of the vulgate includes elisions, slang, colloquialisms, clichés, and a prevalence of short words; the level is characterized further by short sentences and by gross errors in language forms (*lay* for *lie, he don't, between you and I, they was,* and others). When a character in a story or drama uses it, the implication is that the speaker is uneducated and probably from the lower end of the social and economic scale. The informal level of usage, heard in the conversation of educated speakers, is used throughout literature in novels, plays, short stories, and much poetry. It is idiomatic, uses a larger vocabulary and more frequent allusions than the vulgate, and does not depart from accepted language forms. Some poetry and some fiction employ the formal level, addressing a somewhat more limited audience than the other two levels. The three levels are not to be thought of as mutually exclusive. They may overlap, especially when a writer departs deliberately from his customary informal level to characterize as O'Neill does in Yank's lines in *The Hairy Ape,* or as Wilde does, in the opposite direction, in Lady Bracknell's speeches in *The Importance of Being Earnest.* Finding a young man on his knees in front of her daughter, Lady Bracknell says, "Arise, sir, from this semi-recumbent posture." Informal usage might be, "Young man, stand up!" and the vulgate, "On your feet."

---

[14] See Porter G. Perrin, *Writer's Guide and An Index to English,* rev. ed. (Chicago: Scott, Foresman and Company, 1950), pp. 37–55.

"Befuddled" could be said to be a formal word equivalent to "woozy," a vulgate word, or "tipsy," an informal word. Today we might say "Scram!" would be the vulgate equivalent of the formal "Get thee hence!" though, to Shakespeare, the latter would not sound as it does to us.

At this point you might well reread the poems quoted in this chapter, noting what general level of usage the writer has employed and how that level contributes to the feeling of the whole. Good contrast is afforded by the Wordsworth sonnet and the Fearing poem, the latter being largely the plain, low, or vulgate level, which serves the writer's satiric intent. (The informal level, however, overlaps the other.)

In this section we have been talking about diction as an element of style, and we have explored three aspects of it: concrete language, suggestive power of words, and levels of usage. We are now ready to look at structure as an element of style.

Structure: Thought Patterns

Ordinarily we think and speak in word groups or phrases, which function as grammatical and rhetorical units of meaning. True, to an extent the structure of the language itself governs groupings. There are, nevertheless, innumerable ways of shaping a thought, and a writer's choice and preference for certain word-group arrangements create patterns, which are elements of style.

A grammatical phrase is a group of two or more words, without subject or predicate, which, though they serve as sense units, are incomplete or fragmentary in the expression of thought. Words in a phrase are variously arranged, but together they make an aggregate, as do these examples: *before the holiday, hit on the head, his car being stolen, to read a book, will have flunked, the study of history, a commanding stature,* and so on.

Out of the phrase comes the sentence, a word group between end stops, or, as it has been defined, "an independent linguistic form, not included by virtue of any grammatical construction in any larger linguistic form." [15] Sentence structure varies from language to language. English, like most other Indo-European languages, uses a subject-and-predicate construction. In other words, "Reduced to its

---

[15] Charles C. Fries, *The Structure of English* (New York: Harcourt, Brace and Company, Inc., 1952), p. 21.

essence, a good English sentence is a *statement* (in idiomatic word order) *that an agent* (the subject of the sentence) *performed an action* (the verb) *upon something* (the object)." [16] This construction provides the possibility of basic variations that create patterns varying from writer to writer and, indeed, from century to century.[17] In some sentences nouns and verbs greatly outnumber adjectives and adverbs, but in others the opposite is true. In some, phrase is piled on phrase; in others, clause follows clause: *Looking about hesitantly, the little boy, clad in blue jeans, came to the center of the stage;* or, *The little boy was clad in blue jeans; he looked about hesitantly, and then he came to the center of the stage.* Whatever form is used, a successful sentence makes the writer's thought clear and advances the reader's understanding.

Sentences in a paragraph link thoughts and produce a chain of thought; a series of linking paragraphs forms an essay, narrative, or drama. When we were discussing words as ideas, we were examining the smallest denominators of a writer's or a speaker's thought; the next larger units are the phrase, then the sentence, and then the paragraph. A paragraph is a group of related sentences which carry thought forward and develop feeling. The device of indentation signals a transition in thought, either major or minor. A paragraph may be as long or as short as serves the writer's purpose, although it is conventional for each speech in narrative or dramatic dialogue to be set in a separate paragraph. It could be said that the word is to the phrase as the phrase is to the sentence, the sentence to the paragraph, and the paragraph to the fabric of the entire piece of writing.

A stanza of poetry may be likened to a paragraph of prose. Stanzas, too, vary in length; in a given poem the stanzas may all have the same number of lines, but the number of words and the number of thought groups within a stanza will differ, and the close of a stanza may or may not have an end stop. (Generally speaking, a prose paragraph closes with an end stop.) When there is no end stop at a stanza's close, the succeeding stanza will be even more closely linked to the thought of the first than is otherwise the case. An illustration of this is seen in the Dickinson poem quoted earlier in the chapter, whereas in "Sir

----

[16] John Ciardi, "How Does a Poem Mean?" Part Three of *An Introduction to Literature* by Barrows, Heffner, Ciardi, and Douglas (Boston: Houghton Mifflin Company, 1959), p. 787.

[17] See Josephine Miles, *Eras and Modes in English Poetry* (Berkeley: The University of California Press, 1957).

Patrick Spens" each stanza, while carrying the thought forward, is also a self-contained unit.

A reader may "connect" with all the words as separate entities and yet miss their organization, thereby failing in his understanding of the sentence. Short sentences which use the normal word order of agent-action-object offer little difficulty, but more skill is demanded from the reader when the writer uses ellipses, inversions, and many qualifying phrases, and when he separates subject and verb by numerous contributing details. But be it five or fifty-five words long, the main elements of any sentence are subject and predicate (the verb and its dependent words):

The Lord *is my shepherd.*
  S   P

"The" is here a structural word, demanded by English style, and "my" is a content word, qualifying "shepherd." All five words constitute an idea pattern, which in this case is also a sentence.

A reader "connecting" with all the words but not apprehending the thought of the sentence may find the key by isolating the main elements. After he identifies them, the secondary elements, the appositives, and the connectives will ordinarily fall into place. Many an oral interpreter of the Wordsworth sonnet, to which several references have been made in this chapter, has found the words "a sordid boom" troublesome. Do you see that they are equated with "hearts"? Possibly one does not need to know all the labels for the grammatical elements of a sentence or for the syntax, but unless the relationships between the parts and the whole are grasped meaning will not be comprehensible.

Here is a sentence from *Richard II* which demands considerable skill in sensing relationships:

> For that our kingdom's earth should not be soil'd
> With that dear blood which it hath fostered;
> And for our eyes do hate the dire aspect
> Of civil wounds plough'd up with neighbours' sword;
> And for we think the eagle-winged pride
> Of sky-aspiring and ambitious thoughts,
> With rival-hating envy, set on you
> To wake our peace, which in our country's cradle
> Draws the sweet infant breath of gentle sleep;

Which, so rous'd up with bois'trous untun'd drums,
With harsh-resounding trumpets' dreadful bray,
And grating shock of wrathful iron arms,
Might from our quiet confines fright fair Peace
And make us wade even in our kindred's blood;
Therefore, we banish you our territories.

I. iii. 125–139

In this example of a long, complex, compound periodic sentence, the agent-action-object words are "we banish you." What relationship do the word groups set off by semicolons bear to the main elements of the sentence? How is the "for" used in the first, third, and fifth lines? What is the subject of "set"? What is the antecedent of "which" in line ten, and to what verb is it linked? Unless such relationships are firmly grasped, an interpreter voicing the words will fail to make meaning clear to his listener.

Sentences can be studied and analyzed in different ways. We observe varieties in style by noting sentence lengths in number of words, the number and length of the word groups, the omission of one or more elements, the number of clauses and their relationship to one another, the essential and nonessential parts, the order and proportion of the parts, and the relationship of the sentence to what preceded and what follows. Patterns will differ as we move from one writer to another and from one selection to another. In conventional poetry, phrases and sentences fit into line and stanza design, about which more will be said in the next section of this chapter. Free verse and prose sentences make a pattern, but not so highly marked or regular a pattern.

Centuries ago Aristotle observed that a poem (the word is used to denote any piece of imaginative writing) must have a beginning, a middle, and an end. The paragraphs of a story, essay, or drama and the stanzas of a poem may be so grouped; the beginning, or introduction, and the end, or conclusion, are normally brief, and the middle, or body, forms the greatest part of the work. The middle section carries thought and feeling forward to a climax, a point of intensity which may, in a composition of some length, be reached by a series of subclimaxes. In relatively short compositions, the climax may coincide with the close, but in longer works the climax ordinarily is followed by a more relaxed unit, variously called resolution, or denouement.

The end or close, in either case, leaves us with the feeling that we have come "full circle."

Structure: Rhythm

All language is a complex of sound and meaning. In both prose and poetry the total effect of the arrangement of words within word groups, word groups within sentences, sentences within paragraphs or stanzas, and paragraphs or stanzas within the entire composition yields what we call *rhythm*. Rhythm is omnipresent, and yet it eludes easy definition. Its universal importance is indicated by this statement:

Life, in all its forms, is a manifestation of a quickening force sensed as energy. Coexistent with this force, and regulating its flow, is the phenomenon of rhythm. Without its principle of order and proportion all would be chaos. Its presence is revealed in the life patterns and forms of all organic processes. Man and everything that he does are subject to its rules of organization. Nothing escapes. Feelings and thoughts, as well as actions, are subject to this rhythmic scheme.[18]

In what is a half-truth, it has been observed that "we are too familiar with rhythm to recognize it; we know it only in its absence."[19] The unabridged dictionary devotes most of a column to definitions of rhythm; it is said to be "the flow of cadences in written or spoken language," "movement marked by regular recurrence of, or regular alternation in, features, elements, phenomena," and "the regular recurrence of like features in a composition." We see it in the wash of the breakers on the beach, the seasonal flight of birds, the return of day and night, the cycle of the seasons, the phases of the moon, and the myriad other patterns of flux and reflux in nature's universe. We hear it in music and feel it in the dance. We sense it in the difference in riding horseback at a gallop, a trot, a canter, and a walk; the route and distance covered may be the same, but the feeling of the whole ride varies as the rhythm of the gait changes. Frequently psychologists state that the basis of rhythm is within ourselves, in our pulse, our breathing, and our muscular movements with their alternating tension and relaxation. Wilhelm Wundt, noted psychologist, believed that

---

[18] Margaret N. H'Doubler, *Dance: A Creative Art Experience* (Madison: The University of Wisconsin Press, 1957), p. 161.
[19] J. H. Scott and Zilpha E. Chandler, *Phrasal Patterns in English Prose* (New York: The Ronald Press Company, 1932), p. 118.

man's pleasure in rhythm came from the repetition of feelings of tension and from the contrast between feelings of tension and relaxation. Some philosophers say rhythm really exists in the mind, being an organization of impulses, dependent upon the frequency, the duration, and the arrangement of stress and unstress in the stimuli offered. Repetition is a primal principle, and, indeed, one definition is that rhythm is a repeated, recognizable pattern of stress. Critics agree that it is a generic aesthetic trait, giving an essential sense of progression and controlling attention.

In literature rhythm arises from the movement of ideas, from connections between sounds and meanings, and from connections among sounds, silences, and meanings. Not only is there repetition; there is also expectancy, and

This texture of expectations, satisfactions, disappointments, surprisals, which the sequence of syllables brings about, is rhythm. And the sound of words comes to its full power only through rhythm.[20]

The word accent, pause, and sense stress of lines and sentences pile up to establish rhythm. Patterns of rhythm may be loosely or tightly controlled. As a whole, the rhythm of prose is loose and that of poetry less so. When the pattern becomes too definite or insistent, it may obscure meaning. Uniform rhythms, however, can serve to build emotional intensity—witness the beat of a tom-tom or the chant of an Indian dancer or, indeed, the metronome effect of some jazz. The rhythm of literature is an integral part of the experience afforded the reader or listener, and its varieties and nuances are many.

It is often said that what is on the page represents, among other things, a record of the acoustical qualities of language present in the mind of the writer. These qualities are heard in the rise and fall of the voice in speech, which, upon analysis, proves to be a matter of stress, pitch, and juncture. The chapter on voice will develop these ideas much further.[21] For the present let us say that sound-rhythm and sense-rhythm are inextricable, each serving as both cause and effect of the other.

In prose the unit of rhythm, determined by the sense of the passage, is what may be called a speech group. It does not necessarily follow

---

[20] I. A. Richards, *Principles of Literary Criticism* (New York: Harcourt, Brace and Company, Inc., 1924), p. 137.
[21] See pp. 272-280.

punctuation, but it does follow rhetorical emphasis. Within a unit of prose rhythm there may be one stress or several stresses:

Inallspeech*skills* *ha*bitisacontrollingfactor.

Word accent plays a part here, but it does not account for the sentence stress which might require one stress in the first group and one in the second. (Of course, for the sake of meaning one might wish to change this reading to: Inall*speech*skills habit*is*acontrolling-factor. And there are still other possible readings.)

Sometimes words with accented syllables, being subordinate to the thought of the sentence, lose stress, and often, as with single words, the sentence seems to have secondary as well as primary stresses:

One sunny morning when the sea below the cliff was glinting blue and the

white surf creamed on the reef, when even the stone mountains looked

kindly, Mama Torres called out the door of the shack, "Pépé, I have a labor

for thee."

Because of meaning, the underlined words in the sentence—taken from "Flight" by John Steinbeck—seem to require primary stress or rhetorical emphasis, while secondary stress, perhaps, will be given to words marked by the wavy line. Word accent is marked ($'$), and, as you will note, there is some word accent that does not coincide with sense stress.[22]

Baum observes that

The primary rhythm of prose is determined by rhetorical emphases (as distinguished from the conventional or appointed stresses of meter) and is marked by grammatical groups (phrase, clause, sentence, paragraph) with their pauses.

There is also a secondary rhythm which is due partly to the natural alternations of stress and unstress in English speech and partly to our habitual expectation of regularity (as in verse), especially in formal or affective prose. This secondary rhythm appears as latent, half-submerged meter, that is, the sequences of more or less recognizable metrical feet.

. . . They constantly overlap, combine, and interweave in a kind of horizontal harmony and counterpoint. One recognizes them separately only for analysis.

---

[22] For further discussion of accent, see p. 273-274.

In verse, of course, the metrical predominates and is varied by the prose rhythm. In prose the grammatical or rhetorical predominates and may sometimes be enhanced by suggestions of metrical regularity. When neither appears in recognizable form, the language may be said to be a-rhythmic.[23]

As Baum indicates, there are metrical aspects to be observed in the rhythm of poetry. Rhythm is not to be confused with meter, yet meter is the basis of rhythm in conventional prosody. Just as notes of music are fitted into measures of a chosen time (4/4, 3/4, *et cetera*), measures which unite to form a musical phrase, so are the syllables and words of poetry fitted into metrical feet composing lines of different lengths. A metrical foot is the smallest unit in line structure; it consists of one accented syllable and one or more unaccented or lightly accented syllables. The basis of English prosody is said to be the isochronous, or equal time, interval between primary stresses. In the first two lines of the Dickinson poem we have read, these are the metrical stresses:

$$\text{My lífe|closed twíce|befóre|its clóse;|}$$
$$\text{It yét|remáins|to sée|}$$

The first line has four feet and the second, three, each of which is an iamb: one unaccented syllable followed by an accented one. The English language easily falls into this pattern, and, therefore, iambic lines are frequent. In addition, there are three other principal meters:

TROCHAIC:	tróchĕe	áccĕnt	póĕm
ANAPESTIC:	ĭntrŏdúce	rĕcŏlléct	ĕntĕrtáin
DACTYLIC:	íntĕrvăl	páragrăph éasĭlў	

The fact that one or another of these four metrical patterns may prevail throughout a given poem does not mean that there will be no variety of meter. Only in pedestrian verse is there treadmill monotony; the skillful poet occasionally changes stress placement and adds or subtracts syllables within a line of verse, unless the very monotony of unchanging meter will serve his intent. In the sonnet "The World Is Too Much With Us" the prevailing pattern is, of course, iambic, but not the meter of the second, third, and eleventh lines, where the

---

[23] Paull Franklin Baum, . . . *the other harmony of prose* (Durham: Duke University Press, 1952), pp. 214–215.

line begins with a trochee. And in Shakespeare's mature verse, as in *The Tempest*, there is considerable variety in meter and in number of syllables per line. Sections of Vachel Lindsay's "The Congo," on the other hand, make functional use of monotony.

Unlike the dividing line between speech groups, the dividing line between metrical feet can cut across words:

$$\text{Or hear|old Triton|blow|his wreath|ed horn}$$

This is a pentameter, or five-foot, line of five iambs, which together constitute one speech group. As we remarked in the preceding section on thought patterns, some lines of poetry end with the close of the speech group, some with the close of a sentence, and others, because of the predetermined pattern, with an incomplete word group. This sonnet of Keats illustrates these various line endings:

WHEN I HAVE FEARS THAT I MAY CEASE TO BE

John Keats (1795–1821)

When I have fears that I may cease to be
    Before my pen has glean'd my teeming brain,
Before high-pilèd books, in charact'ry,
    Hold like rich garners the full-ripened grain;
When I behold, upon the night's starred face,
    Huge cloudy symbols of a high romance,
And think that I may never live to trace
    Their shadows, with the magic hand of chance;
And when I feel, fair creature of an hour!
    That I shall never look upon thee more,
Never have relish in the faery power
    Of unreflecting love;—then on the shore
Of the wide world I stand alone, and think,
    Till Love and Fame to nothingness do sink.

The entire sonnet, you notice, is one sentence, as is the two-stanza Dickinson poem we read earlier. Occasionally a word group or a sentence of poetry ends *within* the line; such a point of sense pause is called a *caesura*. These pauses contribute to the rhythm of the composition, just as do all others, and the placing of them within the line will set up a pattern of units larger than the smaller ones of metrical foot and line length.

When we speak of line length, we may be referring to the number of metrical feet in the line; occasionally English poetry uses as many as eight, but the usual length is five or fewer. Line length may refer also to the number of syllables or of stresses in the line. All lines of a poem may be identical in length, or corresponding lines within all stanzas may be of the same length. In the ballad stanza, for example, lines one and three are typically four feet and lines two and four, three feet long. Ordinarily there is design in line length, the number of lines to a stanza, and variations in length. (Some of the designs have special names like *sonnet, ballad, rondeau,* and the like.) Here, as in prose, rhythm will not be revealed by marking the meter of a single line or the stresses of a single sentence. Usually the rhythm of a poem reveals itself in the pattern of the entire structure, in the tension between metrical and sense stress, and the placing and length of pauses.

So far, in our discussion of poetic rhythm, we have spoken of highly organized lines with conventional, or set, patterns. There is also free verse, in which lines, varying in length and of no continuous metrical pattern, fall into a pattern of cadence. In other words, the rhythm of free verse tends not to be on a linear basis, but is more akin to that of prose. The writer varies his line length to suit the speech group, he may use frequent recognizable metrical feet or not, and he changes the kind of metrical foot as he wishes, moving at will from iambs to trochees or anything else. Analysis of free verse, nevertheless, yields patterns of stress. Suppose we consider:

THE RED WHEELBARROW

William Carlos Williams (1883–　)

so much depends
upon

a red wheel
barrow

glazed with rain
water

beside the white
chickens

There are both repetitions and variations here. In the first place, we note that there are four two-line stanzas and that the second line in each case is one word, three of them trochees and one an iamb. The line stresses are the same in number in each stanza: 2-1, 2-1, 2-1, 2-1. The first lines of the beginning and the end stanza show the same arrangement of stresses (two iambic feet), but the first lines of the other two vary—one is an unstressed and two stressed syllables, the other a stressed, an unstressed, and a stressed syllable. Both the number of syllables and the number of words in lines show a pattern; the syllable number by lines is 4-2, 3-2, 3-2, and 4-2, while the word number is 3-1 in all stanzas. The lines fall into three speech groups: one of 11 syllables with four sense stresses, one of five with three, and one of six with two. Interestingly enough, the sum of the syllabic length of the last two word groups is the same as the length of the first. One further observation might be made: lines are said to have rising rhythm—or masculine cadence—when they end with an accent, and falling rhythm—or feminine cadence—when they do not. These lines of Williams alternate, the odd numbered ending with stresses (*upon* will weaken its usual stress on the second syllable because it is subordinate to the flow of thought), and the speech groups ending with unstressed syllables, so that the rhythm of the whole seems a falling one.

Rhyme and other sound repetitions set up expectancy in the mind of the reader and listener, contributing to the rhythmic effects. It is doubtful that the more than forty sounds of English and their multiple combinations [24] have meaning in themselves. Is *lullaby*, often called a beautiful word, beautiful because of the repeated [l] sounds or because of all its connotations of warmth, comfort, melody, and affection? Yet it is true that speech sounds vary in duration, pitch, and resonance and that some are musical and others noiselike. Combinations of sound may be pleasing and harmonious or dissonant and disturbing—disturbing, probably because they are difficult to articulate. The English language has its onomatopoetic words, words which in *sound* seem to be what they are in *meaning*: boom, crash, buzz, cut, moan. Modern linguists emphasize the action basis of language, and it is probable that this action is a determinant of rhythm. Imagine saying slowly the words: "Hit him! Hit him! Hit him!" Or try putting a pause between the two words each time. The action of hitting is swift, and, from the phonetic point of view, all the sounds in this

---

24 See p. 281 f.

speech group but [m] are short sounds. The ratio of short to long sounds and of stressed to unstressed syllables is one more factor in tempo and rhythm. Some lines seem to dance, to loiter, to march; they vary in pick-up and in retardation; they have crescendo and diminuendo; they excite us, and they lull us. In our minds, words cannot be separated, however, from the ideas presented and the feelings stirred, and we say again that it is the complex of sound and meaning which results in a variety of rhythms.

This variety is what Northrop Frye says forms

the basis of reading. Let us take a line of poetry at random, say the opening line of Claudio's great speech in *Measure for Measure*: "Ay, but to die, and go we know not where." Here we have, in the first place, the metrical or prosodic rhythm, an iambic pentameter with the first foot reversed. Second, we have the accentual rhythm, in this case a four-stress line. Third, we have the semantic or prose rhythm, the rhythm of sense, which in this case corresponds very closely to the accentual rhythm. Fourth, we have the mimetic rhythm which results from the actor's attempt to catch the mode of speech of a man in imminent fear of death. Mimetic rhythm is of course most important in drama, but it is found in other genres too, as a reader must at least imitate the mood of the piece he is reading. Onomatopoeia is a by-product of mimetic rhythm. Fifth, we have an oracular, meditative, soliloquizing rhythm emerging from the coincidences of the sound pattern . . .

> Ay,
> but to die . . .
> > and go
> > we know
> > > not where.[25]

Levels of Meaning

In our analysis of the literary whole we have thus far examined several keys to meaning and have scrutinized diction and structure as elements of style. Style also includes devices to obtain multiple meanings; among the devices are irony, metaphor, and allusion, of which we already have spoken. Now we are ready to look at the way in which all the words operate together in a given selection to yield a totality of meaning. Blackmur, you recall, told us that the full life of the words

[25] Northrop Frye, ed., *Sound and Poetry* (New York: Columbia University Press, 1957), pp. xxv–xxvii.

is "modified and made unique by the *qualifications* the words perform one upon the other in the poem." We have seen that words function as sense and as sound units. What they, as parts of a whole, symbolize and what they suggest may be called the *conceptual plus*, to be discussed here.

Upon first reading, one may find the literal or first level of meaning in a passage; this level is called basic, primary, or explicit meaning. Complex selections require repeated readings to lead us to multiple, depth, implicit, and symbolic meaning. A symbol is "a person, place, thing, quality, or relationship that is used to stand for something other than itself." There are conventional symbols in life and in art: the flag which stands for country; the cross, for Christ; the sun, for truth; bread, for spiritual sustenance; a stairway, for the ordeals of purgatory. There are also symbols created by the artist to serve his immediate purpose, and, if these are too private, they are obscure to both the skilled and the unskilled observer. In the majority of cases, however, study and analysis dispel the obscurity, make meaningful the symbol, and enhance appreciation.

To arrive at the depth meanings, a reader obviously must first know the words on their literal level. Suppose a word in a line is new to you; you look it up in the dictionary and choose the meaning which, in the context, seems to make sense. Total meaning may still escape you. The Chinese have a proverb, "Lambs have the grace to suckle kneeling." Among the many meanings given by the dictionary for the word *grace*, the one suiting this context is *sense of right*: Lambs have the sense of right to suckle kneeling. Proverbs relate to daily living— what does this one, by implication, really say? What is the meaning beyond the literal denotation of the words?

As with this proverb, so, often, a poem, a story, a drama has meaning greater than the sum of the parts: the sense of the words, the illumination of figurative language, and the effect of the speech sounds. Let us see what meanings we can find in Keats's sonnet:

ON FIRST LOOKING INTO CHAPMAN'S HOMER

Much have I travelled in the realms of gold,
And many goodly states and kingdoms seen;
Round many western islands have I been
Which bards in fealty to Apollo hold.

Oft of one wide expanse had I been told
That deep-browed Homer ruled as his demesne:
Yet did I never breathe its pure serene
Till I heard Chapman speak out loud and bold:
Then felt I like some watcher of the skies
When a new planet swims into his ken;
Or like stout Cortez when with eagle eyes
He stared at the Pacific—and all his men
Looked at each other with a mild surmise—
Silent, upon a peak in Darien.

The sense of the poem on its literal, basic level may be stated thus: Until Keats read Chapman's translation of Homer, he never had experienced the worth of Homer's poetry.

Clearly, the poem is more than this. In the first six lines Keats likens his knowledge and experience of reading poetry to travel, an occupation customarily fraught with excitement and novelty, one which leads us to new ideas and introduces us to new people and folkways. He suggests by "realms of gold" that he has read the "best thoughts of the best minds," inasmuch as gold is our most precious metal. Also gold is a medium of exchange, and it is possible that this figure gives us a connotation of the reciprocity between reader and writer. Gold carries a connotation of value, which further qualifies its use in the line. A further meaning in "realms of gold" is that Keats is familiar with the writings of the Golden Age of Greece—the fifth century B.C., a period of high civilization and art, the era of the great writers Aeschylus, Sophocles, and Euripides. In the second line "goodly states and kingdoms" gives authority, importance, and dimension to what Keats has read. The word "goodly" is close to "godly" in both sound and sight, and this proximity may qualify the phrase. The word "seen" carries more than literal meaning; man's eyes are so important to him that we constantly relate the verb to see with understanding—"I see what you mean," and "I don't see how you solve that equation."

In the next two lines, still using the metaphor of travel, Keats tells us that he has read poets of the western world; the first connotation of "western islands" is probably the islands of the Aegean, and next perhaps England, but the word "western" also suggests exploration and will link itself with Cortez in the last four lines of the sonnet. (A college sophomore, perplexed by these two lines, looked up the word "bards" in the dictionary and only added to his confusion by choosing the meaning "part of the armor of a horse.") The words "in fealty to Apollo" give quality to what Keats has found in the western islands, Apollo being the god of poetry, as well as the god of youth and beauty; the first meaning of "fealty" is fidelity of a feudal tenant to a lord, which links the word to land ownership, an idea repeated in line 6 in the words "Homer ruled as his demesne," *demesne* meaning both a realm of activity and possession of land as one's own. "Deep-brow'd" implies, of course, that Homer is wise and that there is depth to his knowledge.

Taken together the first six lines of the sonnet give dimension to the extent of Keats's reading by the feeling of space given by "realms," "kingdoms," "one wide expanse," and "Much have I travell'd." In line 7, "serene," here used as a noun, also awakens a connotation of dimension, while "breathe" suggests how a reader may "take in" the experience of the literature.

Lines 7 and 8 are the turning point, and it is interesting to note that here Keats changes the sensory image to an auditory one and thereby renews our attention. Attention is further strengthened by the energy of the plosive sounds [p|b|t|d|k|g] in "speak out loud and bold." Moreover, a "loud and bold" sound always arrests attention. The concept of Keats's hearing the author speak implies a nearness and direct rapport in their relationship.

Travel ordinarily terminates in arrival, and Keats, after developing his metaphor of travel, devotes the last six lines of the sonnet to similes descriptive of those rare, breathless moments of intense amazement and excitement when one is overwhelmed by almost unbelievable revelation. Yet here too there is space in the image "watcher of the skies," "the Pacific," and the "peak in Darien." The expanse here, in contrast to that in the earlier lines, is not just immense; it is vast and immeasurable (when Keats wrote these lines comparatively few men had crossed the Pacific and nobody spoke of space travel). The word "stared" means, of course, to look and echoes the word "looking" in the title and "look'd" in line 13 and is a variant of "seen" and "watcher." "Stared" implies incredulity as well as vision. The choice of this word also has a basis in fact: the eagle does not blink, but stares fixedly. In line 13 "wild surmise" adds to the feeling of amazement, and its meaning of "conjecture on scanty evidence" is perhaps significant of the fact that, when Keats wrote the sonnet, he had read only a few passages from Chapman's work. The story is that one night

Understanding the Literary Object 63

Keats's friend Cowden Clarke showed him Chapman's volume, and together they read certain of the famous passages. Long after midnight Keats walked home in the starlight, and between then and ten o'clock that morning he wrote the sonnet, which Clarke found in an envelope on his breakfast table in mid-morning.

Various explanations have been given for Keats's mistake in using the name of Cortez instead of that of Balboa. Even though the substitution seems one he should not have made, the simile is still vivid and functional. "Eagle eyes" adds to the meaning of the whole, carrying out the idea of sharp perception on the part of the discoverer and of movement too, because an eagle drops from heights and takes possession of his quarry.

By title and by lines 7 and 8 Keats shows that a specific experience served as a basis of the experience captured in the sonnet. He has, however, extended the concept and made the sonnet a statement of what writers make available to readers. He states indirectly that treasures await us and that "eagle eyes" are needed to perceive them. He seems to say that reading is an adventure and a journey of exploration, which can lead to unexpected discovery.

Thus we see that much is packed into the fourteen lines of this sonnet, and we note how metaphor, simile, allusion, and symbol unite to yield levels of meaning.

Sidney Cox reports what Robert Frost once told of a conversation with John Dewey about

what it took to produce a work of art. He [Frost] still liked the two words he had so long used: sight and insight . . . "First," he said, "you have to be sure, completely sure, what the *thing* is; what is required is sight and insight. Then . . . you might add one more, if you were generous about the pun . . . : excite. Sight, insight—and—excite." [26]

What Frost says about the producer of art may be said equally of the observer in his perception of the art object. As Cox adds, "You have to get the spark across from the sensation to the significance." This description sums up the process of finding the *conceptual plus*.

---

[26] Sidney Cox, A *Swinger of Birches* (New York: New York University Press, 1957), p. 97.

Conclusion

In this chapter we have examined the writer's contribution to the interpretation event and the reader's understanding and appreciation of the literary object. We found a preliminary step in analysis to be the determination of what we called the situational components of a selection. The situation presented is sometimes *open*, with little definition of speaker and hearer, and sometimes *closed*, with more or less definition of them. Emerging from the synthesis of cognitive and affective elements of the writing is the theme or total comment, clues to which lie in title, information about the author, key lines, and the pervasive feeling of the whole.

Although there is no dichotomy between form and substance, we have used the word *style* to designate details of the writer's workmanship, including diction, structure, and levels of meaning.

A reader will seek to put himself into "possession" of the piece of literature, making use of all the possible means available. Understanding is, indeed, a complex process, and many hurdles block a reader's path to it. As one reads and reads, fortunately, the hurdles diminish, insight quickens, and aesthetic pleasure increases.

In his initial preparation the intepreter is the silent reader, responding aesthetically to the literary object created by the writer. Thorough preparation at this stage strengthens his possibilities of success when he is the reader-become-interpreter. The deeper his own understanding and the richer his own appreciation of the literary object, the more certain he will be of evoking an appropriate aesthetic response from his listeners. Indeed, he cannot put his audience into "possession" of the literature unless he himself has assimilated it.

The next four chapters demonstrate how the tools of analysis from this chapter may be applied to essay, lyric, narrative, and drama. The general framework of analysis, applicable to any selection, rests upon these questions:

Questions for Analysis of the Literary Object

Who is talking?	To whom?	Where?	When?
Writer	All who hear	Anywhere	Anytime
Character	Specified or defined listener	Specific locale	Specified time

Understanding the Literary Object 65

What is the subject? the attitude?

Does the title provide a clue to subject and/or attitude?

Are there key lines which point to subject and attitude?

What do you know about the writer's life and/or general outlook which helps you better understand this work?

How does the selection compare in subject, theme, and style with others by this author?

What are the denotative meanings of the words?

What examples of figurative language do you find?

What are the appeals to sense imagery? How do they contribute to metaphor, simile, etc.?

What allusions do you identify?

What is the general level of language usage in the work?

What is the relation of phrase to sentence, sentence to paragraph or stanza, and paragraph or stanza to the entire work? If the sentences are inverted, long, and involved, can you recast them in normal agent-action-object order?

Is the rhythm tightly or loosely controlled? If tightly, what pattern do you find?

What sound values do you find in the work? What patterns of sound and silence? What sound repetitions?

How do figurative language, imagery, and the sound values of the words aid the development of mood and give clues as to the writer's attitude?

What are the major thought progressions and transitions? Within the major units, what minor transitions do you find?

What are the levels of meaning? What is the total comment?

Part Two

4

Speech and Essay

The perfection which is required of the finished orator is, or rather must be, like the perfection of anything else, partly given by nature, but may also be assisted by art. ∽ PLATO

Good prose is like a window pane. ∽ GEORGE ORWELL

IN CHAPTER 2 WE REVIEWED the traditional forms of literature, and in Chapter 3 we saw what the numerous elements of language contribute to form and meaning. Now we are ready to examine the various modes and structures resulting from the organization of language elements, with special attention to the effects of literary style upon the style of the interpreter.

The rhetorical forms of *speech* and *essay* deal with factual materials, with ideas, and with reasoning from facts and ideas. Differences in these two rhetorical forms spring from the relationship between author and audience. There are limits on the freedom of the speaker, who prepares for a specific audience, purpose, and occasion; there are fewer restrictions for the essayist. The most clearly defined audience for the essay is that furnished by contemporary magazines or journals. Usually the subscribers to a certain magazine have similar tastes and attitudes. The audience least clearly defined for the speaker is that in front of radio sets or television screens. Despite these deviations, we can safely say that the speech is limited in ways that the essay is not: it is meant to be heard in an allotted amount of time and ordinarily is to be heard only once. It must therefore very quickly find common ground and achieve its purpose. Although the essay may be concerned with whatever the author happens to be thinking about, the speech must deal with whatever matter is at hand—a candidate for office, the passage of a piece of legislation, an award, a burial. The effects of this immediacy upon the speaker's style are evident usually in his choice of words, allusions, and connotations, and in his over-all organization.

We have said that the essayist has greater freedom in his choice of subject. Not bound to speak of public questions, he must, nevertheless, through self-revelation, profundity, individuality, humor, some striking attribute of style or turn of mind show that his reactions to his environment are significant. The speech reaches a specific audience, and yet some speeches, by speakers caught up in great currents or gifted in utterance, have lasting interest and appeal. *Individuality* and *universality*, we might say, are characteristic of the speeches and essays suitable for interpretation.

Since our plan is to progress from the modes employing the open situation to the poetic and relatively closed forms, ending with the analysis of a play, the speech is our first concern. We have chosen Winston Churchill's "Dunkirk" because it is an example of a speech which, though prepared for a definite occasion, has become significant for countless persons long after the needs of the occasion have subsided. Some of you, already accustomed to what is known as "rhetorical analysis," will be interested to see the different emphasis in an analysis designed to help the interpreter present a speech as *literature*. Some of the suggestions we shall make would also be useful to a speaker preparing to read (or interpret) his own speech for an audience, but we are not primarily interested in such preparation.

The materials for analysis in this chapter are: "Dunkirk" by Winston Churchill; "Homily for a Troubled Time" by Bernard De Voto; "Young Love" by Hans Zinsser. In the study of each of these selections, we shall use some of the basic tools of analysis set forth in Chapter 3, but the pattern of analysis will be more fully explored for "Dunkirk" than for the two essays. Once established for rhetorical materials, it can be adapted to similar materials without difficulty.

DUNKIRK

Winston Churchill (1874–   )

From the moment when the defenses at Sedan on the Meuse were broken at the end of the second week in May only a rapid retreat to Amiens and the south could have saved the British-French armies who had entered Belgium at the appeal of the Belgian King.

This strategic fact was not immediately realized. The French High Command hoped it would be able to close the gap. The armies of the north were under their orders. Moreover, a retirement of that kind would have involved almost certainly the destruction of a fine Belgian Army of twenty divisions and abandonment of the whole of Belgium.

Therefore, when the force and scope of the German penetration was realized and when the new French Generalissimo, General [Maxime] Weygand, assumed command in place of General Gamelin, an effort was made by the French and British Armies in Belgium to keep holding the right hand of the Belgians and give their own right hand to the newly created French Army which was to advance across the Somme in great strength.

However, the German eruption swept like a sharp scythe south of Amiens to the rear of the armies in the north—eight or nine armored divisions, each with about 400 armored vehicles of different kinds divisible into small self-contained units.

This force cut off all communications between us and the main French Army. It severed our communications for food and ammunition. It ran first through Amiens, afterward through Abbeville, and it shore its way up the coast to Boulogne and Calais, almost to Dunkirk.

Behind this armored and mechanized onslaught came a number of German divisions in lorries, and behind them, again, plodded comparatively slowly the dull, brute mass of the ordinary German Army and German people, always ready to be led to the trampling down in other lands of liberties and comforts they never have known in their own.

I said this armored scythe stroke almost reached Dunkirk— almost but not quite. Boulogne and Calais were scenes of desperate fighting. The guards defended Boulogne for a while and were then withdrawn by orders from this country.

The rifle brigade of the Sixtieth Rifles [Queen Victoria's Rifles], with a battalion of British tanks and 1,000 Frenchmen, in all about 4,000 strong, defended Calais to the last. The British brigadier was given an hour to surrender. He spurned the offer. Four days of intense street fighting passed before the silence reigned in Calais which marked the end of a memorable resistance.

Only thirty unwounded survivors were brought off by the navy, and we do not know the fate of their comrades. Their sacrifice was not, however, in vain. At least two armored divisions which otherwise would have been turned against the B. E. F. had to be sent to overcome them. They have added another page to the glories of the light division.

The time gained enabled the Gravelines water line to be flooded and held by French troops. Thus the port of Dunkirk was held open. When it was found impossible for the armies of the north to reopen their communications through Amiens with the main French armies, only one choice remained. It seemed, indeed, a forlorn hope. The Belgian and French armies were almost surrounded. Their sole line of retreat was to a single port and its neighboring beaches. They were pressed on every side by heavy attacks and were far outnumbered in the air.

When a week ago today I asked the House to fix this afternoon for the occasion of a statement, I feared it would be my hard lot to announce from this box the greatest military disaster of our long history.

I thought, and there were good judges who agreed with me, that perhaps 20,000 or 30,000 men might be re-embarked, but it certainly seemed that the whole French First Army and the whole B. E. F. north of the Amiens-Abbeville gap would be broken up in open field or else have to capitulate for lack of food and ammunition.

These were the hard and heavy tidings I called on the House and nation to prepare themselves for.

The whole root and core and brain of the British Army, around which and upon which we were building and are able to build the great British armies of later years, seemed due to perish upon the field. That was the prospect a week ago, but another blow which might have proved final was still to fall upon us.

The King of the Belgians called upon us to come to his aid. Had not this ruler and his government severed themselves from the Allies who rescued their country from extinction in the late war, and had they not sought refuge in what has been proved to be fatal neutrality, then the French and British armies at the outset might well have saved not only Belgium but perhaps even Holland.

At the last moment, when Belgium was already invaded, King Leopold called upon us to come to his aid, and even at the last moment we came. He and his brave and efficient army of nearly half a million strong guarded our eastern flank; this kept open our only retreat to the sea.

Suddenly, without any prior consultation and with the least possible notice, without the advice of his ministers and on his own personal act, he sent a plenipotentiary to the German Command surrendering his army and exposing our flank and the means of retreat.

I asked the House a week ago to suspend its judgment because the facts were not clear. I do not think there is now any reason why we should not form our own opinions upon this pitiful episode. The surrender of the Belgian Army compelled the British Army at the shortest notice to cover a flank to the sea of more than thirty miles' length which otherwise would have been cut off.

In doing this and closing this flank, contact was lost inevitably between the British and two of three corps forming the First French Army who were then further from the coast than we were. It seemed impossible that large numbers of Allied troops could reach the coast. The enemy attacked on all sides in great strength and fierceness, and their main power, air force, was thrown into the battle.

The enemy began to fire cannon along the beaches by which alone shipping could approach or depart. They sowed magnetic mines in the channels and seas and sent repeated waves of hostile aircraft, sometimes more than 100 strong, to cast bombs on a single pier that remained and on the sand dunes.

Their U-boats, one of which was sunk, and motor launches

took their toll of the vast traffic which now began. For four or five days the intense struggle raged. All armored divisions, or what was left of them, together with great masses of German infantry and artillery, hurled themselves on the ever narrowing and contracting appendix within which the British and French armies fought.

Meanwhile the Royal Navy, with the willing help of countless merchant seamen and a host of volunteers, strained every nerve and every effort and every craft to embark the British and Allied troops.

Over 220 light warships and more than 650 other vessels were engaged. They had to approach this difficult coast, often in adverse weather, under an almost ceaseless hail of bombs and increasing concentration of artillery fire. Nor were the seas themselves free from mines and torpedoes.

It was in conditions such as these that our men carried on with little or no rest for days and nights, moving troops across dangerous waters and bringing with them always the men whom they had rescued. The numbers they brought back are the measure of their devotion and their courage.

Hospital ships, which were plainly marked, were the special target for Nazi bombs, but the men and women aboard them never faltered in their duty.

Meanwhile the R. A. F., who already had been intervening in the battle so far as its range would allow it to go from home bases, now used a part of its main metropolitan fighter strength to strike at German bombers.

The struggle was protracted and fierce. Suddenly the scene has cleared. The crash and thunder has momentarily, but only for the moment, died away. The miracle of deliverance achieved by the valor and perseverence, perfect discipline, faultless service, skill and unconquerable vitality is a manifesto to us all.

The enemy was hurled back by the British and French troops. He was so roughly handled that he dare not molest their departure seriously. The air force decisively defeated the main strength of the German Air Force and inflicted on them a loss of at least four to one.

The navy, using nearly 1,000 ships of all kinds, carried over 335,000 men, French and British, from the jaws of death back to their native land and to the tasks which lie immediately before them.

We must be very careful not to assign to this deliverance attributes of a victory. Wars are not won by evacuations, but there was a victory inside this deliverance which must be noted.

Many of our soldiers coming back have not seen the air force at work. They only saw the bombers which escaped their protective attack. This was a great trial of strength between the British and German Air Forces.

Can you conceive of a greater objective for the power of Germany in the air than to make all evacuations from these beaches impossible and to sink all of the ships, numbering almost 1,000? Could there have been an incentive of greater military importance and significance to the whole purpose of the war?

They tried hard and were beaten back. They were frustrated in their task; we have got the armies away and they have paid fourfold for any losses sustained. Very large formations of German airplanes were turned on several occasions from the attack by a quarter their number of R. A. F. planes and dispersed in different directions. Twelve airplanes have been hunted by two. One airplane was driven into the water and cast away by the charge of a British airplane which had no more ammunition.

All of our types and our pilots have been vindicated. The Hurricane, Spitfires and Defiance have been vindicated. When I consider how much greater would be our advantage in defending the air above this island against overseas attacks, I find in these facts a sure basis on which practical and reassuring thoughts may rest, and I will pay my tribute to these young airmen.

May it not be that the cause of civilization itself will be defended by the skill and devotion of a few thousand airmen? There never has been, I suppose, in all the history of the world such opportunity for youth.

The Knights of the Round Table and the Crusaders have fallen back into distant days, not only distant but prosaic; but these young men are going forth every morning, going forth holding in their hands an instrument of colossal shattering power, of whom it may be said that every morn brought forth a noble chance and every chance brought forth a noble deed. These young men deserve our gratitude, as all brave men who in so many ways and so many occasions are ready and will continue to be ready to give their life and their all to their native land.

I return to the army. In a long series of very fierce battles, now on this front, now on that, fighting on three fronts at once, battles fought by two or three divisions against an equal or sometimes larger number of the enemy, and fought very fiercely on old ground so many of us knew so well, our losses in men exceed 30,000 in killed, wounded and missing. I take this occasion for expressing the sympathy of the House with those who have suffered bereavement or are still anxious.

The President of the Board of Trade [Sir Andrew Duncan] is not here today. His son has been killed, and many here have felt private affliction of the sharpest form, but I would say about the missing—we have had a large number of wounded come home safely to this country—there may be very many reported missing who will come back home some day.

In the confusion of departure it is inevitable that many should be cut off. Against this loss of over 30,000 men we may set the far heavier loss certainly inflicted on the enemy, but our losses in material are enormous. We have perhaps lost one-third of the men we lost in the opening days of the battle on March 21, 1918, but we have lost nearly as many guns—nearly 1,000—and all our transport and all the armored vehicles that were with the army of the north.

These losses will impose further delay on the expansion of our military strength. That expansion has not been proceeding as fast as we had hoped. The best of all we had to give has been given to the B. E. F., and although they had not the number of tanks and some articles of equipment which were desirable they were a very well and finely equipped army. They had the first fruits of all our industry had to give. That has gone and now here is further delay.

How long it will be, how long it will last depends upon the exertions which we make on this island. An effort, the like of which has never been seen in our records, is now being made. Work is proceeding night and day, Sundays and week days.

Capital and labor have cast aside their interests, rights and customs and put everything into the common stock. Already the flow of munitions has leaped forward. There is no reason why we should not in a few months overtake the sudden and serious loss that has come upon us without retarding the development of our general program.

Nevertheless, our thankfulness at the escape of our army with so many men, and the thankfulness of their loved ones, who passed through an agonizing week, must not blind us to the fact that what happened in France and Belgium is a colossal military disaster.

The French Army has been weakened, the Belgian Army has been lost and a large part of those fortified lines upon which so much faith was reposed has gone, and many valuable mining districts and factories have passed into the enemy's possession.

The whole of the channel ports are in his hands, with all the strategic consequences that follow from that, and we must expect another blow to be struck almost immediately at us or at France.

We were told that Hitler has plans for invading the British Isles. This has often been thought of before. When Napoleon lay at Boulogne for a year with his flat-bottomed boats and his Grand Army, some one told him there were bitter weeds in England. There certainly were and a good many more of them have since been returned. The whole question of defense against invasion is powerfully affected by the fact that we have for the time being in this island incomparably more military forces than we had in the last war. But this will not continue. We shall not be content with a defensive war. We have our duty to our Allies.

We have to reconstitute and build up the B. E. F. once again under its gallant Commander in Chief, Lord Gort. All this is en train. But now I feel we must put our defense in this island into such a high state of organization that the fewest possible numbers will be required to give effectual security and that the largest possible potential offensive effort may be released.

On this we are now engaged. It would be very convenient to enter upon this subject in secret sessions. The government would not necessarily be able to reveal any great military secrets, but we should like to have our discussions free and without the restraint imposed by the fact that they would be read the next day by the enemy.

The government would benefit by the views expressed by the House. I understand that some request is to be made on this subject, which will be readily acceded to by the government. We have found it necessary to take measures of increasing stringency, not only against enemy aliens and suspicious characters of other nationalities but also against British subjects who may become a danger or a nuisance should the war be transported to the United Kingdom.

I know there are a great many people affected by the orders which we have made who are passionate enemies of Nazi Germany. I am very sorry for them, but we cannot, under the present circumstances, draw all the distinctions we should like to do. If parachute landings were attempted and fierce fights followed, those unfortunate people would be far better out of the way for their own sake as well as ours.

There is, however, another class for which I feel not the slightest sympathy. Parliament has given us powers to put down fifth column activities with the strongest hand, and we shall use those powers subject to the supervision and correction of the House without hesitation until we are satisfied and more than satisfied that this malignancy in our midst has been effectually stamped out.

Turning once again to the question of invasion, there has, I will observe, never been a period in all those long centuries of which we boast when an absolute guarantee against invasion, still less against serious raids, could have been given to our people. In the days of Napoleon the same wind which might have carried his transports across the Channel might have driven away a blockading fleet. There is always the chance, and it is that chance which has excited and befooled the imaginations of many continental tyrants.

We are assured that novel methods will be adopted, and when we see the originality, malice and ingenuity of aggression which our enemy displays we may certainly prepare ourselves for every kind of novel stratagem and every kind of brutal and treacherous manoeuvre. I think no idea is so outlandish that it should not be considered and viewed with a watchful, but at the same time steady, eye.

We must never forget the solid assurances of sea power and those which belong to air power if they can be locally exercised. I have myself full confidence that if all do their duty and if the best arrangements are made, as they are being made, we shall prove ourselves once again able to defend our island home, ride out the storms of war and outlive the menace of tyranny, if necessary, for years, if necessary, alone.

At any rate, that is what we are going to try to do. That is the resolve of His Majesty's Government, every man of them. That is the will of Parliament and the nation. The British Empire and the French Republic, linked together in their cause and their need, will defend to the death their native soils, aiding each other like good comrades to the utmost of their strength, even though a large tract of Europe and many old and famous States have fallen or may fall into the grip of the Gestapo and all the odious apparatus of Nazi rule.

We shall not flag nor fail. We shall go on to the end. We shall fight in France and on the seas and oceans; we shall fight with growing confidence and growing strength in the air.

We shall defend our island whatever the cost may be; we shall fight on beaches, landing grounds, in fields, in streets and on the hills. We shall never surrender and even if, which I do not for a moment believe, this island or a large part of it were subjugated and starving, then our empire beyond the seas, armed and guarded by the British Fleet, will carry on the struggle until in God's good time the New World, with all its power and might, sets forth to the liberation and rescue of the Old.

The Situation

The disasters that forced Chamberlain's resignation brought Sir Winston Churchill forward to lead the government in the spring of 1940. In the first year of the war with Germany the British people not only stood alone against the enemy, but they had lost faith in their own leadership.

THE SPEAKER. Sir Winston Churchill was well qualified for his task of leading the coalition government which represented the British people during the perilous years of World War II. He had already spent the length of an average life span in military and public service. He had served with the 4th Hussars in India and the Sudan, and had taken command of an infantry battalion during World War I. His government posts included that of First Lord of the Admiralty during World War I, Minister of Munitions, Secretary of State for War, Secretary of State for the Colonies, and Chancellor of the Exchequer. Out of office for a few years, in 1940 he was again First Lord of the Admiralty.

Churchill knew men in and out of affairs, he had a grasp of past [1] and present, and furthermore, he was a thorough patriot. Prior to the onset of World War II, he alone predicted disaster unless steps were taken to stop the dictators on the continent. His description of his personal reaction to becoming prime minister suggests his fitness for the responsibilities ahead of him:

During these last crowded days of the political crisis, my pulse had not quickened at any moment. I took it all as it came. But I cannot conceal from the reader of this truthful account that as I went to bed at about 3 A.M., I was conscious of a profound sense of relief. At last I had the authority to give directions over the whole scene. I felt as if I had been walking with Destiny, and that all my past life had been but a preparation for this hour and this trial. Eleven years in the political wilderness had freed me from ordinary party antagonisms. My warnings over the last six years had been so numerous, so detailed, and were now so terribly vindicated, that no one could gainsay me. I could not be reproached either for making the war or with want of preparation for it. I thought I knew a good deal about it all, and I was sure I should not fail. Therefore, although impatient for the morning, I slept soundly and had no need for cheering dreams. Facts are better than dreams.[2]

Fortunately, Churchill's training in writing and speaking, combined with certain traits of character and habits of mind, fitted him admirably for the position he accepted on May 10, 1940. As a war correspondent in South Africa during the Boer War and later, as the author of several books, among them an account of World War I, he had perfected his written style. In fact, he looked upon writing as his

---

[1] For discussion of Churchill's knowledge and use of history see Charles W. Lomas, "Winston Churchill: Orator-Historian" in *Quarterly Journal of Speech* (April, 1958), pp. 153–160.

[2] From Winston Churchill's *The Gathering Storm* (Boston: Houghton Mifflin Company, 1948), p. 667. Used by permission of the publishers, Houghton Mifflin Company.

chosen calling. He had worked at writing and speaking concomitantly all through his career, and, as leader of the Opposition during the thirties, had participated in the lively parrying of British political debate.

THE AUDIENCE. In "Dunkirk," Sir Winston Churchill was reaching out to make direct contact and to have immediate effect upon his audience, 625 [3] elected members of the House of Commons, sitting in council in a darkened, threatened London. Responsible in large measure for carrying on the war, they looked to the new prime minister for guidance. The speech, broadcast to all the United Kingdom and picked up in the United States and elsewhere in the world, reached a larger audience than the one the prime minister actually faced. The conclusion of the speech reveals Churchill's consciousness of his extended audience, of the British people, and of prospective allies in "the New World."

TIME AND PLACE. We have already mentioned the historic House of Commons where the speech was given. It was the ninth month of World War II, so far an unbroken succession of German victories. Russia, leaning toward Germany, had annexed Latvia, Lithuania, Estonia, and Finland. Hitler had conquered Poland, Denmark, and Norway. On the day Churchill became prime minister, the Nazis attacked Belgium, Luxembourg, and Holland. Soon Belgium surrendered, and Italy under Mussolini joined the war as Germany's ally. It was then that the British evacuated their forces at Dunkirk, a difficult procedure taking from May 26 to June 3. Churchill reported on the episode the day after it was finished and one day before the Germans launched the offensive ending with their occupation of Paris on June 14.

Assimilation of Content

"Dunkirk" brought a heavy burden of bad news: loss of allies, life, and materials. Churchill refused to camouflage the events, but, salvaging every scrap of hope, managed to make future perilous duty seem a privilege. This speech, like others before and after, was a blend of technical information and effective emotional appeals. The prime minister sustained the nation's pride by emphasizing the courage and resourcefulness of the young men of the nation, giving warm praise to the Royal Air Force and the Royal Navy. He urged superhuman effort in

---

[3] Since 1955, after reapportionment, the House of Commons has numbered 630.

defense so that every possible resource could be released for *offense*. His declaration of unyielding resistance was a call to unity within the nation and among uncommitted nations. Yet, as one biographer saw it, Churchill told the truth:

. . . often a great and stirring truth against a background black with menace—in words which, sometimes simple, sometimes magnificent, were exactly right for the thought and feeling which they expressed, and for the time at which they were said.[4]

Achievement of Artistic Form

What words, "sometimes simple, sometimes magnificent," do we find in the "Dunkirk" speech?

SELECTION AND ARRANGEMENT OF WORDS. We note an alternation of short or monosyllabic words with words of three or more syllables. Notice the short, sturdy words in the following passage:

The whole root and core and brain of the British Army, around which and upon which we were building and are able to build the great British armies of later years, seemed due to perish upon the field. That was the prospect a week ago, but another blow which might have proved final was still to fall upon us.

He avoided undue simplicity by careful qualification and distinction, as shown in the underlinings below:

I think no idea is so outlandish that it should not be considered and viewed with a watchful, but at the same time steady, eye

Suddenly, without any prior consultation and with the least possible notice, without the advice of his ministers and on his own personal act

All armored divisions, or what was left of them

Far more dominant than simplicity is the effect of *concreteness*, achieved by specific reference to time, place, numbers, quantities, branches of service, sequence of events. Spatial relations and scenes emerge:

[4] John Henry Robertson, *Winston Churchill*, by John Connell, pseud. (London, New York, and Toronto: Longmans, Green & Co., 1956), p. 32. Published for the British Council and the National Book League, *Writers and Their Work*: No. 80.

. . . the German eruption swept like a sharp scythe south of Amiens to the rear of the armies in the north—eight or nine armored divisions, each with about 400 armored vehicles of different kinds divisible into small self-contained units.

The concreteness is pervaded by vivid imagery, springing from verbs, nouns, and adjectives:

> plodded
> brute mass
> hurled
> contracting appendix within which the British and French
>   armies fought
> crash
> thunder

Figures augment the vividness. We find *simile* in "like a sharp scythe"; *personification* in "silence reigned"; *metaphor* in "ride out the storms of war."

As might be expected, there are allusions designed to gain a reaction from the audience, among them these:

> On old ground so many of us know so well (World War I)
> Many continental tyrants (Hitler and Mussolini)
> Many old and famous States have fallen or may fall (Denmark,
> Norway, Belgium, Holland)

Simplicity, concreteness, and connotative power mark the words employed in "Dunkirk"; their "magnificence" becomes more evident when we examine them with an eye to arrangement. So great was Churchill's skill in this respect that just when you think you see a tendency or pattern, something new emerges. Since we have mentioned short, plain words, one might expect short, simple sentences. On the contrary, we notice an abundance of complex sentences, a sprinkling of compound sentences, and recourse to adjectival and adverbial phrasal modifiers. Subjects, verbs, and objects are often compounded or modified and, more frequently, the objects of prepositions. Here are some of the compounds in the speech:

Compound subjects: Boulogne and Calais; root and core and brain;
                          crash and thunder

Compound objects:	saved not only Belgium but perhaps even Holland; would have involved almost certainly the destruction of a fine Belgian army of twenty divisions and abandonment of the whole of Belgium
Compound prepositional objects:	between us and the main French army; of their devotion and their courage; back to their native land and to the tasks

The effect of these compounds is intensified by Churchill's ability to use balance and subordination to bring out his meaning. *Balance* is the result of the compounds and the use of repetition with *parallel* structure, exemplified by: "ride out the storms of war and outlive the menace of tyranny, if necessary, for years, if necessary, alone," and by "we shall fight in France and on the seas and oceans; we shall fight with growing confidence and growing strength in the air," and by the entire last paragraph of the speech.

The *subordination* is due in part to the frequent use of the periodic sentence, one in which the crux of meaning is reserved for the end. The following are examples of the periodic sentence in Churchill's hands:

When it was found impossible for the armies of the north to re-open their communications through Amiens with the main French armies, only one choice remained.

Had not this ruler and his government severed themselves from the Allies who rescued their country from extinction in the late war, and had they not sought refuge in what has been proved to be fatal neutrality, then the French and British armies at the outset might well have saved not only Belgium but perhaps even Holland.

A survey of Churchill's sentences indicates that despite his well-placed balanced structures, he favored the complex sentence with its causal relations. Doubtless much of the plausibility of the speech rests with these closely reasoned and wrought utterances.

STRUCTURAL DEVELOPMENT. We have suggested that Churchill kept all the parts of his sentences firmly together. He handled total structure in the same decisive way. He was economical of detail. We see the same inevitable relation among paragraphs that we found among sentences. Occasionally he tied paragraphs together with such adverbs as *however, meanwhile, nevertheless,* but more often by repeating a key word or idea. Notice this type of linking between paragraphs three and four, in which the *force* mentioned in the first sentence of paragraph four has been described in paragraph three, and again between the paragraph ending "The surrender of the Belgian Army compelled the British Army at the shortest notice to cover a flank to the sea of more than thirty miles' length which otherwise would have been cut off" and the next paragraph, beginning "In doing this and closing this flank, . . ."

The speech clearly falls into four divisions. First, there is narration of events prior to and during the evacuation of Dunkirk. Second, there is an interpretation of these events: their effect upon Germany, upon future generations, and upon the subsequent conduct of the war at hand. Third, there is a plan of action, a way of dealing with the fear of invasion. Fourth, in conclusion, there is a memorable statement of faith and resolution.

The climactic structure is at once apparent. Yet it is tempered by such transitional statements as the following: "I asked the House a week ago to suspend its judgment because the facts were not clear"; "We must be very careful not to assign to this deliverance attributes of victory." Although the direction is unwavering, these transitions added to the frequent summations keep the emotional tone well within bounds.

Contrast plays a large part in the total effect. Variations in movement from factual to lyrical contribute to the over-all rhythmical effect. To be explicit, the praise of the airmen and of heroic youth is less factual than the paragraphs immediately preceding. But there is a sharp return to direct reporting in "I return to the army." After this transition, there is a gradual reduction of factual matter until the lyrical close is accomplished.

Often there is a contrast between hoped-for results and reality, especially in regard to the enemy: "They tried hard and were beaten back. They were frustrated in their task; we have got the armies away and they have paid fourfold for any losses sustained." Likewise, "Twelve airplanes have been hunted by one" states simply a contrast of numbers.

RHYTHM. Such use of contrast is bound to increase the reader's awareness of the rhythmical values in "Dunkirk." We have already mentioned the juxtaposition of long and short sentences, and the repetition of single words. This last tendency is illustrated in the examples below:

> to keep holding the *right hand* of the Belgians and give their
>   own *right hand* to the newly created French Army . . .
> are *ready* and will continue to be *ready*
> to give *their* life and *their* all to *their* native land
> *if necessary*, for years, *if necessary*, alone.

In the conclusion, there is effective alternation of "fight" and "defend," and additional repetitions throughout, resulting in parallel structure, found in ". . . *that is* what we are going to try to do," "*That is* the resolve . . . ," "*That is* the will of Parliament."

We have already noted that *contrast* in both minor and major divisions heightens the rhythmical movement toward the climax of feeling and appeal. Rhythm implies continuity, for it seldom exists in single lines. Certainly the chronological narrative has a continuous movement, a progression of rises and falls. Many sentences and nearly all of the paragraphs have their own peaks.

The texture is enriched by certain consonances, even alliteration, and by frequent occurrence of open vowels. When spoken, because of the dominance of rising rhythms, some passages are lifted beyond the usual patterns of prose into the realm of poetry. A rearrangement of some of the sentences might look like this:

> We shall defend our island
>   whatever the cost may be;
> We shall fight on beaches,
>   landing grounds,
> In fields, in streets
>   and on the hills.
> We shall never surrender—
>   and even if
> Which I do not for a moment
>   believe—
> This island
>   or a large part of it
> Were subjugated and starving,
> Then—our empire beyond the seas
> Armed and guarded by the British Fleet
>   will carry on the struggle
> Until, in God's good time

The New World
  with all its power and might
Sets forth—
  to the liberation and rescue of the old.

The masculine ending [5] of many cadences, demanding rising rhythm, adds to the measured effect. Such stresses are on the following: "be," "grounds," "streets," "hills," "believe," "seas," "Fleet," "time," "World," "might," "forth," and "old."

It is not unfitting that we use the word "lyrical" for a passage such as this ending, although we, of course, are not suggesting that Churchill moved into metrical *form*. He simply matched his rhythm, the enveloping aspect of style, with his concept. Thus, one might approach "Dunkirk" as an example of the unity obtained by rhythmical organization, or if one chose, as an example of the inevitability of rhythmical form when concept and language merge under the hands of a capable artist.

One need not be told that undoubtedly the oratory of Winston Churchill was the chief ingredient in the valiant endeavor Britain made to endure the Battle of Britain. This speech reconstructs the original situation and the role played by the Prime Minister through his speeches. As interpreters we can never hope to have—nor perhaps desire to have—the kind of attention the Members of the House must have granted to "Dunkirk."

At the same time, by giving a résumé of the early days of World War II, not a labored account, but one containing certain striking essentials, the interpreter can create real interest for "Dunkirk." [6] Beginning with a factual framework and understanding, the interpreter can arrive at a balance, much as Churchill had to, between events and their meaning, or between fact and the evaluation of fact.

The Interpreter's Response

Often because of the personal pronouns in a speech, an interpreter will feel called upon to imitate what he thinks may have been the delivery of the original speaker. Such attempts are sure to be disastrous. Even if we had stenographic reports and tape recordings of every speech in existence, so that our imitations rested on authentic models,

---

[5] See Chapter 3, p. 59.
[6] Or any speech that has quality and originality.

the procedure would be undesirable. We are striving for the essence of the material, not for the hollow echo of voice or mimicry of outward gesture. In the case of Churchill himself, we are told that the crowds came, not to admire him as performer, but to learn and be invigorated by what he had to say. In fact, his was not a "golden" voice, and little has been said of his *appearance* in the act of speaking.

Earlier we commented that Churchill's entire life fitted him for the speaking he did during his terms of office. An omnivorous reader and student of the political scene, he was not inclined to speak without information. It is clear, too, that he never spoke without conviction. An interpreter might try to imitate Churchill's *method of preparation*, but not his delivery. The purpose of the foregoing analysis is to help you with this thorough preparation.

By this time, you have read the speech through several times and are familiar with its movement. You can visualize the physical setting, the House of Commons in wartime. You have responded to what we might call the "universals" in the speech: to the ideals of freedom-holding men, men capable of comradely relationships and resourceful action. You are willing to accept the trust in traditional patriotism and national pride which prevailed above the fears of war and invasion.

The degree of sympathy or identification that you feel, coupled with your awareness of the gravity of the situation Churchill described, may tempt you to begin the speech with too much emotional fervor. The climactic ordering of idea and feeling will be your guide. Attention to the narration of the first twenty-five paragraphs will suggest restraint and the direct personal contact of the open situation. Even in the paragraphs condoling the bereaved and paying tribute to the men of the Royal Air Force, you will want to maintain a comparatively close personal contact with the audience, remembering that the impact of the speech is delayed.

The climb toward the high point of the speech in the conclusion must be modified by careful attention to the relief from tension offered by transitions. As interpreter you must take care not to strike too many hard blows. You will be tempted because of the stirring images and verbs to dwell upon individual sentences, but each must be *assimilated into the total structure*, taking its part in accomplishing *the larger purpose* of the speech. In your effort to give the allusions their due, remember that they were instruments for unifying the audience, but not as important as the problem at hand, and move past them swiftly if you can without slighting the connotations. Reserve your greatest emphasis for the lyrical close.

Churchill's artistry is an infallible guide. When he builds swiftly to the point of a periodic sentence, you do the same. Preserve the balance of the compound constructions, subduing the connectives, of course, and bringing out the concrete nouns. Remember that the speech, though filled with sentiment, is a historic report to highly trained parliamentarians. Beware of any tendency to overplay the emotional aspects to the detriment of the superb reporting of the speech. If you follow the changes from open to closed situation, you will be less inclined to overdo the sentiment.

It seems improbable that interest in the speech could flag, but attention to the contrasts of thought and feeling already indicated will do much to sharpen and vivify the pattern of the whole.

After you have read Chapters 8 and 9, you will want to apply the information acquired there about the use of body and voice in interpretation to the suggestions for interpreting the "Dunkirk" speech.

Since the speech and essay belong to the same family, we shall suggest only the salient features of analysis for the essay, in the hope that the exploration of the speech by Churchill will suffice as a guide for both speech and essay. We shall now examine swiftly in turn "Homily for a Troubled Time" by Bernard De Voto and "Young Love" by Hans Zinsser. In the former, the writer is speaking on a public question; in the latter, the author is speaking frankly of his early loves.

HOMILY FOR A TROUBLED TIME

Bernard De Voto (1897–1955)

Six hundred years ago the plague we now call the Black Death swept over Europe, and at least twenty-five million people died of it, or something more than a fourth of the population of the Continent. In all history there has been no other disaster so great.

There has been no terror so great, either, for nobody could understand what the pestilence was. There was no way to cure it, no way to prevent it or escape it, and men lived in a nightmare of paralyzing panic.

The Black Death has always been the greatest symbol of

human helplessness and of universal fear. Until the present moment and the atom bomb.

In 1348 the plague struck the great Italian city Florence and killed at least sixty per cent of the inhabitants. One whom it spared was a writer named Giovanni Boccaccio, and a few years later he wrote a great book. Called the *Decameron*, it has often been in disrepute because of the robust Latin humor that shocks our more delicate sensibilities. But many scholars have called it the first modern book, and certainly it is the first one that shows the reawakening sunlight which we call the Renaissance, the warmth that means respect for and delight in human experience. It was written in the shadow of an almost universal fear of imminent death, with the end of the world at hand.

Its hundred stories are set in an extremely significant framework. When the plague breaks out in Florence, a small group of people flee to Fiesole, in the hills above the city, and there in a great villa wait for the terror to pass. They are rich, and all the luxuries of the medieval world are at their command. But in the first place they must crowd the fear of the plague out of their minds, and in the second place life on their mountaintop above the stricken city is intolerably barren and empty. So they determine to fill the vacuum by taking turns telling stories.

And what were the stories about? They were about the common, hearty, exuberant, tragic life of Italy. They were stories of adventure, of fortitude, of humor, of youth and age, faith and despair, love and grief—of the daily round of human experience from which the storytellers have fled.

On their sterile promontory, the life they had left behind in Florence preoccupied them—they could no more escape from it than from fear of the plague. If you try to escape from death, you lose life. That is the moral—and the danger—of our obsessive fear today.

At the beginning of the recent depression, a man I knew suddenly became rich. He bought a large estate in a remote but fertile farming country and set out to make it self-sufficient. It was to provide everything necessary for life, flour from his own wheat, meat from his own herds, fish from his own ponds, electricity from his own power plant. All this was because the revolution (the paralyzing but never specifically defined terror of those days) might break out any moment. His plan was entirely unworkable. His power plant would stop operating as soon as the gasoline trucks stopped making deliveries. The mobs he envisioned would overrun his place like locusts. And so on. It was a panic dream, a nightmare. But I wondered, even if his dream of safety could be realized, what his life would be worth to him. Just beyond his high fences his fellow countrymen would be meeting their destiny, warring horribly perhaps, and dying by the thousands—but grappling with the problems of the real world and working out some way of going on. They would be alive. My friend, digesting his dinner in safety, would have no part in their experience. He would be withdrawn from human destiny, and so, while he walked his peaceful fields, he would be dead.

His dream of escape was widespread in those depression days. We all knew people who bought places in the mountains or up the farthest creeks, so they could live untouched by the revolution. One of the most publicized was a man who bought a canyon in the Oregon wilderness and over some years spent a fortune making it, so he thought, an impregnable fortress and an inexhaustible storehouse. Heaven knows how many thousands of gallons of gasoline he stored in underground tanks, how many hundreds of tons of canned and dried and concentrated food he hid in camouflaged vaults, how many motor trucks he bought, how many spare parts, radio tubes, socks, rifles, medical supplies, refrigerators. He thought of everything and bought a hundred of it. Well, someday while he was stalking a revolutionist after the charge had broken against his wall, one whom he had not seen would get a bead on him, or his humble hired hands would take the place from him. And even if that didn't happen, what would be precious about sleeping warm and eating a good meal in a canyon while the nation worked out its fate? An alimentary canal would be preserved for a while; but from the day he set in place the last massive stone of his guard wall, a man would be dead.

Now the fear is of the Bomb. Soon after Hiroshima, a famous scientist arranged to buy an abandoned mineshaft in the Black Hills of South Dakota. He and his family would be safe there, he thought, from the destruction that was to befall the United States. Maybe they would, but they would no longer be a part of the United States or even of humankind. His was an extreme form of a fantasy that is all about us. Real-estate firms in Washington, Pittsburgh, New York, and other metropolises advertise suburban property as being distant enough from industrial and military targets to be beyond the bomb's blast and radiation. Many people have bought houses or shacks in remote locations they think safe. Many others are working out ingenious plans to preserve themselves through the atomic war and enable them to survive when it ends.

The atomic bomb is real. The war we are engaged in, whether or not we call it war, is real. Terrible possibilities are real: that we may be led into a world-wide war, whose duration or even whose outcome we cannot foretell. It is true and real that, if the big war does not come, at best the United States must expect an indefinite period of armament for war, constant vigilance, and a national effort that will forever change and harden the way we live. Fear of these dangers in an age as desperate and precarious as any the world has ever seen is sane, logical, and justified. Fear of real danger is always intelligent and always a valuable weapon with which to combat danger.

But unreal fear is a greater danger than any real danger. We know this very well; but panic tugs at our minds, and the panic is worse than any horror it conjures up. For it could paralyze our thinking and our action.

The essence of our modern despair is that the twentieth century has seen two world wars, after a century in which there were only little wars. But take a thoughtful man when that peaceful century began just after Waterloo, which marked the downfall of Napoleon. Such a man would remember that the eighteenth century fought four world wars, all of them, comparatively, as destructive and as full of agony as ours. The seventeenth century fought three world wars, and each of them, like ours, changed forever everyone's expectation and way of life. The sixteenth century was a whirlpool of almost unceasing war, national, civil, religious. Our philosopher of 1815, looking back through the twenty-five years of world-wide war ended by Waterloo, across the three preceding centuries, on to the ancient world and beyond it to the savagery from which civilization arose—the philosopher might well have believed that war is an inescapable part of the way men live together in society.

Suppose for a moment (though I do not believe it is true) that periodic war is an inescapable part of society, and that we are headed toward our worst world war. Well, China's Great Wall could not keep the invading armies out, any more than the stone walls Londoners built in Samuel Pepys' time could keep the plague out. No nation can live at the bottom of a mine. It would not be a nation but only a cluster of fear-bound and paralyzed polyps.

Yet we are not correctly interpreting this panic if we think of it as national. It is individual, personal, private. If you scrutinize it with care, it turns out to be an abnormal manifestation of a normal fear which is so fundamental a part of life that everyone normally disregards it—the fear of death.

It is every human being's tragic hypochondria. Civilization has increased our expectation of life, but the terms of individual life have not been changed, and any infant born today may die day after tomorrow. Any time one crosses a street, the thin envelope of flesh may be obliterated by an automobile or a falling tile. There is no safety, and our private fear of the atomic bomb is merely a denial that we must keep our final appointment.

Actually, the fear is not of tomorrow but of the day after, and that is its danger—for the fear of death can keep us from living. There is the old question: If you knew you were to die day after tomorrow, what would you do tomorrow? Only one answer has ever been sensible: Just what I would do if I did not know—go to the office, take the children to the park, go on with the job, get married, buy the house, have a baby. All other answers would be folly, and the most foolish of all would be: I would spend my last twenty-four hours at the bottom of an abandoned mine.

We can never surely instill in our children what we have learned from our experience as we can bequeath them money we have saved. But suppose we could, and suppose, too, that there were no threat of war. What would you say to a son or daughter who intended to get married?

You might tell your children that many marriages lead to

Speech and Essay 93

failure and divorce, anguish they could escape by staying single. You might say that all marriages are full of deprivation, disappointment, and sorrow—husbands lose their jobs, savings are used up, homes have to be sold, children are crippled or they die or they grow up and break your heart. How foolish it is to risk all this when all of it can be avoided. But you never do say this. However you phrase it, what you say means that the decency and dignity of life lie not in evading it but in experiencing it as fully as possible. No one, you say, can promise anything surely or foretell what will happen. But make your cast, and no matter what happens, you will have affirmed life. Whatever the bitterness, failure, or tragedy, to act positively and in belief is to be alive, whereas to refrain from acting is to be dead while you still breathe.

Marriage, education, job, career—about none of these can one say anything else. The risk of failure is great, and death in the end is certain. But to refrain from action because of the risk is worse than folly: it is a premature form of the death it envisions. To anyone calculating the odds of life, one of the epitaphs in the Greek Anthology said three thousand years ago all that wisdom can ever say:

> A shipwrecked sailor on this coast
>   Bids you set sail;
> Full many a ship, when ours was lost,
>   Weathered the gale.

Now abandon the supposition that no war or disaster threatens us; face the reality of the world today. What should you do tomorrow if you knew that war was going to break out the day after? Precisely what you would do if you did not know. Go to the office, take the children to the park, get on with the job, get married, buy the house. No one can foretell how much fulfillment you will have, but you will have at least some; whereas you will have none at all if you refrain. To withhold action through fear is to deny life, which is the blackest sin.

It is also simple foolishness. For as you start down the abandoned mineshaft toward your twenty-four hours of safety, the ladder may break under your feet.

Life makes its own price tag. To everyone, the cost of being alive is just what he may be called upon to pay. You pay the amount printed on the tag, and it is a waste of emotion to lament that someone else seems to have got off for less. You cultivate your garden and take whatever crop it produces. Do you think, because fear keeps you from trying for what you want, your neighbors will not take from life whatever it may hold for them? Stop on the sidewalk transfixed by a horrible vision of the Third World War breaking out: all around you people are doing their jobs, shopping, going home to the family, making a date for dinner or the movies. If you pack your family off to the bottom of the mine, it will be the same: the world and its work will be going on. But you will not be part of it.

It will be the same if, while you watch your children playing with the pretty chunks of ore at the bottom of the shaft, the cloud of atomic fire mushrooms over the city from which you have fled. Thousands will be dying there—in pain that is just like any other pain. The rest will be working at the debris, patching up some sort of society, keeping the race going—getting married, begetting children, taking such fulfillment from life as they can, meeting their destiny. You will be meeting yours, too, but with the difference that you will be alone.

"Fellow countrymen, we cannot escape history." Lincoln said that, and at a moment as dark as ours; some would call it darker, for war was here, and the nation seemed likely to die of self-inflicted wounds. Now, as then, we cannot as a people escape destiny, any more than as individuals we can escape death. The United States must pay the sum printed on the tag. If this is an era of darkness, insecurity, and fear, that is the asking price for life, national and personal, in the days of our particular years, and there is no way of not paying the price. There is no Fiesole to which we can flee from the Florence we live in. It may be too bad—but it will be worse if fear of the day after tomorrow paralyzes us in the twenty-four hours that come between.

Fortunately, it will not paralyze the nation or many of us who, as individuals, compose the nation. The panic is private and of the upper levels of the mind, but the deeper levels are wiser. At the base of personality, sheer animal faith in life makes us affirm life. There is always a pistol or a bottle of sleeping pills, but we vote to wake tomorrow and cultivate our garden. Indeed, the affirmation is deeper than personality, for the body has a wisdom that resides in the nerves, the muscles, the very cells. They go on performing their function till death comes. Their function is the maintenance and renewal of human life. So is ours.

What does the asking price buy? At worst it will buy, day after tomorrow, the knowledge that we have lived an additional day—and if fear has not paralyzed us, that we got from it what we could, and did what we could. The knowledge that the United States went out to meet its destiny, acting positively, not refraining from action in panic. That we acted as a sound, sane, resolute people. That as a people we affirmed the life which is in us and were members one of another; and that as individuals we have lived in a decisive time and not shrunk from our part in it. That we stood for the dignity of human experience.

That, at worst. But it is possible that the affirmation of life will be the renewal of life, and that to meet destiny squarely will be to master destiny. We know down to the nerves and cells of our bodies that this is possible, that to act on our faith may be to hold off the big war, prevent the cloud of atomic fire, and usher in an age greater than any we have known before.

The Situation

Bernard De Voto was a professional writer successful as editor, novelist, critic, and historian. He was educated at Harvard University and taught there and at Northwestern University. He served for two years as editor of the *Saturday Review of Literature* [7] and from 1935 until his death in 1955 as editor of *Harper's Magazine* (the section called "The Easy Chair"). De Voto won the Pulitzer prize in history with *Across the Wide Missouri* in 1948 and is also known for his *Mark Twain's America*. A westerner (he was born in Utah), De Voto was an advocate of the conservation of natural resources and brought warmth and knowledge to this and other aspects of the American scene. He was frequently occupied with controversy over current

---

[7] Now published under the title of the *Saturday Review*.

issues. When one surveys De Voto's background, his point of view on the question raised in "Homily for a Troubled Time" seems authoritative.

De Voto wrote to the thoughtful American of our time. The subject has an interest for anyone in the world today, but as we shall see, the author indicated through his allusions and attitude that he had in mind the American audience in particular.

Assimilation of Content

De Voto tried to answer the question: How shall we behave in these days of fear of atomic war? He sought to put the fear of atomic war into historical perspective by speaking of other periods of fear in the history of the world. He dealt directly with the problem of personal fear, seeing the fear of an atomic bomb as an exaggeration of the normal human fear of death. In the case of the atomic bomb, as in all major human problems, one can affirm life by meeting it with faith, or one can deny life by hiding and shrinking from its challenges. De Voto believed that we can affect the direction and progress of our individual and collective destiny by meeting it head-on.

Achievement of Artistic Form

De Voto's style effectively combines informal and formal diction. The essay moves so adroitly from one level to another that one is scarcely surprised to find such phrases as "get a bead on him," "pack your family off," and "asking price" in the same company as: ". . . at best the United States must expect an indefinite period of armament for war, constant vigilance, and a national effort that will forever change and harden the way we live." Allusions to the depression and two world wars add to the sense of reality and familiarity, but even more effective are the references to everyday activities, such as: "go to the office," "take the children to the park," "go on with the job," "get married," "buy the house," "have a baby," "used up," and others. These familiar phrases bring the problem to us, involving us as the activities alluded to involve us.

De Voto achieves vividness mainly through two devices: appropriate imagery and abundant adjectives (sometimes nouns and verbs) in series. Homely sources of imagery are these: "Life makes out its own price tag," "cultivate your garden," and "pretty chunks of ore at the bottom of the shaft." [8] Images of greater elevation are:

> the reawakening sunlight which we call the Renaissance
> mountaintop above the stricken city
> canyon in the Oregon wilderness
> charge had broken against his wall
> whirlpool of almost unceasing war
> envelope of flesh
> cloud of atomic fire mushrooms over the city

Concreteness in series exists in such sentences as: "They were about the common, hearty, exuberant, tragic life of Italy"; "flour from his own wheat, meat from his own herds, fish from his own ponds, electricity from his own power plant"; "It is individual, personal, private"; ". . . all around you people are doing their jobs, shopping, going home to the family, making a date for dinner or the movies." Active participles in sequence again give liveliness to the development in such constructions as: ". . . working at the debris, patching up some sort of society, keeping the race going—getting married, begetting children, taking such fulfillment from life as they can, meeting their destiny."

Repetition plays a minor part in De Voto's plan, but you will wonder at first glance at his use of the commonly overworked words *terror* and *terribly; horror* and *horribly.* What is gained by using these words? How many times does De Voto mention *fear?* This word serves to unify the thought and to enhance the feeling of the essay.

The historical comparisons with which the essay opens are intensified by the recurring contrasts between safety and danger, between life and death. These emotionally tinged contrasts form the framework of the essay. We are also affected by the author's sense of history and chronology: six hundred years ago it was the Black Death; now it is the atomic bomb. Twenty-five years ago it was the depression; now it is the bomb. Other centuries have had wars. Moving backward from the two wars of the twentieth century, De Voto reminds us that there were four world wars in the eighteenth century, three in the seventeenth, and that the sixteenth was a century of almost unceasing war.

We become aware of time in another way. We are reminded of yesterday, today and tomorrow, and of the past, present, and future

---

[8] The first two are examples of metaphor, as well.

of the bomb. Most poignantly we realize the role of time in the life of an individual, committed to the cycle of birth to death.

Early in the essay the recurring theme that a vital force at the roots of life controls human actions becomes prominent. The *Decameron* dealt with a vigorous life which the storytellers hoped to shut out; fleeing from the human lot, be it depression or bomb, is contrary to Nature. We cannot escape life, for "the body has a wisdom that resides in the nerves, the muscles, the very cells." We are encouraged to behave decisively, whether the destiny of our nation is dark, or whether it is to reach "an age greater than any we have known before." This contrast closes the essay.

Another way of discovering just what De Voto is saying would be to note the problem-solving sequence which is present in the essay. The historical background and statement of the problem occupy the first seven paragraphs; the analysis of the problem takes up paragraphs eight through fifteen; the two solutions appear in paragraphs sixteen through twenty-three. Paragraph twenty-four presents De Voto's choice of the two possibilities, and the last two paragraphs envision the future which will follow if his proposal is acted upon. Before presenting the essay to an audience, you will want to make sure of these divisions, but above all, you will want to tie each of the sections together by paying close attention to the guideposts (signatures, if you will) along the way. For instance, the last sentence of paragraph seven signs off the paragraph, but the *next* to the last sentence states the theme clearly for the first time. To which will you give more time and force?

The first sentence of paragraph eight begins on a lower key, with a shift in feeling, but the paragraph builds rapidly. Paragraph nine follows a similar pattern. It is linked to paragraph ten by the one word "Now." Paragraph eleven repeats the idea of the bomb and the idea of war. And so you could proceed through the entire essay, finding the words which bind and the words which separate thoughts, and noting the relative prominence of thoughts. In this way you learn to put together again the divisions which you so carefully made, and when you come to interpret the selection you will give it to your audience as a unit, a *definable form.*

The Interpreter's Response

Although De Voto dealt with a fearsome topic, he managed to end on a high note of courage. Throughout the essay, an ideal type of behavior is implicit, often explicit. Yet the situation remains open throughout, mainly because of the intimacy created by the use of the second-person pronoun, the community of feeling derived from the first-person plural, and the note of practical good sense sustained by the examples. This openness requires the interpreter to maintain close contact with his audience, meeting it much as he would if he were delivering a speech.

The problem raised in "Homily for a Troubled Time" is still unsolved. If, as interpreter, you agree with the solution presented in the essay, you will hope to influence your listeners to accept it also. Many persons dislike facing hard questions, and this problem out of the present "troubled time" is a difficult and unpleasant dilemma. To avoid an unfavorable response from your audience, it would be wise to combine an attitude of rational contemplation with the vivid narrative examples. Alleviations of tension come with such paragraphs as those beginning "The essence of our modern despair" and "It is also simple foolishness." Further relief comes in the two paragraphs immediately following, with their terse closing statements contrasting the behavior of the one who hides with the behavior of the one who participates. Your body must reflect the interplay of tension and release in these ideas.

The author of this essay has, without doubt, written with a skill equaling his earnestness. Without skill in the handling of body and voice, your understanding of his substance will scarcely suffice. As you attain technical skills, the response you make to the written word will become more and more visible and audible to your listeners.

YOUNG LOVE

Hans Zinsser (1878–1940)

The first girl I ever noticed in what, later, I recognized as a sentimental emotion was called Mamie. She was the daughter of a truck driver in my father's chemical factory. We used to play in the large factory yard, where hundreds of barrels of resin were stored on end, and it was great fun to jump from barrel top to barrel top. Mamie had a brother who became a bosom friend, and games of tag on the barrels were organized in which Mamie—being several years younger—was patronizingly allowed to participate. She and her brother were sweet children, amiable and gentle, and I loved them both very dearly. Their lives were hard. At twelve and ten, respectively, they were called upon for severe domestic service, and their poor mother,—a stout, red-faced woman,—kind enough when she was sober, was less so when drunk. Their happy moments were the ones they spent with me, playing on the barrels, but when I went back to my playroom to have my feet dried and to be fed my supper, they went back to a little frame house where dirt, noise, unmerited abuse, and frugal tolerance were their lot.

Mamie was blue-eyed and blonde, with a bright blondeness that shone through the dirt on her face and the squalor of her clothes. And how humbly grateful she was to be allowed to be "It," chasing us over the barrels. There must have been a faint dawning of the endocrines in me even then, baneful prophecy of a long life of struggle, for while I was sorry for Jimmy when I happened to think of being so, there was always a protective tenderness in my heart for Mamie.

One day—it was drizzling—the wet drove us from our playground into a little shed where carboys of sulphuric acid were stored. I dug a nickel out of my pocket and Jimmy was dispatched to the store on the corner to buy some barber-pole candy sticks. Mamie and I sat close together, for we were damp and a little chilly. She stuck up her wet face to be kissed, and I gazed down at her with the warm intention of kissing her. But when I looked into her face, I saw two little rivulets running from Mamie's nose to her pouted upper lip. I had never noticed them before, although I had often observed her sticking her tongue out and upward, whenever she sniffed. For ours was a catarrhal climate. Now I looked and saw. But I have always been proud in later days that, even at this early age, I mastered my repulsion and kissed Mamie on her salty lips. Dear Mamie! What has become of you since? You were a lovely child, in spite of the rivulets on your upper lip, and—no doubt—you deserved more consideration than the world has given you. What happened to me at that moment has never left me since and is perhaps the only achievement that may eventually entitle me to some measure of self-approbation—namely, the mastery of arrogance and disgust by tenderness and pity.

We played in the great court of my father's chemical factory and the atmosphere was redolent with odors of resin, sulphuric acid, and amyl acetate. I never pass a chemical factory or smell amyl acetate without thinking of Mamie and our games on the barrels. Yes, the sense of smell is the most nostalgic of our senses. I recall a charming lady from the West who stayed with us in New York, but left suddenly—long before she had intended to. She was in the recently cleaned bathroom one morning and, smelling the household ammonia, got so homesick for her twins that she couldn't stand it and had to go home.

2

It is strange that after all these years I should remember their names. They were called Galeoti, and came from Florence; and the name of the English governess was Miss Satterthwaite. For a month, in the late spring, we played together, the two little girls and I, in the garden of the hotel at Pegli, on the Italian Riviera. Everything was bursting into flower, and the garden had bushes blazing with white and red; there were gravel walks, and a fountain with a spout in the middle, and goldfish which were fed conscientiously every morning by the fat proprietress. We skipped and laughed in the garden, for the little Galeoti girls—one of them my age, the other two years younger, which would make her ten—were merry and great chatterboxes in a mixture of Italian and English that was frequently corrected by the governess. We took long walks together into the hills, and came home with great bunches of violets. Late in the afternoon, Miss Satterthwaite often read to us. Among other things, she read an English translation of De Amicis. She was only a child herself, about seventeen, I should judge, and pretty as blonde, high-colored British girls so often are at that age. To me, she seemed a young goddess. I sat very quiet when she read, and followed her about like a little dog. She was very lonely—probably it was the first time she had been away from home and isolated, as a young English governess would be in an Italian family. The parents Galeoti were away most of the time on excursions and at night played cards with my father and mother and other people in the hotel, drinking large quantities of *Asti spumante* and having very jolly times, as we children could hear after we had gone to bed.

I slept in a room that faced the garden, and the warm fragrance from many flowers and shrubs came into my window. I used to pretend that I was going to bed outside, among the bushes. One night, I remember I could not sleep because the moon was white in the window; and, feeling restless and adventurous, I tiptoed through the hall and crept out into the garden. There, on a bench, Miss Satterthwaite was sitting, and when I slipped up beside her, I saw that she was weeping. I was very sorry for her, but she took my hand between hers and told me that it was only the moonlight, that she had felt lonesome and was crying only because it was so terribly beautiful. And suddenly she said: "Hush!" and I heard my first nightingale. But it was a great disappointment. I was thinking of Miss Satterthwaite and the terrible grief I thought she was enduring when she led me to the door and told me to be a good boy and go to bed.

3

Of course I have been more or less in love all my life. But in the golden, adolescent days I fell in and out much faster than I did later. A look, a touch of the hand, a word, or—as in one case—only the sound of a snatch of song heard through a window on a summer night, and I was off on the new, sometimes before I was out of the old. Even this was not embarrassing, because the ladies in question had been fallen in love with, adored in half a dozen execrable sonnets, taken on honeymoons to Spanish castles that I kept always ready and fully equipped for such purposes, and dropped again for a new love before they themselves had become aware that they were participating in a romantic adventure. I used them, so to speak, as lay figures for my sentimental education. It did me a lot of good, and them no harm.

There was Marie-Louise, the New York society girl, ten years older than I, indeed approaching thirty, an accomplished musician with a magnificent, almost Wagnerian soprano, but a figure pathologically—that is, incapacitatingly—fat. She would have made four of me, and she thought I was "a nice boy but a little funny."

There was Maud, the harness maker's daughter, a young Diana, but always suspecting melodramatic perils to her virtue from the rich man's son.

There was the Smith girl, who really had no particular attractions except that she lived in a hotel across the lake and tempted my Hero and Leander complex by sitting out on the wharf with a lantern at night; knowing that I would swim across a half mile of cold, black, starlit water just because of the stage setting. I might have been drowned half a dozen times, and no one the wiser till the next day; and when I did arrive and sat dripping and cold on the dock, we had nothing to say to each other—she, because she was a stupid little doll, and I because I was blown. Yet even she served a purpose, and I used to swim home and climb up the hill through the woods, half-frozen but feeling elatedly heroic and devoted.

There was—but why catalogue them? They were all appropriate in their individual ways, and played passive, usually unconscious rôles in my development. Unlike François Villon, I know more or less what life made of them—poor things. Not one turned out to be a princess, and those I've seen within the last ten years had become just as one would have expected— quite commonplace, with no signs whatever of having lived for a time in a cloud-swept castle somewhere between Barcelona and Bourg Madame.

In all this there was—I should say, in my own justification— a minimum of the physical. In defense of romanticism, which in so many of its aspects appears silly and affected, one should not underestimate the service it does, at a certain age, in sublimating into its lovely hocus-pocus what might otherwise, and, in its absence, often does, become a gross or careless attitude toward physical love. The romanticism which had me in its grip at that age was associated with hard riding, frugal living,— as far as food and drink were concerned,—and intellectual intoxication, under George Woodberry's influence, with the English romantic poets and their idealization of love. The cult of physical hardness helped considerably in keeping this state of mind from becoming, as it might so easily have done, a morbid one; for by instinct I knew the wisdom of Guarnerius's prescription for love-melancholy: "To go with haircloth, etc., as monks do, but above all to fast."

Also, the ladies as a rule were far from sentimental themselves. One of them, now the mother of four and the still attractive grandmother of two or three,—Ella,—how lovely, but, withal, how sensible she was! She was the daughter of the principal of a well-known boys' boarding school, and had an apartment of her own, on the corner of the big barrack-like school building, high above the road. I used to serenade her at night, riding under her window on my big gray horse, Harry, and singing softly to the twang of a lute—with many a sour chord, for Harry was young and lively. The first time, Ella came to the window for a moment in a lovely pink nightgown. The second time, she didn't come to the window at all. She pretended to be asleep, and didn't mention my visit the next day. The third time, just as I was really finding my voice, the window just above her own was thrown open and a bucket of cold soapsuds came smack down on my horse's head. For a mile, I just hung on, trying not to drop the lute. I was halfway to Shruboak before I had the horse under control. Ella didn't mention this the next day, either. The boy who threw the water was, I believe, the one whom she married a few years later. I trust she had little comfort of him. He had a depraved sense of humor.

4

There was a chestnut girl, who lived over the grocery store in the village. In those days, I classified girls as chestnut, sorrel, or bay. Her father was quite a celebrity. He was very old, a carpenter by trade, and had fought in the Civil War. When my father once complimented him on his hale-and-hearty appearance, and asked him how he had managed to live to such a healthy old age, he made a remark which I then thought original with him: "Ye want to know why I've lived so long, mister? Well, it's because I had sense enough to run like hell at the second battle o' Bull Run." Pansy was the apple of his eye. She was pretty, in the slightly oversolid, bucolic manner, and was what was called "pert" in her conversation. On warm summer evenings, when the roads were fragrant with locust blossoms, I often rode down to the store to sit on the piazza with her and the old man, who would tell us stories of what was still known as "the War." He often told the same tale, but since he was a great liar and never told it the same way twice, it was never stale. Pansy was amorously inclined, and in this case, at least, any ideas I got into my head were initiated by her. She was something of a local belle, and had acquired the habit, in a gently bovine manner, of exercising, in male company, beguilements which were highly effective with the young farmer boys, grooms, and store clerks throughout the township. This is not to insinuate that she was not a thoroughly nice girl, and if I was flattered and inclined to dangerous plays of imagination in her regard, I was probably like the foolish one of the verse:—

> *Stultus quando videt*
> *Quod pulchra puellula ridet*
> *Tum fatuus credit*
> *Se quod amare velit—*

which is to say that when a fool sees a fair maid smile at him, he thinks it love when it's only flirtation. At any rate, Pansy in her way was a dear girl, and I might have made a fool of myself with her as with others had it not been for one of those fortunate flashes of common sense which have so often snatched me, by mere accident, from precipices of imbecility.

One evening we were sitting on the porch. The old man had talked himself to sleep, and began to snooze right in the middle of the Wilderness. Invention had tired him. Pansy and I were sitting closer together than the temperature warranted, and her arm was pressed caressingly against my shoulder. There was a crescent moon, and a gentle breeze enfolded us with the fragrance of the honeysuckle vine. If her head had followed her arm at that moment, God knows what might have happened. But Pansy, though—I still truly believe—a good girl, possibly intent on a bolder yet—I insist—entirely innocent (innocent in the conventional sense) attack upon my emotions, asked me suddenly whether I would like to see their new calf. It *was so darling*, she said, and had such lovely eyes and such a soft, wet nose. It was a temptation, for the calf of course was in the barn; and the barn was isolated and dark and full of hay. I fell, and said I'd love to see the calf. Merely for convention's sake, I think, Pansy lighted a stable lantern, so that we might at least fulfill the ostensible purpose of really looking at the calf. Oh, how sweet and aphrodisiacally caressing is the odor of a cowbarn at night, with its indescribable blending of clover, cow manure, sour milk, and animal! A gentle tremor ascended my spine as I stepped over the threshold, and I drew Pansy's soft form closer to my side as we stumbled over the rough boards by the dim and swinging light in her hand. I had lost all interest in the calf, and dear Pansy I believe had completely forgotten it. Yet we dared not *not* look at it— half craving, half dreading what might happen when we had seen it. But here Pallas Athene—ever my guardian goddess— intervened. Pansy walked into the stall, put her chubby arm about the calf's neck, and held the stable lantern at arm's length in front of her. And here they were—both confronting me, the dim rays of the lantern illuminating both their faces. Fascinated, I gazed upon them. They appeared like two sisters —helpless, bovine, kindly; infinite vacuity looked out at me from these two pairs of large, swimming eyes. The expression of Pansy's warm and moist lips was not more invitingly tender than the soft, velvety nozzle of the calf. There they stood,— poor innocents,—two calves together; and I gazed and gazed, hypnotically held in the light of the lamp, until I did not know which was Pansy and which calf. And I bent down and kissed the calf tenderly on the nose. Then I went out quietly, and untied my horse from the hitching post. Pansy followed me out. There were tears in her eyes when she said good-night, as I mounted and rode away—sadly, but not without a sense of relief.

The Situation

In "Homily for a Troubled Time" the author, who sought to influence our thinking in regard to a vital issue in our lives, needed to be respected as a person of substance and intelligence. Hans Zinsser was not striving directly to persuade us of anything, and yet his personal and professional stature add interest to "Young Love." Reminiscences of this *kind* are rare, despite the ubiquitousness of reminiscences on this *subject*. We come through the essay feeling that a discerning individual, looking back over tender moments in his youth, has shed light on episodes in our own lives. Furthermore, we respect the intellectual fiber that keeps these memories from being flabby pieces of sentimentality. Images and allusions pop up which indicate that medical and bacteriological specialization may be useful outside the office and laboratory. Some of you may be familiar with the biography —in reality autobiography—from which this essay is taken [9] or with *Rats, Lice, and History*, a study of the influence of plagues on civilization. Dr. Zinsser taught at Harvard, Stanford, and Columbia and served on the American Red Cross Sanitary Commission to Serbia in World War I, besides being a colonel in the medical corps from 1917–1919, and sanitary commissioner in 1923 for the health section of the League of Nations in Russia to study cholera.

Assimilation of Content

The author was recalling humorously the loves of his adolescent years. He used a light touch throughout, laughing at himself as he remembered that "the ladies as a rule were far from sentimental themselves." In paragraph eleven he disclosed his attitude toward his romanticism and linked all the loves together in this justification of his tendency to fall in and out of love.

Beyond its value as a pleasure-giving essay, the account presents a clear picture of a certain mode of life in the latter years of the nineteenth century.

Achievement of Artistic Form

The precision with which Zinsser conveyed his impressions holds our interest from beginning to end. Careful observation and scientific training, combined with literary knowledge, give us surprising images and allusions. Notice from the world of science: "the endocrines in me," "catarrhal climate," "household ammonia," "pathologically fat." Do you react fully to the literary and artistic allusions: "almost Wagnerian soprano," "a young Diana," "Hero and Leander complex,"

---

[9] *As I Remember Him: The Biography of R. S.* (Boston: Little, Brown and Company, 1940).

"François Villon," "George Woodberry's influence," "Guarnerius," and the four lines of Latin verse?

Zinsser's concreteness helps us to see each girl clearly as an individual. He did not seem to repeat a certain type, but to appreciate different kinds of beauty and character! His comfortable social position gave him experiences that affected his choice of words. For instance, owning a horse made it easy for him to think of the coloring of his girls in relation to the coloring of horses: chestnut, sorrel, or bay. His travels in Europe created fresh experiences which he recollected so fully that he leads us unsuspectingly to terms that may be unfamiliar, such as: *Asti spumante,* and "somewhere between Barcelona and Bourg Madame."

The structure is loose, episodic, and not strictly chronological. With all its concreteness and vividness, the essay has a leisurely, almost dreamlike quality. This is due in part to the juxtaposition of *then* and *now,* in part to the sprinkling of sentiment, and in part to descriptions of beautiful scenes. The garden and locale of Florence, the revelation of imaginary castles, the fondness of lovers for evening—all these suggestions of sentiment tempt us to say that it took years for Zinsser to attain his height of objectivity and see the humor in the events he recounted.

Although episodic, the essay has a climax. Undoubtedly the final episode, portrayed at greater length and containing stronger humor, is climactic. Yet with a few introductory remarks it could be read without the preceding sections quite satisfactorily.

The Interpreter's Response

At first thought, one might consider "Young Love" a clear-cut example of direct communication. Is it not, after all, a true account of personal experience simply related? As a whole, it belongs to the open situation, but its parts vary in regard to openness, or directness. To read the passages of tenderness or simulated tenderness effectively, one must retreat slightly from the audience. The eyes should not be focused at the audience directly when reading, for example, "Dear Mamie! What has become of you since?" (after all, she's not in the audience!) and in the bits of dialogue, whether direct or indirect discourse. The humorous effect of the last episode would be augmented if "Oh, how sweet and aphrodisiacally caressing is the odor of a cowbarn at night, with its indescribable blending of clover, cow manure, sour milk, and animal" were read as though it were seriously nostalgic.

Since Zinsser is laughing at himself, the interpreter can emphasize the let-down which accompanies each little affair without appearing to be unsympathetic. Sympathy develops as we come to know that the author expresses a large measure of understanding for each object of love and *forgives himself* for all his foolish devotions. The contrast between his lot and Mamie's, his pity for what disgusted him in Mamie, his refusal to attribute anything but noble motives to the girls he remembers—these marks of kindliness endear the author to us.

We have said that the last episode may be read separately. There are several possible combinations: Sections 3 and 4, Sections 1, 3 and 4, Sections 1 and 3, or all four sections, with parts of 3 omitted. Care must be taken when the entire essay is read that each episode retains its individuality, but that the details do not impede the progression. With any cutting of paragraphs or sections, it is necessary to adjust emphasis by changes in rate, pitch, and loudness so that all parts bear their true relation to the whole and a climax is accurately attained.

Episodic though "Young Love" is, the interpreter must in any reading of it, full or curtailed, establish the "right" tone indicative of attitude—a blend of mellow humor and thoughtful observation. Probably the first real assurance that the touch is light comes in paragraph two, with "There must have been a faint dawning of the endocrines in me even then, . . ." Each section ends with a humorous comment or happening, and each girl, with the exception of Mamie, is dismissed with disillusioning, salty sense. If the interpreter is aware of this build in reverse, he is likely to make his audience aware of it, too. When he has mastered the selection, he will be revealing a humane, warm personality and suggesting a point of view toward young love.

For all of the rhetorical selections, the interpreter finds himself in a relatively open situation, communicating ideas and feelings directly to his audience. We have pointed out that even in such an open situation, emotional fervor or a mood of recollection can move material toward closure. *Variety in one's interpretation* comes from *responding to the variety in the materials themselves*, not from interjecting certain vocal or physical actions in an attempt to enliven one's delivery. Awareness of changes in the openness or closure of the situation is an important aspect of interpretative style. For all rhetorical materials, in addition, there must be absolute clarity in the progression of the thought. Narrative or illustrative passages are effective when properly subordinated in order to support and not to overwhelm the outline of the thesis. Success in interpreting rhetorical materials comes with the ability to achieve emphasis by means of vocal and bodily force, to bring out the contrasts by use of shading in loudness and pitch, and to enliven the whole interpretation with appropriate responses to the rhythmic values suggested by the choice and arrangement of words. Further help in adapting one's means to proper ends will come as we analyze poetic materials and learn more about the physical and vocal means at our disposal.

Selections for Interpretation

RADIO AND TELEVISION DIALOG

John Crosby (1912–)

After examining the drama again—Broadway, movies, radio, television—I've decided to issue the Crosby Pocket Handbook which will come out from time to time and will settle barroom arguments among dialog writers.

You get a couple dialog writers, they're discussing a scene where the girl realizes she's got cancer, her husband is saying, "Joanna, you look like a ghost. What . . . ?" The correct line for her, of course, is "I'm tired, just tired, that's all." That's now official.

Any deviation, like deviations from any ceremony, will be considered blasphemous and the penalty therefore will be court-martial or, at the very least, the tab on the next drink.

Dialog writing has become a matter as ceremonious as Japanese drama. We had better codify these things so that everyone knows what to expect in given situations. Following are the proper lines for given situations. I've omitted some of the situations since we all know them well:

"Doctor, you've got to pull her through. You've got to. She's all I have."

"Son . . . , you'd better get some rest."

Then there's the tense moment in the detective drama. Here, depending on the circumstances and the way the plot is shaping up, there are two opposite ways of handling the problem:

"Tell him, Joe! Tell him. If you won't say where you were at the hour of the murder, I will!"

"Maisie, you don't know what you're saying."

"Inspector, Joe was with me. In—my boudoir."

Or there's the other side of the coin.

"I was with you all evening—you know I was, Maisie! I was with you. Go on! Tell them!"

"Inspector, I never saw this man before in my life."

The scene where the girl is lost, heartbroken, and broke in the bus station and Cary Grant happens through and helps her out:

"Why are you—a stranger—doing all this for me?"

The problems of maternity, paternity, and what might be described as the You Were Almost My Daughter gambit have to be treated fairly extensively:

"Jennifer, 20 years ago I loved a woman. She never knew. I never told her. Because—well, that woman was your mother. And it was your father that she loved. So I went away—it doesn't matter where. But tonight she lives again—in all her loveliness, in you, my child. And that is why—but this is a night for youth and gaiety and love. Back to the ball with you both! I will join you later—later—later."

The absent or deceased parent gambit:

A—"How proud your mother would have been to see you in your graduation dress!"

B—"Bill, you can't quit! You've got to keep fighting this thing. Mother would have wanted it this way."

C—"And that man was—your father."

Bereavement or imminent bereavement? Well, naturally we have to cover that:

"Oh God, I'm just a little boy seven years old and maybe I've been bad but don't let my dog Rover die. I'll be a good boy, God. Thank you God. Goodby God. Amen."

You want some goodby music? Here it is:

"I guess I've led a pretty hard life, Miss Milly. There ain't many laws I ain't broke. But I'd just like you to know—well, since that night I met you—well, I been trying to go straight, anyway. I know I ain't fit to be speaking to you like this—but I wanted you to know. So, well, I guess this is goodbye."

Most of these classic lines were penned in 1933 by Nunnally Johnson. It just goes to show nothing has changed very much in the spoken drama in seventeen years.

WHY I NEVER BAWL OUT A WAITRESS

Harry Golden (1902–   )

I have a rule against registering complaints in a restaurant; because I know that there are at least four billion suns in the Milky Way—which is only one galaxy. Many of these suns are thousands of times larger than our own, and vast millions of them have whole planetary systems, including literally billions of satellites, and all of this revolves at the rate of about a million miles an hour, like a huge oval pinwheel. Our own sun and its planets, which includes the earth, are on the edge of this wheel. This is only our own small corner of the universe, so why do not these billions of revolving and rotating suns and planets collide? The answer is, the space is so unbelievably vast that if we reduced the suns and the planets in correct mathematical proportion with relation to the distances between them, each sun would be a speck of dust, two, three, and four thousand miles away from its nearest neighbor. And, mind you, this is only the Milky Way—our own small corner— our own galaxy. How many galaxies are there? Billions. Billions of galaxies spaced at about one million light-years apart (one light-year is about six trillion miles). Within the range of our biggest telescopes there are at least one hundred million separate galaxies such as our own Milky Way, and that is not all, by any means. The scientists have found that the further you go out into space with the telescopes the thicker the galaxies become, and there are billions of billions as yet uncovered to the scientist's camera and the astrophysicist's calculations.

When you think of all this, it's silly to worry whether the waitress brought you string beans instead of limas.

MY MOTHER AND GOD

Harry Golden (1902–   )

My father was an intellectual and our home was filled with talk. We are a vocal people to begin with, and it was not unusual for intellectuals to spend hours discussing the meaning of a single sentence in the Law, or for that matter, a single word. We are the greatest hairsplitters in the world. A pilpul is what they call these complicated discussions. But my father went far beyond the Biblical text. He was at home with Henry George, and Eugene V. Debs, and Benjamin Franklin, and the rationalists of the past. He conducted a sort of philosophy discussion group every Saturday afternoon. Five or six of the men would be gathered around the table and my mother was busy serving them. She walked on tiptoe not to disturb the great men, as she brought the platters of boiled potatoes or haiseh bubbes (chick-peas), and silently went her way. But there was always a trace of a smile on her face, if not cynical, certainly one of amusement.

My mother, I would say, was a primitive woman. She spoke only Yiddish. She could read the prayers out of the book but that was all. She spent all her time cooking, cleaning, sewing; sewing for the family as well as professionally for the neighbors. I think my intellectual father guessed at my mother's "amusement." I have had the feeling that he knew that she was not overly impressed. My mother, of course, thought all those discussions were nonsense. What does a person need but God? And she had God. Sometimes I smile at all the goings-on over the radio about God. Whose God are they talking about anyway—what do they know about God? My mother talked with God all the time, actual conversations. She would send you on an errand and as you were ready to dart off into the crowded, dangerous streets, she turned her face upward and said: "Now see that he's all right." She smiled at the boy, but was dead serious when she spoke to Him. She gave the impression that this was a matter-of-fact relationship, part of the covenant. "In the home that boy is my obligation but once he is out on the street, that is Your department and be sure to see to it." And she never permitted a single expression involving the future to be uttered without that covering clause, "With God's help." And this had to follow hard upon the original assertion. Thus if you ran down the hallway saying, "I'll go to the library tomorrow," she chased after you to make sure that there was no great lapse between your stated intention and the follow-up, "With God's help."

I do not know of any people *less* chauvinistic than the Jews. Just imagine if another race had produced the Ten Commandments, for instance. Think of the place that event would have held in history? But the Jews have always insisted that they had nothing to do with any of these wonderful things. God merely used them to establish His moral code among the peoples of the world. This idea influenced our entire history and every phase of our lives. If a dish happened to turn out well, do you think my mother would take credit for it? Not at all. She said it was an act of God. God helped her cook and sew and clean. And sometimes you have to wonder about it. I am thinking of Mother's potato latkes (pancakes) and holishkas (chopped beef and spices rolled in cabbage leaves and cooked in a sweet-and-sour raisin sauce) and kreplach (small portions of dough folded around chopped beef, boiled, and then dropped into a steaming hot platter of golden chicken soup), and I will say this, "If God did not really help her prepare those dishes (as she claimed), how is it that I haven't been able to find anything equal to them in all these years?" This is the kind of evidence that would even stand up in a court of law.

ORATION AT HIS BROTHER'S GRAVE

Robert Ingersoll (1833–1899)

My Friends:—I am going to do that which the dead oft promised he would do for me.

The loved and loving brother, husband, father, friend died where manhood's morning almost touches noon, and while the shadows still were falling toward the west.

He had not passed on life's highway the stone that marks the highest point, but, being weary for a moment, he lay down by the wayside, and, using his burden for a pillow, fell into that dreamless sleep that kisses down his eyelids still. While yet in love with life and raptured with the world he passed to silence and pathetic dust.

Yet, after all, it may be best, just in the happiest, sunniest hour of all the voyage, while eager winds are kissing every sail, to dash against the unseen rock, and in an instant hear the billows roar above a sunken ship. For, whether in midsea or 'mong the breakers of the farther shore, a wreck at last must mark the end of each and all. And every life, no matter if its hour is rich with love and every moment jeweled with joy, will, at its close, become a tragedy as sad and deep and dark as can be woven of the warp and woof of mystery and death.

This brave and tender man in every storm of life was oak and rock, but in the sunshine he was vine and flower. He was the friend of all heroic souls. He climbed the heights and left all superstitions far below, while on his forehead fell the golden dawning of the grander day.

He loved the beautiful, and was with color, form, and music touched to tears. He sided with the weak, and with a willing hand gave alms; with loyal heart and with purest hands he faithfully discharged all public trusts.

He was a worshiper of liberty, a friend of the oppressed. A thousand times I have heard him quote these words: "For justice all places, a temple, and all seasons, summer." He believed that happiness was the only good, reason the only torch, justice the only worship, humanity the only religion, and love the only priest. He added to the sum of human joy; and were every one to whom he did some loving service to bring a blossom to his grave, he would sleep to-night beneath a wilderness of flowers.

Life is a narrow vale between the cold and barren peaks of two eternities. We strive in vain to look beyond the heights. We cry aloud, and the only answer is the echo of our wailing cry. From the voiceless lips of the unreplying dead there comes no word; but in the night of death hope sees a star, and listening love can hear the rustle of a wing.

He who sleeps here, when dying, mistaking the approach of death for the return of health, whispered with his latest breath: "I am better now." Let us believe, in spite of doubts and dogmas, and tears and fears, that these dear words are true of all the countless dead.

And now to you who have been chosen, from among the many men he loved, to do the last sad office for the dead, we give this sacred dust. Speech cannot contain our love. There was, there is, no greater, stronger, manlier man.

DEFINITION OF "A NICE PERSON"

Sydney Smith (1771–1845)

A nice person is neither too tall nor too short, looks clean and cheerful, has no prominent feature, makes no difficulties, is never misplaced, sits bodkin, is never foolishly affronted, and is void of affectations.

A nice person helps you well at dinner, understands you, is always gratefully received by young and old, Whig and Tory, grave and gay.

There is something in the very air of a nice person which inspires you with confidence, makes you talk, and talk without fear of malicious misrepresentation; you feel that you are reposing upon a nature which God has made kind, and created for the benefit and happiness of society. It has the effect upon the mind which soft air and a fine climate has upon the body.

A nice person is clear of little, trumpery passions, acknowledges superiority, delights in talent, shelters humility, pardons adversity, forgives deficiency, respects all men's rights, never stops the bottle, is never long and never wrong, always knows the day of the month, the name of every body at table, and never gives pain to any human being.

If any body is wanted for a party, a nice person is the first thought of; when the child is christened, when the daughter is married—all the joys of life are communicated to nice people; the hand of the dying man is always held out to a nice person.

A nice person never knocks over wine or melted butter, does not tread upon the dog's foot, or molest the family cat, eats soup without noise, laughs in the right place, and has a watchful and attentive eye.

5

Lyric

Blood, imagination, and intellect running together . . . ᴄᴧ
WILLIAM BUTLER YEATS

Out of the slimy mud of words, out of the sleet and hail of verbal imprecisions,
Approximate thoughts and feelings, words that have taken the place of thoughts and feelings,
There spring the perfect order of speech, and the beauty of incantation. ᴄᴧ T. S. ELIOT

IN PRECEDING CHAPTERS we have made distinctions between poetical and rhetorical forms, but have seen that certain developmental tendencies may occasionally overshadow differences and cause *poetic* and *rhetoric* to merge. When we examine the sub-forms of poetic, we find the same tendency to overlapping. But since we are not bent on classification, but upon the discovery and enjoyment of the work of art, we can accept conventional classifications for the convenience that they afford us and spend the greater part of our time looking closely at the works themselves. It is this close look which will provide us as interpreters with the clues to style and performance.

The ideas and factual materials which occupied the foreground of *rhetoric* recede in poetic forms. Consequently, we need to spend much less time upon the situational aspects so vital to the speech and often to the essay; instead, we shall attempt to get close to the inner life of the work, its texture, organization, and rhythm serving as guides. The one aspect of the situation which remains central is the question of directness, or, as we have said, the degree of openness in a given situation. In Chapter 2 we have placed lyric at a middle point in respect to openness, with narrative and drama progressively less open. Following this progression, it is natural to move from the essay to the lyric poem, thence to narrative, and finally to drama. Accordingly, we have arranged the three lyric poems to be dealt with in this chapter as follows:

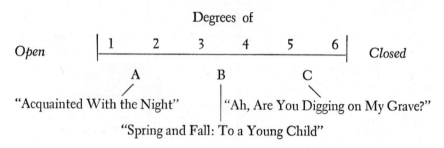

ACQUAINTED WITH THE NIGHT

Robert Frost (1875–   )

I have been one acquainted with the night.
I have walked out in rain—and back in rain.
I have outwalked the furthest city light.

I have looked down the saddest city lane.
I have passed by the watchman on his beat
And dropped my eyes, unwilling to explain.

I have stood still and stopped the sound of feet
When far away an interrupted cry
Came over houses from another street,

But not to call me back or say good-bye;
And further still at an unearthly height,
One luminary clock against the sky

Proclaimed the time was neither wrong nor right.
I have been one acquainted with the night.

The Situation

We start with this poem by Robert Frost because it is close to the open form of the essay in certain respects. The speaker seems to expect understanding from an audience outside the situation of the poem and not specifically defined. However, the speaker is not necessarily the author. Frost may have taken many such night walks as he describes, but as a poet he was not limited to actual experience or bound by the events he recorded. In other words, we need not seek to locate the experience of the poem through reference to Frost's biography. Sometimes, if the interpreter's study of the script leaves him puzzling over allusions or artistic intention, biographical orientation is profitable for him, but here it is sufficient to know that the poem is open speech about a highly personal and humanly significant experience. The degree of indirectness, which moves "Acquainted With the Night" into the realm of poetry, is achieved by rhythmic pattern, significant images, and enveloping scene. Also contributing to indirectness are suggestion, rather than complete revelation, and the employment of past tense.

Assimilation of Content

The depth of this deceptively simple lyric becomes apparent when we try to express its paraphrasable content. We might say something like this: "The speaker has found himself solitary in the world of men and nature alike and has come to feel that the soul of man is doomed to loneliness." We see at once that we have not captured the whole of the poem. We have left out the prominent image of the "luminary clock." Shall we begin again? "The night walk symbolizes man's isolation and the temporal limits of his existence." We still have not indicated the measure of quietness, the resignation to an indifferent world, that colors the poem. We look at the lyric with new respect. What gives distinction to these lines about a night walk in the rain?

The individual acquainted with the night is one who has looked squarely at the starkness of existence. Yet he does not look upon his lone moments as the total of his life. The tense of the verb "have been" suggests that the speaker has accepted the night and the aloneness and moved on. Like the clock, he refrains from making a judgment. Why was he walking in the rain at night? Why was he alone? The poem gains additional depth if one equates mankind with "city light" and "city lane," and the natural universe with "night" and "rain." The light of the city was insufficient for the speaker, and the city itself offered little of human comfort or help. Even the inter-rupted cry was not meant for his ears. He proceeded alone, his only light the luminous dial of a clock that measured off the limits of his days and the indifferent progress of time. "Time," like "city light," "night," and "rain," has a second meaning besides its surface meaning. It can apply to the era in which the individual found himself, the period of the world's history.

Achievement of Artistic Form

Although we never lose our awareness of time, the poem moves spatially, too. We walk along the city streets, out beyond the city, back into the city, where we look up to the clock that dominates man's night and day. The structure and internal organization of the poem work together to convey the rhythms of walking, of hesitations, of decisions. The language is familiar, there are few symbols, but the poem is carefully designed. The organization owes a good deal to repetition, sometimes exact, sometimes partially identical, but always cumulative in feeling. The poem begins and ends with the same words; the third repeats the second line with slight change.[1] Line 4 repeats the subject-verb, or agent-action, order used in the first three lines as well as the word "city," but this time "city" modifies "lane," not "light." Line 7 brings us to a halt, then turns us from the outward action and scene to the inner.

As the outward action decreases, the image of sound takes over and dominates four lines, to be immediately succeeded in lines 10 to 12 by kinesthetic imagery. Since each group of three lines contains a different image, the images provide both expectancy and variety and play their part in the total rhythmic effect.

In the first six lines, the agent-action order, the mid-line pause, and the lurking syncopation of lines 1, 3, 4, and 5 all contribute to marked symmetry. To counteract this symmetry and avoid monotony, the poet provided textural variety through contrasting long vowel with short

---

[1] Elizabeth Drew says of this structure, "This is a sonnet, but the poet has intensified the atmosphere of unrelatedness by breaking up the close-knit form into triplets." See her *Poetry, A Modern Guide to Its Understanding and Enjoyment* (New York: Dell Pub-lishing Co., 1959), p. 145. © Copyright, 1959, by Elizabeth Drew. Published by the Dell Publishing Co., Inc., and reprinted by permission of the publishers.

vowel, voiced consonant with unvoiced consonant. We find these contrasts in the first line, where "one" with its length and resonance stands next to "acquainted" with its two unvoiced consonants; and in the eighth line, where the long vowels in "far away" and "cry" balance the short ones in "interrupted."

The quietness of the night scene is implicit in the total sound pattern, with its numerous repetitions of the unvoiced (*t*) and the palatal (*k*). The rhyme scheme firmly binds the sounds together in the following way:

aba contains two *a*'s and one *b*.
bcb contains two *b*'s and one *c*.
cdc contains two *c*'s and one *d*.
ded contains two *d*'s and one *e*.
ee rounds off the succession of two old sounds and one new sound.

Alliteration in lines 4 (*s*), 7 (*s*), 10 (*b*), and 13 (*r*) joins with repeated (*n*'s) and (*m*'s) within syllables to enrich the design. The several instances of assonance are built on one sound, long (*i*), more accurately known as the diphthong (*ay*), dominant in lines 1, 3, 6, and 13.

Taken together, the repetitions of words and sounds and the carefully planned rhymes yield a pattern of sound which, by intensifying the feeling, enhances the theme. In translating meaning for an audience, the interpreter must be keenly aware of what the poet has done to objectify meaning.

SPRING AND FALL: TO A YOUNG CHILD

Gerard Manley Hopkins (1844–1889)

Margaret, are you grieving
Over Goldengrove unleaving?
Leaves, like the things of man, you
With your fresh thoughts care for, can you?
Ah! as the heart grows older
It will come to such sights colder
By and by, nor spare a sigh
Though worlds of wanwood leafmeal lie;
And yet you will weep and know why.

Now no matter, child, the name:
Sorrow's springs are the same.
Nor mouth had, no nor mind, expressed
What heart heard of, ghost guessed:
It is the blight man was born for,
It is Margaret you mourn for.

The Situation

Our study of "Acquainted With the Night" moved us a step away from the completely open situation and across the threshold of poetic form. Now, in "Spring and Fall: To a Young Child," we move still farther along the continuum toward the closed situation.

The speaker in "Spring and Fall: To a Young Child" might well be the poet himself, but he is identified only by his age: he is older than the one he addresses. The speaker muses, partly to the child, partly to himself. We shall later discuss the archaisms, emotional intensity, and technical devices which add to the indirectness of the lyric. We visualize a young child, a girl, in the September wood, a child touched with sadness at the sight of fallen leaves. The child and the scene are so vivid that we seem to be overhearing a conversation, not a monologue. It could be argued that the poem contains signs of response from the child, that some expression, though unworded, prompted the speaker to utter lines 5 and 10.

Assimilation of Content

Many poets have written of the swift passage of time, the swing of the seasons, and the shortness of human life. Hopkins characteristically connects the earth's cycle and the human cycle, and with one stroke makes his point: Margaret, you are not mourning for the "worlds of wanwood," but for the self that they symbolize. Hopkins presents Margaret, a human being, at a moment of interaction with the physical world outside herself. Knowing that Hopkins sought an unadulterated vision of nature in order to experience full sensuous awareness of it, we find his choice of a child extremely apt. With her awareness, the child has intuitive knowledge [2] of the ephemeral nature of beauty in the physical world.

[2] Expressed in lines 12 and 13 before the return to the main theme in lines 14 and 15.

As we reread the poem, we discover that implied imagery carries on a mysterious, subterranean current of meaning. There are implied oppositions: nature and man, in lines 3 and 4; the spring, which is the child's age, and the fall, which is the speaker's age, in the title; mouth and mind (knowledge) against heart and spirit (innocence) in lines 12 and 13. Throughout, the fresh view of youth is contrasted with the knowledge of age. From these oppositions comes much of the symbolic force of the lyric. But the likenesses between nature and man help to unify the poem. Plants and man alike are subject to an invisible "blight" or force; *springs* which are a natural flow of water from the earth may also suggest the natural flow of feeling in man. The faded leaves at the feet of bare trees may symbolize crumbling emotional and moral worlds. Change in nature parallels change in man, but change means transience, and death comes to objects in nature and to man. Thus, death in the "worlds of wanwood" brings a premonition of death to the child.

The vocabulary of the poet needs close attention. The economical compounding of meaning into single words, as in line 2, the archaic meaning of "ghost," and the symbolism of the compounding in line 8 —all these demand study. Without close reading, Hopkins' individual devices for achieving dynamic movement may impede understanding and appreciation.

Achievement of Artistic Form

The basic design of this poem, and one often used by Hopkins, is a description followed by a comment. Such a statement of case followed by interpretation might be labeled rhetorical, but Hopkins himself preferred to call it a movement from *sense pattern* to *inner form*. The poem moves temporally from a moment of present contemplation to a projected future, and then returns to the present with the thrust of the last line. The aphorism, "Sorrow's springs are the same," holds the weight of the poem, but enlargement comes from the secondary meaning, that a sense of the transience of beauty and life is intuitive.[3]

The poet achieved an effect of spontaneity despite his known concern for technique by his use of direct address and question, the inversions of colloquial, intimate speech, and the use of monosyllabic words. Despite the intensity of the poem, there is surprising realism, illus-

[3] See reference to intuitive knowledge, page 124.

trated by "Now no matter, child, the name:" overriding childish attempts at explanation. Spontaneity and intensity are both increased by the remarkable *economy* of Hopkins' style. He drops articles and relative pronouns, combines adjectives with nouns ("Golden-grove," "wanwood"), substitutes ejaculation for subordinations or stated transitions, and deftly conceives epithets and aphorisms.[4] Adjectives with sensory appeals—*golden, fresh, older, colder, wan*—and participles suggesting activity—*grieving, unleaving, expressed, guessed*—vivify and emphasize meaning.

Hopkins was a theorist as well as a serious poet, and he labored to describe his poetic processes.[5] As a poet, he exploits fully the resources of his medium: he employs word repetitions, rhyme, alliteration, and assonance; he forms unexpected compounds; he resorts to archaic usages of familiar words and finds original ways of handling conventional metrical patterns.

In "Spring and Fall: To a Young Child," Hopkins finds simple rhyming couplets serviceable. Often he uses full word repetitions to gain his effect at the ends of lines: "you, can you," "born for, mourn for"; but he varies the scheme at the point of greatest desolation, and we find lines 7, 8, and 9 constituting a triplet, ending with the diphthong in "sigh," "lie," and "why."

An easy way to "scan" "Spring and Fall: To a Young Child" (or any poem, for that matter) is to set down a slant mark for each syllable, line by line, in this fashion:

```
⊽ / ⊽ ⊽ / ⊽ /
⊽ / ⊽ / ⊽ / ⊽ /
/ / / / / / /
/ / / / / / / /
```

Then read the poem with your normal sense-feeling stresses and conventional pronunciation and place a horizontal mark above each syllable that receives stress. You will discover that "Spring and Fall: To a Young Child" is basically a four-stress, trochaic line, but that, no matter how many syllables each contains, the feet are of equal length,

---

[4] In certain sonnets ("God's Grandeur," "The Windhover," and "Pied Beauty"), these characteristic devices are striking in effect.

[5] See Preface to *Poems and Prose of Gerard Manley Hopkins*. Introduction by W. H. Gardner (Baltimore: Penguin Books, Inc., 1954).

and a one-syllable foot will take as much reading time as a four-syllable foot. Pauses, or extended quantity, take the time of the extra syllable.[6] When Hopkins wanted additional emphasis, he placed an accent mark above the syllable he thought should receive emphasis, and editions of his work include these markings from his manuscripts. In the poem at hand, you will notice them in lines 1, 3, 5, 11, and 14. Considering them carefully, do you believe that they add to or detract from your reading of the poem?

The addition of alliteration to these stressed syllables is unmistakably attention-getting, and "Spring and Fall: To a Young Child" is richly alliterative. Some examples are:

grieving, Goldengrove	*g*'s	lines 1, 2
unleaving, leaves, like	*l*'s	lines 2, 3
fresh, for	*f*'s	line 4
care, can	*k*'s	line 4

If you follow through the poem, you will find others. The *w*'s, *l*'s, and *g*'s are especially noteworthy. Assonances in lines 2, 5, 6, and 8 are part of the textural detail.

Hopkins manipulates the flow of sound, reversing the metrical foot (with the effect that strong stresses end a foot which normally would end with light stress), or truncating several feet to achieve successive heavy stresses or monosyllables, side by side: "fresh thoughts care," "heart grows old(er)," "such sights cold(er)," "you will weep," "springs are," "what heart heard," "ghost guessed." The emphasis of these stresses does not slow the movement of the lines, for Hopkins conceived the total metrical pattern so clearly that his lines are tied fast together by *enjambment* and *anacrusis*.[7]

Understanding of the situation and contents, with all its implications, must be augmented by consideration of these technical values if the interpreter is to give the poem an appropriate reading. In particular, there must be recognition of the time values which Hopkins worked out so conscientiously.

---

[6] In addition to Hopkins' Preface, see Harold Whitehall, "Sprung Rhythm," in The Kenyon Critics, *Gerard Manley Hopkins* (Norfolk, Connecticut: New Directions Books, 1945). See also Chapter 3 above, especially p. 56.

[7] Enjambment occurs in the following lines: 3 and 4; 5 and 6; 7 and 8; 12 and 13. Anacrusis is illustrated in lines 4, 8, and 9. Hopkins speaks of "rove over" lines.

AH, ARE YOU DIGGING ON MY GRAVE?

Thomas Hardy (1840–1928)

"Ah, are you digging on my grave
    My loved one?—planting rue?"
—"No: yesterday he went to wed
One of the brightest wealth has bred.
'It cannot hurt her now,' he said,
    'That I should not be true.' "

"Then who is digging on my grave?
    My nearest dearest kin?"
—"Ah, no: they sit and think, 'What use!
What good will planting flowers produce?
No tendance of her mound can loose
    Her spirit from Death's gin.' "

"But some one digs upon my grave?
    My enemy?—prodding sly?"
—"Nay: when she heard you had passed the Gate
That shuts on all flesh soon or late,
She thought you no more worth her hate.
    And cares not where you lie."

"Then, who is digging on my grave?
    Say—since I have not guessed!"
—"O it is I, my mistress dear,
Your little dog, who still lives near,
And much I hope my movements here
    Have not disturbed your rest?"

"Ah, yes! *You* dig upon my grave . . .
    Why flashed it not on me
That one true heart was left behind!
What feeling do we ever find
To equal among human kind
    A dog's fidelity!"

"Mistress, I dug upon your grave
    To bury a bone, in case
I should be hungry near this spot
When passing on my daily trot.
I am sorry, but I quite forgot
    It was your resting-place."

The Situation

Thomas Hardy wrote novels out of the literary tradition in which he was nurtured, but when he turned to poetry, he cast off tradition. His reactions to events in the world and his mode of expressing them were highly individualized.

In this poem, as in others, Hardy pierces sentimentality and self-deception. The true facts of existence are a contrast to an individual's hopes and desires, and the result is an ironic comment. Despite its insistence on realism, the poem calls upon our powers of willing belief, for one of the speakers is dead, and the other is a dog. The situation is moving further toward closure, for the dialogue is evenly divided between the two speakers, and there is no recognition of other listeners. The first speaker's identity is established in the first three lines: she is dead and speaking from her grave. We are not sure of the second speaker's identity until we reach the fourth stanza. Then we become acutely aware of the rural scene, the forlorn grave, and the little creature whose digging has disturbed the sleeper. The indirectness is achieved in part by dialogue and scene, in part by the music of the lines. We are further held by the demand upon our imaginations and compelled to give credence to the incredible—the personification of the animal who also serves as the local newspaper.[8]

Assimilation of Content

This poem, like Hopkins' poem above, makes a comment, but we cannot find the lines which contain it. We know only that the stanzas leave us with the impression that the individual, once dead, is soon forgotten by those who remain behind. The lover, the family, even the enemy, find their daily business all-absorbing. The poem seems at first to be probing into the subject of mourning, but upon reflection, we see that the larger subject of the individual's place in the universe is being looked at, in a situation where mourning would be appropriate. At first we are shaken and disillusioned with the face of reality, which the poet wipes clean of sentimentality. It is only when we begin to understand that the healthy flow of life above the grave is necessary

---

[8] In other poems, as well, Hardy endowed members of the animal kingdom with human attributes.

that we can accept the poet's negation of individual desire for permanence.

The characterization of the dead woman helps us, too, to accept the poet's picture of reality. She seems self-centered, if not selfish, and a bit shallow. Yet she is redeemed by her affectionate nature. The dog, too, is affectionate, and although normally we do not expect more than affection from a dog, we find this one understanding and apologetic like a human being confessing a fault. The loving feelings give the poem tenderness and redeem it from absolute defeat. Somehow, too, we feel that the whole conversation is as temporal as life above the grave, and that the sadness is only a whim of the dead and will not last long.

The development of the incident is clear and swift. The dead woman is disturbed by someone digging on her grave. Her first question receives an answer that hurts and surprises her: her lover, whom she most of all hoped would be at her grave, was wed just yesterday to a wealthy beauty. Her second question reveals that her family is resigned to her death. Preferring enmity to oblivion, she is jarred to hear that she no longer has an enemy. At this point, she is happy to settle for the possibility that her pet dog alone has remained true; but she is not allowed even such slight comfort. In all honesty, the little dog confesses that his practical concern for his own future appetite was his motive for being present. He, too, had "quite forgot" that his mistress lay there in her final sleep.

Achievement of Artistic Form

The poem answers an unstated question: Who remembers me (or Who is faithful to me) now that I am dead? The faithfulness of the pet dog would, after all, be an unoriginal solution, but it gives the dead woman comfort to cling to this answer as long as she can. The answer that no one remembers is postponed until the last two lines, which completely reverse the seemingly straightforward movement of the preceding five stanzas. This is actually a second reverse movement, the first one coming in stanza four precipitated the climax of feeling in stanza five. The dead woman has been insistent up to this point that another human being must be at her grave, but in stanza four she learns that her little dog is digging on her grave. Her outburst of gratitude is the strongest expression of positive feeling in the lyric. You will notice that the emphasis of the poem is arrived at by a change in the proportioning of the dialogue. In each of the first four stanzas the mistress has a two-line question and the dog a four-line answer; but in stanza five, praising the dog's fidelity, only the mistress speaks. Again, with the second reversal in stanza six, only the dog speaks.

The exchange and line divisions of which we just spoke also give variety to the lyric. The behavior of the lover, the kinfolk, and the rival enriches our understanding of the dead mistress's previous life and character. Structural unity reflects the interrelationship of thought and feeling: the six-line stanzas maintain an ingenious rhyme scheme (a—b—c—c—c—b), and the short trimeter lines (second and sixth in each stanza) are the apex of feeling stated in the lines immediately preceding them.

These parts of the rhythmical organization are buried in the easy conversational give-and-take of the speakers. There is only one inversion, and its coming in the fifth stanza ("Why flashed it not on me?") suggests that the poet used it for emphasis at this focal point of feeling. Most of the words are Anglo-Saxon and monosyllabic, but when the words contain more than one syllable, they are out of familiar speech. The use of "tendance" and the archaic meaning of "gin" (snare or trap) do not offend in this context, but seem, on the contrary, to add credibility to the situation.

The lyric has music as well as suspense. Close examination of its sound structure reveals that, in addition to adhering strictly to the rhyme scheme, Hardy generously uses word repetition, alliteration, and assonance. There is, you will notice, the little altered refrain of "digging on my grave" in each stanza. Can you think of any associations making the preponderance of dental sounds (t's and d's) significant?

Patterned and musical though it is, the poem moves dynamically to excite and hold our attention, and the interpreter must find the means to reproduce it faithfully without loss of energy.

The Interpreter's Response

In our discussion of the three lyrics above,[9] we have stressed the importance of complete understanding, believing that only by this

---

[9] We have leaned heavily on The Kenyon Critics, *Gerard Manley Hopkins*, mentioned on page 127, for explication of Hopkins' purpose and technique. Cecil Maurice Bowra's *The Lyrical Poetry of Thomas Hardy* (Nottingham, University College, 1946), Byron Foundation Lecture, proved helpful in our analysis of Hardy's lyric.

means can there be a truly satisfying interpretation. We have seen each lyric as an expression of an individual consciousness, and we have become acquainted with each poet's use of his medium. Now we must ask ourselves how we can utilize what we have done. Probably the interpreter finds his greatest challenge in these rhythmical forms made up of image, feeling, and melody.

It can be seen that for all poems, the interpreter can profitably ask himself four questions:

1. What is the essence of the poetic experience with which we are here concerned?
2. What situational aspects affect the attitude of the interpreter?
3. What physical responses does the poem require?
4. What vocal responses does the poem require?

In answering the first question, we provide ourselves with a sound basis for developing responsiveness. In each of our analyses we have set forth what we considered to be the essence of each poem; we have discussed the situation; and we have looked carefully at the poetic form in order to better understand interpretative form. All that remains is the concrete adaptation of the poem into voice and action. But this can be difficult. The interpreter must take care that his physical and vocal responses fulfill the poem, but do not overwhelm or falsify it.

It is unlikely that an interpreter will fail to identify himself with the situations and experiences of the lyrics under consideration. We may even go so far as to say that any good poem, given careful attention, will reveal some aspect of familiar, or at least comprehensible, human experience. Some modicum of experience from the interpreter's own life will furnish a starting point. For each of the three lyrics, the internal situation demands withdrawal from direct, open speech with one's listeners. In "Acquainted With the Night," the withdrawal is motivated by the meditative tone and the speaker's solitary state; in "Spring and Fall: To a Young Child," the withdrawal is a blend of autumnal mood and overheard conversation, intimate, lively speech with the child in the poem as the main listener; in "Ah, Are You Digging on My Grave?" the dialogue, like that in a play, keeps the audience outside in the role of observer.

The interpreter's body controls our primary impression of directness or indirectness, and the eyes are especially important in establishing the details of a situation. In Frost's poem, the eyes and head will convey the impression of stillness by responding to the cues for listening in lines 8 and 9. Throughout the entire lyric, the body will be poised and quiet, and direct eye contact with any member of the audience will be incidental if, indeed, it occurs at all. It is as though the speaker were thinking aloud in the presence of others. In Hopkins' poem, in addition to suggesting the revelation of feeling in the presence of others, the interpreter needs in some way to indicate that the child is not in the audience, but in the memory of the speaker or perhaps in a scene shared by the speaker. He can do this in several ways, perhaps indicating by the angle of his head that he is addressing someone else. He might, for example, look to the center for his first four lines and a little to the side for the next four lines, returning to center on line 9. For the last two lines, the address could be generalized by enlarging one's eye span, and perhaps by some sign of elevation or expansion. In the Hardy poem, the use of angles of address will convey the change of speakers and remove the situation from the realm of the audience.

Bodily alignment, the angle of the head, the lift or turn of the chin can reflect the directness or indirectness of mental attitude and the interplay of speakers. It is hardly necessary to say, perhaps, that such physical adjustments will be subtle, accommodated to the rhythmical movement of the lines and to the other elements of expression. The quality and melody of the voice will in themselves convey a sense of situation.

The emotional quality of the lyrics is proportional to the effectiveness of their sound patterns. In each case we have pointed out contrast and variation in feeling and the part played by mellifluous combinations, vowel lengths, and carefully marked pauses in communicating these changes. Vocal response to the poem's texture is normally a sign of one's understanding and sympathy and, as we shall see in Chapter 9, cannot be achieved apart from response to meaning.

Contributing also to the interpreter's success in communicating the emotional quality of these, or any lyrics, is the concentration and single-mindedness that permits him to strike the "right" note with the first word of the poem. These lyrics are comparatively brief, concentrated and tightly organized. There is no time after the title has been pronounced to "get into the mood."

In Chapters 8 and 9 we shall be much more specific about the use of body and voice to convey meaning. Yet we shall not depart from the admonition that all clues to physical and vocal response are within the work to be interpreted. For example, in "Acquainted With the Night," the aspects of the situation—night, rain, empty streets, echoing footsteps—convey the loneness of the individual, which is the essence of the poetic situation. In "Spring and Fall: To a Young Child," the images "Goldengrove unleaving" and "worlds of wanwood leafmeal lie" suggest the "blight that man was born for." In "Ah, Are You Digging on My Grave?" the images stirred by "rue," "grave," "mound," "resting-place" and the triviality of the mistress's concerns point up the final irony. Equally important in each case is the rhythmic frame, clearly set forth, but softened by variations in tempo. The parts and the combination of parts into each whole can yield full meaning when fully expressed through voice and body.

Exercise

Test your recognition of situational aspects after reading the lyrics at the close of the chapter by placing their titles under the following heads:
1. The speaker addresses an undefined audience.
2. The speaker addresses a defined, passive audience or listener.
3. The speaker addresses a defined, responsive audience.
4. The speaker receives answers or engages in dialogue with a second speaker within the poem.
5. The address shifts within the piece.

Glossary of Terms

ALLITERATION: Sometimes called "initial rhyme"; the repetition of initial consonant sounds (refers primarily to accented syllables) in close proximity. Modern practice is to avoid more than two alliterative sounds in sequence.
   Example: "when *l*ilacs *l*ast in the dooryard bloom'd."

ANACRUSIS: The placing of an unstressed syllable at the beginning of a line, but not counting it as part of the first foot.
   Example: "*To an* unsettled fancy, cure thy brains."

ASSONANCE: Sometimes called "interior rhyme"; the identity of vowel sounds in accented syllables without identity of consonants following.
   Example: the lonely m*o*ated grange; r*i*m of the r*i*dge.

CONSONANCE: May be used to mean any pleasing combination of sounds. More often (and in this chapter) used to mean that the consonants of corresponding syllables are identical, though vowels are different. Different from *alliteration* in that it applies to unaccented syllables as well.

> *Example:* spelled, spilled.

ENJAMBMENT: Running of the thought from one line or couplet into the next.

> *Example:* "Nothing of him that doth fade,
>   But doth suffer a sea change
>   Into something rich and strange."

FOOT: A metrical unit containing one stressed and one or more unstressed syllables.

> *Example:* "To the lonely sea and the sky" (line contains three feet, the first with three syllables, the second with two, and the third with three).

RHYME: A correspondence of sound or sounds at the ends of words or syllables.

> *Example:* blow, grow; potato, Plato; pattering, scattering. *Rhyme depends on sound, not on spelling.*

MASCULINE RHYME: Occurs when the syllables that are rhymed are the last syllables of the words in question, or monosyllables.

> *Example:* devote, connote; the *deep*, to *creep*.

FEMININE RHYME: Occurs when the syllables that are rhymed are followed by identical unaccented syllables.

> *Example:* fighting, biting; tenderly, slenderly.
> (The second example may also be called triple rhyme.)

STANZA: Two or more lines tied together by thought and feeling as well as by metrical elements such as meter and rhyme. Usually recurrent.

TROCHAIC FOOT: A two-syllable foot with the stress on the first syllable.

> *Example:* table, donkey, Arthur.
> (Other feet are iambic, anapestic, dactylic.)

Selections for Interpretation

DOVER BEACH

Matthew Arnold (1822–1888)

The sea is calm to-night.
The tide is full, the moon lies fair
Upon the straits;—on the French coast the light
Gleams and is gone; the cliffs of England stand
Glimmering and vast, out in the tranquil bay.

Come to the window, sweet is the night-air!
Only, from the long line of spray
Where the sea meets the moon-blanch'd land,
Listen! you hear the grating roar
Of pebbles which the waves draw back, and fling,
At their return, up the high strand,
Begin, and cease, and then again begin,
With tremulous cadence slow, and bring
The eternal note of sadness in.

Sophocles long ago
Heard it on the Aegean, and it brought
Into his mind the turbid ebb and flow
Of human misery; we
Find also in the sound a thought,
Hearing it by this distant northern sea.

The Sea of Faith
Was once, too, at the full, and round earth's shore
Lay like the folds of a bright girdle furl'd.
But now I only hear
Its melancholy, long, withdrawing roar,
Retreating, to the breath
Of the night-wind, down the vast edges drear
And naked shingles of the world.

Ah, love, let us be true
To one another! for the world, which seems
To lie before us like a land of dreams,
So various, so beautiful, so new,
Hath really neither joy, nor love, nor light,
Nor certitude, nor peace, nor help for pain;
And we are here as on a darkling plain
Swept with confused alarms of struggle and flight,
Where ignorant armies clash by night.

MUSEE DES BEAUX ARTS

W. H. Auden (1907–   )

About suffering they were never wrong,
The Old Masters: how well they understood
Its human position; how it takes place
While someone else is eating or opening a window or just
    walking dully along;
How, when the aged are reverently, passionately waiting
For the miraculous birth, there always must be
Children who did not specially want it to happen, skating
On a pond at the edge of the wood:
They never forgot
That even the dreadful martyrdom must run its course
Anyhow in a corner, some untidy spot
Where the dogs go on with their doggy life and the torturer's
    horse
Scratches its innocent behind on a tree.

In Brueghel's *Icarus*, for instance: how everything turns away
Quite leisurely from the disaster; the ploughman may
Have heard the splash, the forsaken cry,
But for him it was not an important failure; the sun shone
As it had to on the white legs disappearing into the green
Water; and the expensive delicate ship that must have seen
Something amazing, a boy falling out of the sky,
Had somewhere to get to and sailed calmly on.

TARANTELLA

Hilaire Belloc (1870–1953)

Do you remember an Inn,
Miranda?
Do you remember an Inn?
And the tedding and the spreading
Of the straw for a bedding,
And the fleas that tease in the High Pyrenees,
And the wine that tasted of the tar?
And the cheers and the jeers of the young muleteers
(Under the vine of the dark verandah)?

Do you remember an Inn, Miranda,
Do you remember an Inn?
And the cheers and the jeers of the young muleteers
Who hadn't got a penny,
And who weren't paying any,
And the hammer at the doors and the din?
And the *hip! hop! hap!*
Of the clap
Of the hands to the twirl and the swirl
Of the girl gone chancing,
Glancing,
Dancing,
Backing and advancing,
Snapping of the clapper to the spin
Out and in—
And the *ting, tong, tang* of the guitar!
Do you remember an Inn,
Miranda?
Do you remember an Inn?

 Never more;
 Miranda,
 Never more.
 Only the high peaks hoar:
 And Aragon a torrent at the door.
 No sound
 In the walls of the halls where falls
 The tread
 Of the feet of the dead to the ground,
 No sound:
 But the boom
 Of the far waterfall like doom.

IN WESTMINSTER ABBEY

John Betjeman (1907–   )

Let me take this other glove off
 As the *vox humana* swells,
And the beauteous fields of Eden
 Bask beneath the Abbey bells.

Here, where England's statesmen lie,
Listen to a lady's cry.

Gracious Lord, oh bomb the Germans.
　　Spare their women for Thy sake,
And if that is not too easy
　　We will pardon Thy mistake.
But, gracious Lord, whate'er shall be,
Don't let anyone bomb me.

Keep our Empire undismembered
　　Guide our Forces by Thy Hand,
Gallant blacks from far Jamaica,
　　Honduras and Togoland;
Protect them Lord in all their fights,
And, even more, protect the whites.

Think of what our Nation stands for,
　　Books from Boots' and country lanes,
Free speech, free passes, class distinction,
　　Democracy and proper drains.
Lord, put beneath Thy special care
One-eighty-nine Cadogan Square.

Although dear Lord I am a sinner,
　　I have done no major crime;
Now I'll come to Evening Service
　　Whensoever I have time.
So, Lord, reserve for me a crown,
And do not let my shares go down.

I will labour for Thy Kingdom,
　　Help our lads to win the war,
Send white feathers to the cowards
　　Join the Women's Army Corps,
Then wash the Steps around Thy Throne
In the Eternal Safety Zone.

Now I feel a little better,
　　What a treat to hear Thy Word,
Where the bones of leading statesmen,
　　Have so often been interr'd.
And now, dear Lord, I cannot wait
Because I have a luncheon date.

From *The Holy Bible*

Remember now thy Creator in the days of thy youth, while the evil days come not, nor the years draw nigh, when thou shalt say, I have no pleasure in them;

While the sun, or the light, or the moon, or the stars, be not darkened, nor the clouds return after the rain:

In the day when the keepers of the house shall tremble, and the strong men shall bow themselves, and the grinders cease because they are few, and those that look out of the windows be darkened,

And the doors shall be shut in the streets, when the sound of the grinding is low, and he shall rise up at the voice of the bird, and all the daughters of musick shall be brought low;

Also *when* they shall be afraid of *that which is* high, and fears *shall be* in the way, and the almond tree shall flourish, and the grasshopper shall be a burden, and desire shall fail: because man goeth to his long home, and the mourners go about the streets:

Or ever the silver cord be loosed, or the golden bowl be broken, or the pitcher be broken at the fountain, or the wheel broken at the cistern.

Then shall the dust return to the earth as it was: and the Spirit shall return unto God who gave it.

Vanity of vanities, saith the preacher; all *is* vanity.

And moreover, because the preacher was wise, he still taught the people knowledge; yea, he gave good heed, and sought out, *and* set in order many proverbs.

The preacher sought to find out acceptable words: and *that which was* written *was* upright, *even* words of truth.

The words of the wise *are* as goads, and as nails fastened *by* the masters of assemblies, *which* are given from one shepherd.

And further, by these, my son, be admonished: of making many books *there is* no end; and much study *is* a weariness of the flesh.

Let us hear the conclusion of the whole matter: Fear God, and keep his commandments: for this *is* the whole *duty* of man.

For God shall bring every work into judgment, with every secret thing, whether *it be* good, or whether *it be* evil.

SONG

John Donne (1573–1631)

Go and catch a falling star,
  Get with child a mandrake root,
Tell me where all past years are,
  Or who cleft the Devil's foot,
Teach me to hear Mermaids singing,
Or to keep off envy's stinging,
    And find
    What wind
Serves to advance an honest mind.

If thou be'st born to strange sights,
  Things invisible to see,
Ride ten thousand days and nights,
  Till age snow white hairs on thee,
Thou, when thou return'st, will tell me
All strange wonders that befell thee,
    And swear
    No where
Lives a woman true, and fair.

If thou find'st one, let me know,
  Such a Pilgrimage were sweet;
Yet do not, I would not go,
  Though at next door we might meet;
Though she were true, when you met her,
And last, till you write your letter,
    Yet she
    Will be
False, ere I come, to two, or three.

MACAVITY: THE MYSTERY CAT

T. S. Eliot (1888–   )

Macavity's a Mystery Cat; he's called the Hidden Paw—
For he's the master criminal who can defy the Law.
He's the bafflement of Scotland Yard, the Flying Squad's
  despair;
For when they reach the scene of crime—*Macavity's not there!*

Lyric   141

Macavity, Macavity, there's no one like Macavity,
He's broken every human law, he breaks the law of gravity.
His powers of levitation would make a fakir stare,
And when you reach the scene of crime—*Macavity's not there!*
You may seek him in the basement, you may look up in the
air—
But I tell you once and once again—*Macavity's not there!*

Macavity's a ginger cat, he's very tall and thin;
You would know him if you saw him, for his eyes are sunken
in.
His brow is deeply lined with thought, his head is highly
domed;
His coat is dusty from neglect, his whiskers are uncombed.
He sways his head from side to side, with movements like a
snake;
And when you think he's half asleep, he's always wide awake.

Macavity, Macavity, there's no one like Macavity,
For he's a fiend in feline shape, a monster of depravity.
You may meet him in a by-street, you may see him in the
square—
But when a crime's discovered, then *Macavity's not there!*

He's outwardly respectable. (They say he cheats at cards.)
And his footprints are not found in any file of Scotland Yard's.
And when the larder's looted, or the jewel-case is rifled,
And when the milk is missing, or another Peke's been stifled,
Or the greenhouse glass is broken, and the trellis past repair—
Ay, there's the wonder of the thing! *Macavity's not there!*

And when the Foreign Office find a Treaty's gone astray,
Or the Admiralty lose some plans and drawings by the way,
There may be a scrap of paper in the hall or on the stair—
But it's useless to investigate—*Macavity's not there!*
And when the loss has been disclosed, the Secret Service say:
"It *must* have been Macavity!"—but he's a mile away.
You'll be sure to find him resting, or a-licking of his thumbs,
Or engaged in doing complicated long division sums.

Macavity, Macavity, there's no one like Macavity,
There never was a Cat of such deceitfulness and suavity.
He always has an alibi, and one or two to spare:
At whatever time the deed took place—MACAVITY
    WASN'T THERE!

And they say that all the Cats whose wicked deeds are widely
    known
(I might mention Mungojerrie, I might mention Griddlebone)
Are nothing more than agents for the Cat who all the time
Just controls their operations: the Napoleon of Crime!

TO AN ATHLETE DYING YOUNG

A. E. Housman (1859–1936)

The time you won your town the race
We chaired you through the market-place;
Man and boy stood cheering by,
And home we brought you shoulder-high.

To-day, the road all runners come,
Shoulder-high we bring you home,
And set you at your threshold down,
Townsman of a stiller town.

Smart lad, to slip betimes away
From fields where glory does not stay
And early though the laurel grows
It withers quicker than the rose.

Eyes the shady night has shut
Cannot see the record cut
And silence sounds no worse than cheers
After earth has stopped the ears:

Now you will not swell the rout
Of lads that wore their honours out,
Runners whom renown outran
And the name died before the man.

To set, before its echoes fade,
The fleet foot on the sill of shade,
And hold to the low lintel up
The still-defended challenge-cup,

And round that early-laurelled head
Will flock to gaze the strengthless dead,
And find unwithered on its curls
The garland briefer than a girl's.

POETRY

Juan Ramon Jimenez (1881–1958)

When first she came to me chastely,
Dressed in her innocence only,
As a little girl I loved her truly.

Then she took to adorning herself
With all sorts of finery
And I hated her not knowing why.

At last she became a queen,
Gaudily hung with jewelry . . .
What bitter contrariness and how senseless!

But once more she began undressing
And I smiled upon her.

She was left in her slip,
Her former innocence
And again I believed in her.

And she took off her slip, too,
And appeared quite naked . . .
Oh naked poetry, my lifelong passion,
Now you are mine forever!

Marianne Moore (1887–   )

I, too, dislike it: there are things that are important
      beyond all this fiddle.
Reading it, however, with a perfect contempt for it, one
      discovers in
it after all, a place for the genuine.
   Hands that can grasp, eyes
   that can dilate, hair that can rise
     if it must, these things are important not because a

high-sounding interpretation can be put upon them but
      because they are
useful. When they become so derivative as to become
      unintelligible,
the same thing may be said for all of us, that we
   do not admire what
   we cannot understand: the bat
     holding on upside down or in quest of something to

eat, elephants pushing, a wild horse taking a roll, a tire-
      less wolf under
a tree, the immovable critic twitching his skin like a
      horse that feels a flea, the base-
ball fan, the statistician—case after case
   could be cited did
   one wish it; nor is it valid
     to discriminate against 'business documents and

school-books'; all these phenomena are important. One
      must make a distinction
however: when dragged into prominence by half poets,
      the result is not poetry,
nor till the poets among us can be
   'literalists of
   the imagination'—above
     insolence and triviality and can present

for inspection, imaginary gardens with real toads in them,
          shall we have
   it. In the meantime, if you demand on the one hand,
   the raw material of poetry in
      all its rawness and
        that which is on the other hand
          genuine, then you are interested in poetry.

AND DEATH SHALL HAVE NO DOMINION

Dylan Thomas (1914–1953)

And death shall have no dominion.
Dead men naked they shall be one
With the man in the wind and the west moon;
When their bones are picked clean and the clean bones gone,
They shall have stars at elbow and foot;
Though they go mad they shall be sane,
Though they sink through the sea they shall rise again;
Though lovers be lost love shall not;
And death shall have no dominion.

And death shall have no dominion.
Under the windings of the sea
They lying long shall not die windily;
Twisting on racks when sinews give way,
Strapped to a wheel, yet they shall not break;
Faith in their hands shall snap in two,
And the unicorn evils run them through;
Split all ends up they shan't crack;
And death shall have no dominion.

And death shall have no dominion.
No more may gulls cry at their ears
Or waves break loud on the seashores;
Where blew a flower may a flower no more
Lift its head to the blows of the rain;
Though they be mad and dead as nails,
Heads of the characters hammer through daisies;
Break in the sun till the sun breaks down,
And death shall have no dominion.

6

Narrative

> *"The proper stuff of fiction" does not exist; everything is the proper stuff of fiction, every feeling, every thought; every quality of brain and spirit is drawn upon; no perception comes amiss.* ∽
> VIRGINIA WOOLF

> *The novel is the book of life.* ∽ D. H. LAWRENCE

IN CHAPTER 5 WE FOUND in three lyric poems that paraphrasable content was only a portion of the whole poem. We saw images clarify and vivify meaning and felt pleasure in rhythmical movement. We are to find images and rhythmic patterns again in narrative writing, but working in relation to the traditional parts of narrative: setting, plot, character, and dialogue.[1] To appreciate and communicate "the inner life" of a narrative selection, the interpreter must understand the interplay of all these elements.

You will recall that a variety of narrative materials [2] awaits the interpreter, from novel and novelette to narrative verse and ballad. For the sample analysis, we have chosen a short story by John Steinbeck in which all the narrative elements are active and integrated to form

---

[1] See the end of this chapter for brief definitions of these traditional parts of narrative.
[2] See Chapter 2.

a unified whole. Our approach to this story, "Flight," will serve as a method of study for longer stories and novels; combined with the lyric analysis, it will serve for narrative verse.

FLIGHT

John Steinbeck (1902–   )

About fifteen miles below Monterey, on the wild coast, the Torres family had their farm, a few sloping acres above a cliff that dropped to the brown reefs and to the hissing white waters of the ocean. Behind the farm the stone mountains stood up against the sky. The farm buildings huddled like little clinging aphids on the mountain skirts, crouched low to the ground as though the wind might blow them into the sea. The little shack, the rattling, rotting barn were gray-bitten with sea salt, beaten by the damp wind until they had taken on the color of the granite hills. Two horses, a red cow and a red calf, half a dozen pigs and a flock of lean, multicolored chickens stocked the place. A little corn was raised on the sterile slope, and it grew short and thick under the wind, and all the cobs formed on the landward sides of the stalks.

Mama Torres, a lean, dry woman with ancient eyes, had ruled the farm for ten years, ever since her husband tripped over a stone in the field one day and fell full length on a rattlesnake. When one is bitten on the chest there is not much that can be done.

Mama Torres had three children, two undersized black ones of twelve and fourteen, Emilio and Rosy, whom Mama kept fishing on the rocks below the farm when the sea was kind and when the truant officer was in some distant part of Monterey County. And there was Pepé, the tall smiling son of nineteen, a gentle, affectionate boy, but very lazy. Pepé had a tall head, pointed at the top, and from its peak, coarse black hair grew down like a thatch all around. Over his smiling little eyes Mama cut a straight bang so he could see. Pepé had sharp Indian cheekbones and an eagle nose, but his mouth was as sweet and shapely as a girl's mouth, and his chin was fragile and chiseled. He was loose and gangling, all legs and feet and wrists, and he was very lazy. Mama thought him fine and brave, but she never told him so. She said, "Some lazy cow must have got into thy father's family, else how could I have a son like thee." And she said, "When I carried thee, a sneaking lazy coyote came out of the brush and looked at me one day. That must have made thee so."

Pepé smiled sheepishly and stabbed at the ground with his knife to keep the blade sharp and free from rust. It was his inheritance, that knife, his father's knife. The long heavy blade folded back into the black handle. There was a button on the handle. When Pepé pressed the button, the blade leaped out ready for use. The knife was with Pepé always, for it had been his father's knife.

One sunny morning when the sea below the cliff was glinting and blue and the white surf creamed on the reef, when even the stone mountains looked kindly, Mama Torres called out the door of the shack, "Pepé, I have a labor for thee."

There was no answer. Mama listened. From behind the barn she heard a burst of laughter. She lifted her full long skirt and walked in the direction of the noise.

Pepé was sitting on the ground with his back against a box. His white teeth glistened. On either side of him stood the two black ones, tense and expectant. Fifteen feet away a redwood post was set in the ground. Pepé's right hand lay limply in his lap, and in the palm the big black knife rested. The blade was closed back into the handle. Pepé looked smiling at the sky.

Suddenly Emilio cried, "Ya!"

Pepé's wrist flicked like the head of a snake. The blade seemed to fly open in mid-air, and with a thump the point dug into the redwood post, and the black handle quivered. The three burst into excited laughter. Rosy ran to the post and pulled out the knife and brought it back to Pepé. He closed the blade and settled the knife carefully in his listless palm again. He grinned self-consciously at the sky.

"Ya!"

The heavy knife lanced out and sunk into the post again. Mama moved forward like a ship and scattered the play.

"All day you do foolish things with the knife, like a toy-baby," she stormed. "Get up on thy huge feet that eat up shoes. Get up!" She took him by one loose shoulder and hoisted at him. Pepé grinned sheepishly and came half-heartedly to his feet. "Look!" Mama cried. "Big lazy, you must catch the horse and put on him thy father's saddle. You must ride to Monterey. The medicine bottle is empty. There is no salt. Go thou now, Peanut! Catch the horse."

A revolution took place in the relaxed figure of Pepé. "To Monterey, me? Alone? Sí, Mama."

She scowled at him. "Do not think, big sheep, that you will buy candy. No, I will give you only enough for the medicine and the salt."

Pepé smiled. "Mama, you will put the hatband on the hat?"

She relented then. "Yes, Pepé. You may wear the hatband."

His voice grew insinuating. "And the green handkerchief, Mama?"

"Yes, if you go quickly and return with no trouble, the silk green handkerchief will go. If you make sure to take off the handkerchief when you eat so no spot may fall on it. . . ."

"Sí, Mama. I will be careful. I am a man."

"Thou? A man? Thou art a peanut."

He went into the rickety barn and brought out a rope, and he walked agilely enough up the hill to catch the horse.

When he was ready and mounted before the door, mounted on his father's saddle that was so old that the oaken frame showed through torn leather in many places, then Mama brought out the round black hat with the tooled leather band, and she reached up and knotted the green silk handkerchief about his neck. Pepé's blue denim coat was much darker than his jeans, for it had been washed much less often.

Mama handed up the big medicine bottle and the silver coins. "That for the medicine," she said, "and that for the salt. That for a candle to burn for the papa. That for *dulces* for the little ones. Our friend Mrs. Rodriguez will give you dinner and maybe a bed for the night. When you go to the church say only ten Paternosters and only twenty-five Ave Marias. Oh! I know, big coyote. You would sit there flapping your mouth over Aves all day while you looked at the candles and the holy pictures. That is not good devotion to stare at the pretty things."

The black hat, covering the high pointed head and black thatched hair of Pepé, gave him dignity and age. He sat the rangy horse well. Mama thought how handsome he was, dark and lean and tall. "I would not send thee now alone, thou little one, except for the medicine," she said softly. "It is not good to have no medicine, for who knows when the toothache will come or the sadness of the stomach. These things are."

"Adios, Mama," Pepé cried. "I will come back soon. You may send me often alone. I am a man."

"Thou art a foolish chicken."

He straightened his shoulders, flipped the reins against the horse's shoulder and rode away. He turned once and saw that they still watched him, Emilio and Rosy and Mama. Pepé grinned with pride and gladness and lifted the tough buckskin horse to a trot.

When he had dropped out of sight over a little dip in the road, Mama turned to the black ones, but she spoke to herself. "He is nearly a man now," she said. "It will be a nice thing to have a man in the house again." Her eyes sharpened on the children. "Go to the rocks now. The tide is going out. There will be abalones to be found." She put the iron hooks into their hands and saw them down the steep trail to the reefs. She brought the smooth stone *metate* to the doorway and sat grinding her corn to flour and looking occasionally at the road over which Pepé had gone. The noonday came and then the afternoon, when the little ones beat the abalones on a rock to make them tender and Mama patted the tortillas to make them thin. They ate their dinner as the red sun was plunging down toward the ocean. They sat on the doorsteps and watched the big white moon come over the mountain tops.

Mama said, "He is now at the house of our friend Mrs. Rodriguez. She will give him nice things to eat and maybe a present."

Emilio said, "Some day I too will ride to Monterey for medicine. Did Pepé come to be a man today?"

Mama said wisely, "A boy gets to be a man when a man is needed. Remember this thing. I have known boys forty years old because there was no need for a man."

Soon afterwards they retired, Mama in her big oak bed on one side of the room, Emilio and Rosy in their boxes full of straw and sheepskins on the other side of the room.

The moon went over the sky and the surf roared on the rocks. The roosters crowed the first call. The surf subsided to a whispering surge against the reef. The moon dropped toward the sea. The roosters crowed again.

The moon was near down to the water when Pepé rode on a winded horse to his home flat. His dog bounced out and circled the horse yelping with pleasure. Pepé slid off the saddle to the ground. The weathered little shack was silver in the moonlight and the square shadow of it was black to the north and east. Against the east the piling mountains were misty with light; their tops melted into the sky.

Pepé walked wearily up the three steps and into the house. It was dark inside. There was a rustle in the corner.

Mama cried out from her bed. "Who comes? Pepé, is it thou?"

"Sí, Mama."

"Did you get the medicine?"

"Sí, Mama."

"Well, go to sleep, then. I thought you would be sleeping at the house of Mrs. Rodriguez." Pepé stood silently in the dark room. "Why do you stand there, Pepé? Did you drink wine?"

"Sí, Mama."

"Well, go to bed then and sleep out the wine."

His voice was tired and patient, but very firm. "Light the candle, Mama. I must go away into the mountains."

"What is this, Pepé? You are crazy." Mama struck a sulphur match and held the little blue burr until the flame spread up the stick. She set light to the candle on the floor beside her bed. "Now, Pepé, what is this you say?" She looked anxiously into his face.

He was changed. The fragile quality seemed to have gone from his chin. His mouth was less full than it had been, the lines of the lips were straighter, but in his eyes the greatest change had taken place. There was no laughter in them any more, nor any bashfulness. They were sharp and bright and purposeful.

He told her in a tired monotone, told her everything just as it had happened. A few people came into the kitchen of Mrs. Rodriguez. There was wine to drink. Pepé drank wine. The little quarrel—the man started toward Pepé and then the knife —it went almost by itself. It flew, it darted before Pepé knew it. As he talked, Mama's face grew stern, and it seemed to grow more lean. Pepé finished. "I am a man now, Mama. The man said names to me I could not allow."

Mama nodded. "Yes, thou art a man, my poor little Pepé. Thou art a man. I have seen it coming on thee. I have watched you throwing the knife into the post, and I have been afraid." For a moment her face had softened, but now it grew stern again. "Come! We must get you ready. Go. Awaken Emilio and Rosy. Go quickly."

Pepé stepped over to the corner where his brother and sister slept among the sheepskins. He leaned down and shook them gently. "Come, Rosy! Come, Emilio! The mama says you must arise."

The little black ones sat up and rubbed their eyes in the candlelight. Mama was out of bed now, her long black skirt over her nightgown. "Emilio," she cried. "Go up and catch the other horse for Pepé. Quickly, now! Quickly!" Emilio put his legs in his overalls and stumbled sleepily out the door.

"You heard no one behind you on the road?" Mama demanded.

"No, Mama. I listened carefully. No one was on the road."

Mama darted like a bird about the room. From a nail on the wall she took a canvas water bag and threw it on the floor. She stripped a blanket from her bed and rolled it into a tight tube and tied the ends with string. From a box beside the stove she lifted a flour sack half full of black stringy jerky. "Your father's black coat, Pepé. Here, put it on."

Pepé stood in the middle of the floor watching her activity. She reached behind the door and brought out the rifle, a long 38–56, worn shiny the whole length of the barrel. Pepé took it from her and held it in the crook of his elbow. Mama brought a little leather bag and counted the cartridges into his hand. "Only ten left," she warned. "You must not waste them."

Emilio put his head in the door. "'Qui 'st 'l caballo, Mama."

"Put on the saddle from the other horse. Tie on the blanket. Here, tie the jerky to the saddle horn."

Still Pepé stood silently watching his mother's frantic activity. His chin looked hard, and his sweet mouth was drawn and thin. His little eyes followed Mama about the room almost suspiciously.

Rosy asked softly, "Where goes Pepé?"

Mama's eyes were fierce. "Pepé goes on a journey. Pepé is a man now. He has a man's thing to do."

Pepé straightened his shoulders. His mouth changed until he looked very much like Mama.

At last the preparation was finished. The loaded horse stood outside the door. The water bag dripped a line of moisture down the bay shoulder.

The moonlight was being thinned by the dawn and the big white moon was near down to the sea. The family stood by the shack. Mama confronted Pepé. "Look, my son! Do not stop until it is dark again. Do not sleep even though you are tired. Take care of the horse in order that he may not stop of weariness. Remember to be careful with the bullets—there are only ten. Do not fill thy stomach with jerky or it will make thee sick. Eat a little jerky and fill thy stomach with grass. When thou comest to the high mountains, if thou seest any of the dark watching men, go not near to them nor try to speak to them. And forget not thy prayers." She put her lean hands on Pepé's shoulders, stood on her toes and kissed him formally on both cheeks, and Pepé kissed her on both cheeks. Then he went to Emilio and Rosy and kissed both of their cheeks.

Pepé turned back to Mama. He seemed to look for a little softness, a little weakness in her. His eyes were searching, but Mama's face remained fierce. "Go now," she said. "Do not wait to be caught like a chicken."

Pepé pulled himself into the saddle. "I am a man," he said.

It was the first dawn when he rode up the hill toward the little canyon which let a trail into the mountains. Moonlight and daylight fought with each other, and the two warring qualities made it difficult to see. Before Pepé had gone a hundred yards, the outlines of his figure were misty; and long before he entered the canyon, he had become a gray, indefinite shadow.

Mama stood stiffly in front of her doorstep, and on either side of her stood Emilio and Rosy. They cast furtive glances at Mama now and then.

When the gray shape of Pepé melted into the hillside and

disappeared, Mama relaxed. She began the high, whining keen of the death wail. "Our beautiful—our brave," she cried. "Our protector, our son is gone." Emilio and Rosy moaned beside her. "Our beautiful—our brave, he is gone." It was the formal wail. It rose to a high piercing whine and subsided to a moan. Mama raised it three times and then she turned and went into the house and shut the door.

Emilio and Rosy stood wondering in the dawn. They heard Mama whimpering in the house. They went out to sit on the cliff above the ocean. They touched shoulders. "When did Pepé come to be a man?" Emilio asked.

"Last night," said Rosy. "Last night in Monterey." The ocean clouds turned red with the sun that was behind the mountains.

"We will have no breakfast," said Emilio. "Mama will not want to cook." Rosy did not answer him. "Where is Pepé gone?" he asked.

Rosy looked around at him. She drew her knowledge from the quiet air. "He has gone on a journey. He will never come back."

"Is he dead? Do you think he is dead?"

Rosy looked back at the ocean again. A little steamer, drawing a line of smoke sat on the edge of the horizon. "He is not dead," Rosy explained. "Not yet."

Pepé rested the big rifle across the saddle in front of him. He let the horse walk up the hill and he didn't look back. The stony slope took on a coat of short brush so that Pepé found the entrance to a trail and entered it.

When he came to the canyon opening, he swung once in his saddle and looked back, but the houses were swallowed in the misty light. Pepé jerked forward again. The high shoulder of the canyon closed in on him. His horse stretched out its neck and sighed and settled to the trail.

It was a well-worn path, dark soft leaf-mold earth strewn with broken pieces of sandstone. The trail rounded the shoulder of the canyon and dropped steeply into the bed of the stream. In the shallows the water ran smoothly, glinting in the first morning sun. Small round stones on the bottom were as brown as rust with sun moss. In the sand along the edges of the stream the tall, rich wild mint grew, while in the water itself, the cress, old and tough, had gone to heavy seed.

The path went into the stream and emerged on the other side. The horse sloshed into the water and stopped. Pepé dropped his bridle and let the beast drink of the running water.

Soon the canyon sides became steep and the first giant sentinel redwoods guarded the trail, great round red trunks bearing foliage as green and lacy as ferns. Once Pepé was among the trees, the sun was lost. A perfumed and purple light lay in the pale green of the underbrush. Gooseberry bushes and blackberries and tall ferns lined the stream, and overhead the branches of the redwoods met and cut off the sky.

Pepé drank from the water bag, and he reached into the flour sack and brought out a black string of jerky. His white teeth gnawed at the string until the tough meat parted. He chewed slowly and drank occasionally from the water bag. His little eyes were slumberous and tired, but the muscles of his face were hard set. The earth of the trail was black now. It gave up a hollow sound under the walking hoofbeats.

The stream fell more sharply. Little waterfalls splashed on the stones. Five-fingered ferns hung over the water and dripped spray from their fingertips. Pepé rode half over in his saddle, dangling one leg loosely. He picked a bay leaf from a tree beside the way and put it into his mouth for a moment to flavor the dry jerky. He held the gun loosely across the pommel.

Suddenly he squared in his saddle, swung the horse from the trail and kicked it hurriedly up behind a big redwood tree. He pulled up the reins tight against the bit to keep the horse from whinnying. His face was intent and his nostrils quivered a little.

A hollow pounding came down the trail, and a horseman rode by, a fat man with red cheeks and a white stubble beard. His horse put down its head and blubbered at the trail when it came to the place where Pepé had turned off. "Hold up!" said the man and he pulled up his horse's head.

When the last sound of the hoofs died away, Pepé came back into the trail again. He did not relax in the saddle any more. He lifted the big rifle and swung the lever to throw a shell into the chamber, and then he let down the hammer to half cock.

The trail grew very steep. Now the redwood trees were smaller and their tops were dead, bitten dead where the wind reached them. The horse plodded on; the sun went slowly overhead and started down toward the afternoon.

Where the stream came out of a side canyon, the trail left it. Pepé dismounted and watered his horse and filled up his water bag. As soon as the trail had parted from the stream, the trees were gone and only the thick brittle sage and manzanita and chaparral edged the trail. And the soft black earth was gone, too, leaving only the light tan broken rock for the trail bed. Lizards scampered away into the brush as the horse rattled over the little stones.

Pepé turned in his saddle and looked back. He was in the open now: he could be seen from a distance. As he ascended the trail the country grew more rough and terrible and dry. The way wound about the bases of great square rocks. Little gray rabbits skittered in the brush. A bird made a monotonous high creaking. Eastward the bare rock mountaintops were pale and powder-dry under the dropping sun. The horse plodded up and up the trail toward a little V in the ridge which was the pass.

Pepé looked suspiciously back every minute or so, and his eyes sought the tops of the ridges ahead. Once, on a white barren spur, he saw a black figure for a moment, but he looked quickly away, for it was one of the dark watchers. No one knew who the watchers were, nor where they lived, but it was better to ignore them and never to show interest in them. They did not bother one who stayed on the trail and minded his own business.

The air was parched and full of light dust blown by the breeze from the eroding mountains. Pepé drank sparingly from his bag and corked it tightly and hung it on the horn again. The trail moved up the dry shale hillside, avoiding rocks, dropping under clefts, climbing in and out of old water scars. When he arrived at the little pass he stopped and looked back for a long time. No dark watchers were to be seen now. The trail behind was empty. Only the high tops of the redwoods indicated where the stream flowed.

Pepé rode on through the pass. His little eyes were nearly closed with weariness, but his face was stern, relentless and manly. The high mountain wind coasted sighing through the pass and whistled on the edges of the big blocks of broken granite. In the air, a red-tailed hawk sailed over close to the ridge and screamed angrily. Pepé went slowly through the broken jagged pass and looked down on the other side.

The trail dropped quickly, staggering among broken rock. At the bottom of the slope there was a dark crease, thick with brush, and on the other side of the crease a little flat, in which a grove of oak trees grew. A scar of green grass cut across the flat. And behind the flat another mountain rose, desolate with dead rocks and starving little black bushes. Pepé drank from the bag again for the air was so dry that it encrusted his nostrils and burned his lips. He put the horse down the trail. The hooves slipped and struggled on the steep way, starting little stones that rolled off into the brush. The sun was gone behind the westward mountain now, but still it glowed brilliantly on the oaks and on the grassy flat. The rocks and the hillsides still sent up waves of the heat they had gathered from the day's sun.

Pepé looked up to the top of the next dry withered ridge. He saw a dark form against the sky, a man's figure standing on top of a rock, and he glanced away quickly not to appear curious. When a moment later he looked up again, the figure was gone.

Downward the trail was quickly covered. Sometimes the horse floundered for footing, sometimes set his feet and slid a little way. They came at last to the bottom where the dark chaparral was higher than Pepé's head. He held up his rifle on one side and his arm on the other to shield his face from the sharp brittle fingers of the brush.

Up and out of the crease he rode, and up a little cliff. The grassy flat was before him, and the round comfortable oaks. For a moment he studied the trail down which he had come, but there was no movement and no sound from it. Finally he rode out over the flat, to the green streak, and at the upper end of the damp he found a little spring welling out of the earth and dropping into a dug basin before it seeped out over the flat.

Pepé filled his bag first, and then he let the thirsty horse drink out of the pool. He led the horse to the clump of oaks, and in the middle of the grove, fairly protected from sight on all sides, he took off the saddle and the bridle and laid them on the ground. The horse stretched his jaws sideways and yawned. Pepé knotted the lead rope about the horse's neck and tied him to a sapling among the oaks, where he could graze in a fairly large circle.

When the horse was gnawing hungrily at the dry grass, Pepé went to the saddle and took a black string of jerky from the sack and strolled to an oak tree on the edge of the grove, from under which he could watch the trail. He sat down in the crisp dry oak leaves and automatically felt for his big black knife to cut the jerky, but he had no knife. He leaned back on his elbow and gnawed at the tough strong meat. His face was blank, but it was a man's face.

The bright evening light washed the eastern ridge, but the valley was darkening. Doves flew down from the hills to the spring, and the quail came running out of the brush and joined them, calling clearly to one another.

Out of the corner of his eye Pepé saw a shadow grow out of the bushy crease. He turned his head slowly. A big spotted wildcat was creeping toward the spring, belly to the ground, moving like thought.

Pepé cocked his rifle and edged the muzzle slowly around. Then he looked apprehensively up the trail and dropped the hammer again. From the ground beside him he picked an oak twig and threw it toward the spring. The quail flew up with a roar and the doves whistled away. The big cat stood up: for a long moment he looked at Pepé with cold yellow eyes, and then fearlessly walked back into the gulch.

The dusk gathered quickly in the deep valley. Pepé muttered his prayers, put his head down on his arm and went instantly to sleep.

The moon came up and filled the valley with cold blue light, and the wind swept rustling down from the peaks. The owls worked up and down the slopes looking for rabbits. Down in the brush of the gulch a coyote gabbled. The oak trees whispered softly in the night breeze.

Pepé started up, listening. His horse had whinnied. The moon was just slipping behind the western ridge, leaving the valley in darkness behind it. Pepé sat tensely gripping his rifle.

From far up the trail he heard an answering whinny and the crash of shod hooves on the broken rock. He jumped to his feet, ran to his horse and led it under the trees. He threw on the saddle and cinched it tight for the steep trail, caught the unwilling head and forced the bit into the mouth. He felt the saddle to make sure the water bag and the sack of jerky were there. Then he mounted and turned up the hill.

It was velvet dark. The horse found the entrance to the trail where it left the flat, and started up, stumbling and slipping on the rocks. Pepé's hand rose up to his head. His hat was gone. He had left it under the oak tree.

The horse had struggled far up the trail when the first change of dawn came into the air, a steel grayness as light mixed thoroughly with dark. Gradually the sharp snaggled edge of the ridge stood out above them, rotten granite tortured and eaten by the winds of time. Pepé had dropped his reins on the horn, leaving direction to the horse. The brush grabbed at his legs in the dark until one knee of his jeans was ripped.

Gradually the light flowed down over the ridge. The starved brush and rocks stood out in the half light, strange and lonely in high perspective. Then there came warmth into the light. Pepé drew up and looked back, but he could see nothing in the darker valley below. The sky turned blue over the coming sun. In the waste of the mountainside, the poor dry brush grew only three feet high. Here and there, big outcroppings of unrotted granite stood up like moldering houses. Pepé relaxed a little. He drank from his water bag and bit off a piece of jerky. A single eagle flew over, high in the light.

Without warning Pepé's horse screamed and fell on its side. He was almost down before the rifle crash echoed up from the valley. From a hole behind the struggling shoulder, a stream of bright crimson blood pumped and stopped and pumped and stopped. The hooves threshed on the ground. Pepé lay half stunned beside the horse. He looked slowly down the hill. A piece of sage clipped off beside his head and another crash echoed up from side to side of the canyon. Pepé flung himself frantically behind a bush.

He crawled up the hill on his knees and one hand. His right hand held the rifle up off the ground and pushed it ahead of him. He moved with the instinctive care of an animal. Rapidly he wormed his way toward one of the big outcroppings of granite on the hill above him. Where the brush was high he doubled up and ran, but where the cover was slight he wriggled forward on his stomach, pushing the rifle ahead of him. In the last little distance there was no cover at all. Pepé poised and then he darted across the space and flashed around the corner of the rock.

He leaned panting against the stone. When his breath came easier he moved along behind the big rock until he came to a narrow split that offered a thin section of vision down the hill. Pepé lay on his stomach and pushed the rifle barrel through the slit and waited.

The sun reddened the western ridges now. Already the buzzards were settling down toward the place where the horse lay. A small brown bird scratched in the dead sage leaves directly in front of the rifle muzzle. The coasting eagle flew back toward the rising sun.

Pepé saw a little movement in the brush far below. His grip tightened on the gun. A little brown doe stepped daintily out on the trail and crossed it and disappeared into the brush again. For a long time Pepé waited. Far below he could see the little flat and the oak trees and the slash of green. Suddenly his eyes flashed back at the trail again. A quarter of a mile down there had been a quick movement in the chaparral. The rifle swung over. The front sight nestled in the V of the rear sight. Pepé studied for a moment and then raised the rear sight a notch. The little movement in the brush came again. The sight settled on it. Pepé squeezed the trigger. The explosion crashed down the mountain and up the other side, and came rattling back. The whole side of the slope grew still. No more movement. And then a white streak cut into the granite of the slit and a bullet whined away and a crash sounded up from below. Pepé felt a sharp pain in his right hand. A sliver of granite was sticking out from between his first and second knuckles and the point protruded from his palm. Carefully he pulled out the sliver of stone. The wound bled evenly and gently. No vein or artery was cut.

Pepé looked into a little dusty cave in the rock and gathered a handful of spider web, and he pressed the mass into the cut, plastering the soft web into the blood. The flow stopped almost at once.

The rifle was on the ground. Pepé picked it up, levered a new shell into the chamber. And then he slid into the brush on his stomach. Far to the right he crawled, and then up the hill, moving slowly and carefully, crawling to cover and resting and then crawling again.

In the mountains the sun is high in its arc before it penetrates the gorges. The hot face looked over the hill and brought instant heat with it. The white light beat on the rocks and reflected from them and rose up quivering from the earth again, and the rocks and bushes seemed to quiver behind the air.

Pepé crawled in the general direction of the ridge peak, zigzagging for cover. The deep cut between his knuckles began to throb. He crawled close to a rattlesnake before he saw it, and when it raised its dry head and made a soft beginning whir, he backed up and took another way. The quick gray lizards flashed in front of him, raising a tiny line of dust. He found another mass of spider web and pressed it against his throbbing hand.

Pepé was pushing the rifle with his left hand now. Little drops of sweat ran to the ends of his coarse black hair and rolled down his cheeks. His lips and tongue were growing thick and heavy. His lips writhed to draw saliva into his mouth. His little dark eyes were uneasy and suspicious. Once when a gray lizard paused in front of him on the parched ground and turned its head sideways he crushed it flat with a stone.

When the sun slid past noon he had not gone a mile. He crawled exhaustedly a last hundred yards to a patch of high sharp manzanita, crawled desperately, and when the patch was reached he wriggled in among the tough gnarly trunks and dropped his head on his left arm. There was little shade in the meager brush, but there was cover and safety. Pepé went to sleep as he lay and the sun beat on his back. A few little birds hopped close to him and peered and hopped away. Pepé squirmed in his sleep and he raised and dropped his wounded hand again and again.

The sun went down behind the peaks and the cool evening came, and then the dark. A coyote yelled from the hillside, Pepé started awake and looked about with misty eyes. His hand was swollen and heavy; a little thread of pain ran up the inside of his arm and settled in a pocket in his armpit. He peered about and then stood up, for the mountains were black and the moon had not yet risen. Pepé stood up in the dark. The coat of his father pressed on his arm. His tongue was swollen until it nearly filled his mouth. He wriggled out of the coat and dropped it in the brush, and then he struggled up the hill, falling over rocks and tearing his way through the brush. The rifle knocked against stones as he went. Little dry avalanches of gravel and shattered stone went whispering down the hill behind him.

After a while the old moon came up and showed the jagged ridge top ahead of him. By moonlight Pepé traveled more easily. He bent forward so that his throbbing arm hung away from his body. The journey uphill was made in dashes and rests, a frantic rush up a few yards and then a rest. The wind coasted down the slope rattling the dry stems of the bushes.

The moon was at meridian when Pepé came at last to the sharp backbone of the ridge top. On the last hundred yards of the rise no soil had clung under the wearing winds. The way was on solid rock. He clambered to the top and looked down on the other side. There was a draw like the last below him, misty with moonlight, brushed with dry struggling sage and chaparral. On the other side the hill rose up sharply and at the top the jagged rotten teeth of the mountain showed against the sky. At the bottom of the cut the brush was thick and dark.

Pepé stumbled down the hill. His throat was almost closed with thirst. At first he tried to run, but immediately he fell and rolled. After that he went more carefully. The moon was just disappearing behind the mountains when he came to the bottom. He crawled into the heavy brush feeling with his fingers for water. There was no water in the bed of the stream, only damp earth. Pepé laid his gun down and scooped up a handful of mud and put it in his mouth, and then he spluttered and scraped the earth from his tongue with his finger, for the mud drew at his mouth like a poultice. He dug a hole in the stream bed with his fingers, dug a little basin to catch water; but before it was very deep his head fell forward on the damp ground and he slept.

The dawn came and the heat of the day fell on the earth,

and still Pepé slept. Late in the afternoon his head jerked up. He looked slowly around. His eyes were slits of wariness. Twenty feet away in the heavy brush a big tawny mountain lion stood looking at him. Its long thick tail waved gracefully, its ears were erect with interest, not laid back dangerously. The lion squatted down on its stomach and watched him.

Pepé looked at the hole he had dug in the earth. A half inch of muddy water had collected in the bottom. He tore the sleeve from his hurt arm, with his teeth ripped out a little square, soaked it in the water and put it in his mouth. Over and over he filled the cloth and sucked it.

Still the lion sat and watched him. The evening came down but there was no movement on the hills. No birds visited the dry bottom of the cut. Pepé looked occasionally at the lion. The eyes of the yellow beast drooped as though he were about to sleep. He yawned and his long thin red tongue curled out. Suddenly his head jerked around and his nostrils quivered. His big tail lashed. He stood up and slunk like a tawny shadow into the thick brush.

A moment later Pepé heard the sound, the faint far crash of horses' hooves on gravel. And he heard something else, a high whining yelp of a dog.

Pepé took his rifle in his left hand and he glided into the brush almost as quietly as the lion had. In the darkening evening he crouched up the hill toward the next ridge. Only when the dark came did he stand up. His energy was short. Once it was dark he fell over the rocks and slipped to his knees on the steep slope, but he moved on and on up the hill, climbing and scrabbling over the broken hillside.

When he was far up toward the top, he lay down and slept for a little while. The withered moon, shining on his face, awakened him. He stood up and moved up the hill. Fifty yards away he stopped and turned back, for he had forgotten his rifle. He walked heavily down and poked about in the brush, but he could not find his gun. At last he lay down to rest. The pocket of pain in his armpit had grown more sharp. His arm seemed to swell out and fall with every heartbeat. There was no position lying down where the heavy arm did not press against his armpit.

With the effort of a hurt beast, Pepé got up and moved

again toward the top of the ridge. He held his swollen arm away from his body with his left hand. Up the steep hill he dragged himself, a few steps and a rest, and a few more steps. At last he was nearing the top. The moon showed the uneven sharp back of it against the sky.

Pepé's brain spun in a big spiral up and away from him. He slumped to the ground and lay still. The rock ridge top was only a hundred feet above him.

The moon moved over the sky. Pepé half turned on his back. His tongue tried to make words, but only a thick hissing came from between his lips.

When the dawn came, Pepé pulled himself up. His eyes were sane again. He drew his great puffed arm in front of him and looked at the angry wound. The black line ran up from his wrist to his armpit. Automatically he reached in his pocket for the big black knife, but it was not there. His eyes searched the ground. He picked up a sharp blade of stone and scraped at the wound, sawed at the proud flesh and then squeezed the green juice out in big drops. Instantly he threw back his head and whined like a dog. His whole right side shuddered at the pain, but the pain cleared his head.

In the gray light he struggled up the last slope to the ridge and crawled over and lay down behind a line of rocks. Below him lay a deep canyon exactly like the last, waterless and desolate. There was no flat, no oak trees, not even heavy brush in the bottom of it. And on the other side a sharp ridge stood up, thinly brushed with starving sage, littered with broken granite. Strewn over the hill there were giant outcroppings, and on the top the granite teeth stood out against the sky.

The new day was light now. The flame of the sun came over the ridge and fell on Pepé where he lay on the ground. His coarse black hair was littered with twigs and bits of spider web. His eyes had retreated back into his head. Between his lips the tip of his black tongue showed.

He sat up and dragged his great arm into his lap and nursed it, rocking his body and moaning in his throat. He threw back his head and looked up into the pale sky. A big black bird circled nearly out of sight, and far to the left another was sailing near.

He lifted his head to listen, for a familiar sound had come

to him from the valley he had climbed out of; it was the crying yelp of hounds, excited and feverish, on a trail.

Pepé bowed his head quickly. He tried to speak rapid words but only a thick hiss came from his lips. He drew a shaky cross on his breast with his left hand. It was a long struggle to get to his feet. He crawled slowly and mechanically to the top of a big rock on the ridge peak. Once there, he arose slowly, swaying to his feet, and stood erect. Far below he could see the dark brush where he had slept. He braced his feet and stood there, black against the morning sky.

There came a ripping sound at his feet. A piece of stone flew up and a bullet droned off into the next gorge. The hollow crash echoed up from below. Pepé looked down for a moment and then pulled himself straight again.

His body jarred back. His left hand fluttered helplessly toward his breast. The second crash sounded from below. Pepé swung forward and toppled from the rock. His body struck and rolled over and over, starting a little avalanche. And when at last he stopped against a bush, the avalanche slid slowly down and covered up his head.

The Situation

In "Flight," the speaker (whom we shall call narrator) addresses any willing listener. His vision is limited, first, to the Torres family farm and, second, to the mountain canyons of Pepé's flight. The intimate family scene draws us close to the characters and makes us especially aware of Mama's force and influence. The focus upon Pepé in the second half of the story heightens suspense and tightens the plot. During this half of the story, we never get inside Pepé's mind, yet we infer his reactions from his reported behavior, and our sympathy is stirred. Despite the seeming directness of the account of Pepé's flight, the enveloping emotion and suspense move it toward closure. Throughout the story, the alternation of swift summary, description, and scene provides changes from directness to indirectness, or from openness to closure.

Summary . . . . Open Situation
Description . . . . Less open situation
Scene . . . . Comparative closure

Place and time are important components of the situation, in the sense that environmental factors markedly influence the lives of the characters. The background for "Flight" is authoritative in its detail, as well it might be, for Steinbeck was born in Salinas and knew the California coastal region north to Santa Cruz and south to the Big Sur. The narrative of the Torres family is set in recent times in the mountainous region bordering the Pacific, a region of a certain beauty, but not a region of fertility. To farm there meant a struggle, and we feel that the Torres family have been conditioned by the isolation and poverty in which they live. In fact, we see these physical influences making the events of the story possible. Nature and inheritance are Pepé's antagonists, and the whole family is at the mercy of the wind that stunts the corn and the ocean salt that attacks the flimsy buildings. Some years before, a rattlesnake has bitten the father.

In orderly fashion, the author sketches the background. First the sterile acres between mountains and sea, then the Torres family, are described. We pick up two necessary pointers immediately: mention of the truant officer is a reminder that the law touches these remote districts; and the emphasis—six sentences are devoted to it—upon Pepé's knife, the knife that had been his father's, hints of death. We grow suspicious that "the sunny morning when the sea below the cliff was glinting and blue" will not last, and that darker things await the Torres family.

Assimilation of Content

THE PLOT (WITH MARGINAL SYNOPSIS):

Pepé accepts responsibility.	Mama Torres finds Pepé, her oldest, trying his skill with his knife. She sends him off to Monterey to buy salt and medicine, but has to coax him by letting him wear the round black hat and tooled hatband, and the green silk handkerchief.
The family awaits Pepé's return.	After he is gone, riding proudly in his father's saddle, Mama tells Emilio and Rosy that a boy gets to be a man when a man is needed.
Pepé returns.	Toward morning of that night, Pepé returns.
Pepé says goodbye a second time.	Pepé had gone to the home of Mrs. Rodriguez in Monterey, as planned, but there in her kitchen, drinking wine with strangers, Pepé had thrown his knife in anger at a man who called him names.

Now Pepé must go away to hide in the mountains. Mama hurries his departure. They load the fresh horse, and bolstered by Mama's strength, Pepé says in farewell, "I am a man."

Mama and the two younger children wail after he has gone, and Rosy speaks their resignation: "He has gone on a journey. He will never come back."

It looks as though Pepé has a chance, but mishaps take place in rapid succession. After a day of watchful haste, he camps by a spring. Wakened by his horse's whinny, he hears an answering whinny and hooves on the rock. Hurrying to get away, he leaves his *hat* behind him under the oak tree where he had slept.

Soon his horse is shot from under him, and he spends that day climbing, crawling, hiding like the animals and wild creatures around him.

Toward sundown he sees a movement below him in the chaparral and fires his rifle. Soon after, a bullet from below splinters a piece of granite from a boulder and sends it flying into his right hand.

Wild animals shadow him. He hears baying hounds on his trail. He drops the heavy *coat* (his father's) in the brush.

During the second night out, after a day of thirst and pain, he leaves his *rifle* at one of his resting places, and his feeble search for it is fruitless.

At dawn of the third day, crazed with pain from his swollen, infected arm, and unable to speak for thirst, Pepé hears the yelp of the hounds below him on the trail. He crawls to the top of a big rock on a peak and stands straight against the sky. There are two rifle shots from below. The second one sends Pepé rolling forward down the slope, where at last he stops against a bush, and an avalanche slides down to cover up his head.

In "Flight," as in all good stories, the end is a direct outcome of the beginning. We have alluded to the dark aspects of nature which give coloring to the story, and we have noted the foreshadowing of death in the knife. Our expectation of disaster is fulfilled by Pepé's contact with the external world. The conventional trappings of manhood—hat, scarf, and knife—pleased his vanity and gave him a sense of power. But they were inadequate weapons against civilization and its conventions. Mama's need forced Pepé to accept his inheritance of male responsibility prematurely, in a world for which he was totally unprepared. The main question of the story is: Can Pepé assume the full responsibility of manhood?

In his own world, Pepé's story would have been different. But before he had grown used to the idea of being a man, he was brought up against another way of living and judging. When he returned from Monterey, he was changed. Mama and Rosy both said he was a man. Pepé said he was a man. Later, in flight, one by one, the symbols of manhood dropped from him: he had no knife, he forgot his hat, he dropped the coat of his father, he lost his rifle. One might conclude that Pepé lost his claim to manhood as he lost the symbols of manhood, and that the narrative is one of total defeat. Another interpretation is that although the first claim to manhood was premature, Pepé's real maturity came at the moment of his death, when his full realization of his plight caused him to expose himself to the bullets from below. Then, after much suffering, he showed himself strong.

The title becomes more meaningful as we penetrate the story. *Flight* means first of all Pepé's flight from the law which he doesn't understand fully; second, it could mean his flight from civilization and reduction to an animal state. This second theme is suggested in the many references to Pepé's animal-like movements and by the behavior of the lion and other creatures who give him slight attention. Yet just before his death, Pepé drew a shaky cross with his left hand. At least one of the symbols of civilization remained. A third connotation of *flight* is that Pepé was running away from his own manhood because the burden of the consequences was too heavy.

Pepé immediately becomes the center of our attention, arousing sympathy because he appears to be the instrument of forces outside his control. His careless boyhood, his living within the family circle and accepting unquestioningly the primitive standards of life and thought held by his mother, gave him little preparation for his first harsh contact with a world holding different standards. A full description of the family group and their reactions to him round out Pepé's characterization. The affection, faith, and admiration of Mama, Emilio, and Rosy influence us to look favorably upon Pepé, and when, in the death wail, they expressed their sorrow over his departure, our involvement increases.

The knowledge we receive of the family group serves another function in the narrative: it not only deepens our understanding of Pepé's character, but lends credibility to the early scenes and provides motivation for ensuing action. We see that Mama had molded Pepé's character long before she started him on his trip to Monterey. Involved in the plot, too, were Emilio, who caught the horse for the flight, and Rosy, who predicted Pepé's death.

The dialogue is simple, mixed with colloquial Spanish and stilted phrasing, with inversions. It does little to distinguish among characters, but is useful in two other respects: it advances the plot and suggests the primitive outlook of the Torres family, so little touched by the currents of civilization around them. The repetitions, the use of "thee," the use of epithet, and the use of expletive are evidences of this primitivism and assist the reader-interpreter to visualize his characters, especially Pepé, against the setting.

Achievement of Artistic Form

We have mentioned alternations of summary, description, and scene in the structure of "Flight," and we have given a brief outline of its plot. You will notice that each of the marginal comments [3] indicates a scene and that the first half of the story contains five scenes and the last half, six. But much of the story is description, and summary is used sparingly. Our involvement in Pepé's flight depends upon a concreteness not possible in summary as it is conceived here. Basically, the story is climactic, its energy increasing until it culminates in the last scene; but the break between the two halves of the story and the lowered excitement of Pepé's first hours of flight create a plateau in the movement toward climax of feeling. Contrast is a minor structural element, apparent in the conflict between Pepé's primitive world and the external world, as well as in the contrast between Pepé as boy and Pepé as man. We have seen a smiling son, very lazy, with a mouth "as sweet and shapely as a girl's mouth, and his chin . . . fragile and chiseled," change into an unsmiling man, pushing his strength to its limits, with the muscles of his face "hard set." Smaller contrasts exist among the various aspects of nature, large and small, hot and cold, dark and light. What we see as artistic totality is made

---

[3] See pages 167–168 of this chapter.

up of plot line and theme, both enriched by symbolism and secondary theme.

Steinbeck makes the stark, pathetic story bearable by furnishing us with pleasing sensuous and rhythmic elements. His sentences are varied in length and arrangement. Often the paragraphs are climactic, rounded off with a sentence like a musical coda or signature. Paragraphs illustrating this effect are those beginning:

> The air was parched and full of light dust . . .
> When the horse was gnawing hungrily . . .
> Pepé started up, listening.
> Gradually the light flowed down over the ridge.
> Pepé saw a little movement in the brush . . .

Steinbeck employs repetition in words, phrases, and clauses, achieving emphasis by this means in such passages as these:

> The knife was with Pepé always, for it had been his father's knife.
>
> The moon went over the sky and the surf roared on the rocks. The roosters crowed the first call. The surf subsided to a whispering surge against the reef. The moon dropped toward the sea. The roosters crowed again.
>
> She . . . stood on her toes and kissed him formally on both cheeks, and Pepé kissed her on both cheeks. Then he went to Emilio and Rosy and kissed both of their cheeks.

You will notice in the last two passages above that parallel structure complements the effect of the word repetitions. Other examples of parallelism and repetition are these:

> Up and out of the crease he rode, and up a little cliff.
>
> Where the brush was high he doubled up and ran, but where the cover was slight he wriggled forward on his stomach, . . .

Steinbeck's use of repetition as a device includes the repetition of vowels and consonants. We expect assonantal and consonantal repetitions to be held to a minimum in prose, and yet in "Flight" there are such passages as these:

> Now the redwood trees were smaller and their tops were dead, bitten dead where the wind reached them. The horse plodded on; the sun went slowly overhead and started down toward the afternoon.
>
> (*e* in *redwood, dead,* and *overhead; d* used six times)

The wind coasted down the slope . . .
  (use of *o*)
There was a draw like the last below him misty with moonlight, brushed with dry struggling sage and chaparral.
  (*l* in *like, last, below, moonlight, struggling, chaparral;*
  m in *misty, moonlight*)

These musical characteristics of "Flight" and other narratives by Steinbeck have led to the observation that his style has a Biblical flavor.

The story abounds in images and figures. There is scarcely a sentence
without an appeal to one or more of the senses. Some of the images
are these:

> great round red trunks bearing foliage as green
>   and lacy as ferns
> a scar of green grass cut across the flat [4]
> dark watching men
> purple light
> redtailed hawk
> black knife

Many of the numerous visual appeals are made to color. *Black* and
gray may seem dominant, but there are *yellow* eyes, *dark* earth, *red*
sun, and *white* moon. The verbs, appealing to the kinesthetic sense,
contribute to tension: Mama *darted*; Pepé *swung* the horse from the
trail and *kicked* it hurriedly up behind a big redwood tree; lizards
scampered, rabbits *skittered*; the horse *plodded*; the lion's head *jerked*;
Pepé *glided* into the brush; his body *jarred* back; his left hand *fluttered* helplessly. Examining the images for their primary appeals not
only gives us a vivid awareness of scene and action, but an intensified
response to the theme. For example, images highlight the similarity
between Pepé's movement and those of the wild creatures about him.
Likewise, from the specific image *black* we feel a deepening of tragedy:
black hair, *black* tongue, *black* bird, *black* against the morning sky.
Kinesthetic imagery mingles with figures, expressed in verbs and participles, such as wind *coasted*, trail *staggering*, light *washed*, brush
grabbed. A symbolic meaning develops mainly from these images and
figures, and we appreciate the artistry which wove them into a patterned structure. In the last paragraph, embodying the pathos of
Pepé's struggle, his helplessness, and the final kindness of nature,

---

[4] This is also metaphorical.

which in spite of its indifference has proved more kindly than men, the "inner life" of the narrative is made manifest in sensuous language.

The Interpreter's Response

Traditionally a sequence of events with characters enacting them is the heart of narrative, and thus the first requirement in the interpretation of much narrative is to present clearly the plot line and characters. The well-defined plot in "Flight" lends itself to oral presentation. The scenes in the first half of the story require emphasis and a gradual building up of excitement; the excitement is less at the beginning of the second half than it was at the end of the first half, but the entire second half is pitched high and reaches a great height at the end. Probably the sentences completing the movement toward despair are these: "The moon moved over the sky. Pepé half turned on his back. His tongue tried to make words, but only a thick hissing came from between his lips." The acute images in the paragraphs which follow bring us surely and irrevocably to the conclusion.

The details of the flight and the seeming monotony of the struggle through mountainous terrain are a problem for the interpreter, who must keep the listeners' interest by realizing the changing images in the unfolding scenes. Alertness to each new element will include attention again to kinesthetic, or motor imagery, to all words alluding to the passage of time, and to adverbs, adjectives, and verbs offering cues to muscle tone and pace. Although the pace of the second half is bound to be more rapid than that of the first half, with its dialogue and scenes of lower tension, the story as a whole calls for deliberateness.[5]

At the outset great care must be taken to present the scene and family, and yet the first two paragraphs must move swiftly enough to start the action going. Because of its length, the description of Pepé stands out, but parts of it must be emphasized, especially his age, his smiling, his gentle, affectionate, indolent nature, his sweet mouth. As the tale is told, his mouth is an index to the changes in him; it becomes unsmiling, stern, determined, and finally dry, swollen, and misshapen with thirst and pain. Emilio and Rosy require little distinguishing before their last scene, for they are hardly more than agents

---

[5] Suggestions as to pace must of necessity be relative. Probably all competent interpreters use a pace unattainable for beginners. Personal characteristics, diction, and factors in the audience situation all enter into timing.

for action and theme; but Mama ought to be presented carefully. Her ambivalence regarding her son, her affection masked by scolding, her hard-won wisdom, her brisk capability in practical matters have significance.

The usual method for interpreting dialogue is to assign each character an angle of address and use it consistently each time the character speaks.[6] Accompanying this convention is another, fast becoming the rule for interpretation, and that is the visualization of scene, not on the stage, but out beyond the audience. Complying with these two conventions for dialogue and otherwise facing the audience rather directly for summary and description help the interpreter immeasurably to clarify scene, identify character, and at the same time maintain contact with his audience. Recollection of the open and closed situation will aid him in tying all parts of the narrative together purposefully.

To read "Flight" for story and characterization would not suffice. We must suggest its supplementary theme. In fact, it can be taken as a symbolic presentation of a boy's struggles to assume the burdens of manhood. In its blending of the attributes of nature with the characters and theme, the story is complex rather than simple, and its overtones must be given vocal expression. It is the interpreter's task to approximate the author's style, with its shading, contrasts in tension, and balanced movement. Only by faithfully attending to connotations, proportioning, and climactic development can he achieve the spirit and form of the original.

Glossary of Terms[7]

SETTING: A sense of *time* and *place*. May be suggested or fully presented. Place and time affect each other. A narrative of California in 1848 evokes a different feeling from that of a narrative of California, 1948. Some authors rely heavily on place (e.g., William Faulkner, Willa Cather, Thomas Hardy).

---

6 See Chapter 7.

7 We have drawn upon the following sources in assembling these definitions:

Phyllis Bentley, *Some Observations on the Art of Narrative* (New York: The Macmillan Company, 1947).

Cleanth Brooks and Robert Penn Warren, *Modern Rhetoric*, 2nd ed. (New York: Harcourt, Brace and Company, Inc., 1958).

E. M. Forster, *Aspects of the Novel* (New York: Harcourt, Brace and Company, Inc., 1927).

Caroline Gordon, *How to Read a Novel* (New York: The Viking Press, Inc., 1957).

Fred Benjamin Millett, *Reading Fiction* (New York: Harper & Brothers, 1950).

POINT OF VIEW: Used to mean the position from which the narrator—not the author—viewed the action he relates.

In Chapter 3 we spoke of point of view in relation to the teller of the story. The teller may be designated as "I" and speak from the first-person point of view or as "he" or "she" and speak from the third-person point of view. The third person may be limited to either a major or minor character in the story, or may be outside the story, with what is called an omniscient view. (The omniscient view is rarely found in modern narrative writing.)

PLOT: The relation of all parts of a narrative in an articulated skeleton: exposition, development, turning point, climax, denouement, in order.

Exposition tells us time, place, and problem or question.

Development contains series of events to turning point.

Turning point is the place at which events take a new direction.

Climax is the point at which events engender highest or most intense feeling.

Denouement brings us to a satisfying ending. Sometimes there is little exposition; often the turning point and climax are combined and there is no denouement. Sometimes the chronology is inverted, and an event or a series of events precedes exposition. Stories postponing exposition are said to begin *in medias res.*

CHARACTERS: Events happen to and around certain persons. Plots without characters would be useless.

DIALOGUE: Contributes to plausibility of plot and characterizations. It must seem to be the normal speech of given characters, yet always advance the story and add to our knowledge of the one speaking.

SCENE: A full presentation of action, with movement, speech, gesture. Unbroken sequence in time and place. Generally used for crises.

SUMMARY: The author moves swiftly through time and space. Likely to be used for minor parts, low in action and feeling, but necessary for logical development and continuity.

Like other sub-forms the narrative may be simple or complex; it may be primitive, as are the folk tale and ballad; it may be purely a record of action, as some detective stories are; it may be strong in thematic implications, as are *Cry, the Beloved Country* by Alan Paton and "Xingu" by Edith Wharton; or it may be strongly symbolic, as is "La Belle Dame sans Merci," or *Portrait of the Artist as a Young Man.*

THE HANGMAN'S TREE

An American version of an old ballad

"Slack your rope, hangs-a-man,
O slack it for a while.
I think I see my father coming,
Riding many a mile."

"O father, have you brought me gold?
Or have you paid my fee?
Or have you come to see me hanging
On the gallows tree?"
"I have not brought you gold.
I have not paid your fee.
But I have come to see you hanging
On the gallows tree."

"Slack your rope, hangs-a-man,
O slack it for a while.
I think I see my mother coming,
Riding many a mile."

"O mother have you brought me gold?
Or have you paid my fee?
Or have you come to see me hanging
On the gallows tree?"
"I have not brought you gold.
I have not paid your fee.
But I have come to see you hanging
On the gallows tree."

"Slack your rope, hangs-a-man,
O slack it for a while,
I think I see my true love coming,
Riding many a mile."

"O true love, have you brought me gold?
Or have you paid my fee?

Or have you come to see me hanging
On the gallows tree?"
"Yes, I have brought you gold.
Yes, I have paid your fee.
Nor have I come to see you hanging
On the gallows tree."

THE YOUNG MAN WHO FLEW PAST

Arcadii Averchenco (1881–1925)

This sad and tragic history began thus:

Three persons, in three different poses, were carrying on an animated conversation on the sixth floor of a large stone house.

The woman, with plump, beautiful arms, was holding a bed sheet to her breast, forgetting that a bed sheet could not do double duty and cover her shapely bare knees at the same time. The woman was crying, and in the intervals between sobs she was saying:

"Oh John! I swear to you I'm not guilty! He set my head in a whirl, he seduced me—and, I assure you, all against my will! I resisted—"

One of the men, still in his hat and overcoat, was gesticulating wildly and speaking reproachfully to the third person in the room:

"Scoundrel! I'm going to show you right now that you will perish like a cur and the law will be on my side! You shall pay for this meek victim! You reptile! You base seducer!"

The third in this room was a young man who, although not dressed with the greatest meticulousness at the present moment, bore himself, nevertheless, with great dignity.

"I? Why, I have not done anything—I . . . ." he protested, gazing sadly into an empty corner of the room.

"You haven't? Take this, then, you scoundrel!"

The powerful man in the overcoat flung open the window giving out upon the street, gathered the young man who was none too meticulously dressed into his arms, and heaved him out.

Finding himself flying through the air, the young man

bashfully buttoned his vest, and whispered to himself in consolation:

"Never mind! Our failures merely serve to harden us!"

And he kept on flying downward.

He had not yet had time to reach the next floor (the fifth) in his flight, when a deep sigh issued from his breast.

A recollection of the woman whom he had just left poisoned with its bitterness all the delight in the sensation of flying.

"My God!" thought the young man. "Why, I loved her! And she could not find the courage even to confess everything to her husband! God be with her! Now I can feel that she is distant, and indifferent to me."

With this last thought, he had already reached the fifth floor and, as he flew past a window he peeked in, prompted by curiosity.

A young man was sitting reading a book at a lopsided table, his head propped up in his hands.

Seeing him, the young man who was flying past recalled his life; recalled that heretofore he had passed all his days in worldly distractions, forgetful of learning and books; and he felt drawn to the light of knowledge, to the discovery of nature's mysteries with a searching mind, drawn to admiration before the genius of the great masters of words.

"Dear, beloved student!" he wanted to cry out to the man reading, "you have awakened within me all my dormant aspirations, and cured me of the empty infatuation with the vanities of life, which have led me to such a grievous disenchantment on the sixth floor. . . ."

But, not wishing to distract the student from his studies, the young man refrained from calling out, flying down to the fourth floor instead, and here his thoughts took a different turn.

His heart contracted with a strange, sweet pain, while his head grew dizzy—from delight and admiration.

A young woman was sitting at the window of the fourth floor and, with a sewing machine before her, was at work upon something.

But her beautiful white hands had forgotten about work at the present moment, and her eyes—blue as cornflowers—were afar off, pensive and dreamy.

The young man could not take his eyes off this vision, and some new feeling, great and mighty, spread and grew within his heart.

And he understood that all his former encounters with women had been no more than empty infatuations, and that only now he understood that strange, mysterious word—Love.

And he was attracted to the quiet, domestic life; to the endearments of a being beloved beyond words; to a smiling existence, joyous and peaceful.

The next story, past which he was flying at the present moment, confirmed him still more in his inclination.

In the window of the third floor he saw a mother who, singing a quiet lullaby and laughing, was bouncing a plump, smiling baby; love, and a kind, motherly pride were sparkling in her eyes.

"I, too, want to marry the girl on the fourth floor, and have just such rosy, plump children as the one on the third floor," mused the young man, "and I would devote myself entirely to my family and find my happiness in this self-sacrifice."

But the second floor was now approaching. And the picture which the young man saw in a window of this floor forced his heart to contract again.

A man with disheveled hair and wandering gaze was seated at a luxurious writing table. He was gazing at a photograph in a frame before him; at the same time, he was writing with his right hand, and holding a revolver in his left, pressing its muzzle to his temple.

"Stop, madman!" the young man wanted to call out. "Life is so beautiful!" But some instinctive feeling restrained him.

The luxurious appointments of the room, its richness and comfort, led the young man to reflect that there is something else in life which could disrupt even all this comfort and contentment, as well as a whole family; something of the utmost force—mighty, terrific . . .

"What can it be?" he wondered with a heavy heart. And, as if on purpose, Life gave him a harsh, unceremonious answer in a window of the first floor, which he had now reached.

Nearly concealed by the draperies, a young man was sitting at the window, sans coat and vest, a half-dressed woman was sitting on his knees, lovingly entwining the head of her beloved with her round, rosy arms, and passionately hugging him to her magnificent bosom . . .

The young man who was flying past remembered that he had seen this woman (well-dressed) out walking with her husband—but this man was decidedly not her husband. Her husband was older, with curly black hair, half-gray, while this man had beautiful fair hair.

And the young man recalled his former plans: of studying, after the student's example; of marrying the girl on the fourth floor; of a peaceful, domestic life, à la the third—and once more his heart was heavily oppressed.

He perceived all the ephemerality, all the uncertainty of the happiness of which he had dreamed; beheld, in the near future, a whole procession of young men with beautiful fair hair about his wife and himself; remembered the torments of the man on the second floor, and the measures which he had taken to free himself from these torments—and he understood.

"After all I have witnessed, living is not worth while! It is both foolish and tormenting," thought the young man, with a sickly, sardonic smile; and, contracting his eyebrows, he determinedly finished his flight to the very sidewalk.

Nor did his heart tremble when he touched the flagging of the pavement with his hands, and, breaking these now useless members, he dashed out his brains against the hard, indifferent stone.

And, when the curious gathered around his motionless body, it never occurred to any of them what a complex drama the young man had lived through just a few moments before.

THE LAMENT

Anton Chekhov (1860–1904)

IT IS TWILIGHT. A thick wet snow is slowly twirling around the newly lighted street lamps, and lying in soft thin layers on roofs, on horses' backs, on people's shoulders and hats. The cabdriver Iona Potapov is quite white, and looks like a phantom; he is bent double as far as a human body can bend double; he is seated on his box; he never makes a move. If a whole snowdrift fell on him, it seems as if he would not find it necessary to shake it off. His little horse is also quite white, and remains motionless; its immobility, its angularity, and its straight wooden-looking legs, even close by, give it the appearance of a gingerbread horse worth a *kopek*. It is, no doubt, plunged in deep thought. If you were snatched from the plow, from your usual gray surroundings, and were thrown into this slough full of monstrous lights, unceasing noise, and hurrying people, you too would find it difficult not to think.

Iona and his little horse have not moved from their place for a long while. They left their yard before dinner, and up to now, not a fare. The evening mist is descending over the town, the white lights of the lamps replacing brighter rays, and the hubbub of the street getting louder. "Cabby for Viborg way!" suddenly hears Iona. "Cabby!"

Iona jumps, and through his snow-covered eyelashes sees an officer in a greatcoat, with his hood over his head.

"Viborg way!" the officer repeats. "Are you asleep, eh? Viborg way!"

With a nod of assent Iona picks up the reins, in consequence of which layers of snow slip off the horse's back and neck. The officer seats himself in the sleigh, the cabdriver smacks his lips to encourage his horse, stretches out his neck like a swan, sits up, and, more from habit than necessity, brandishes his whip. The little horse also stretches its neck, bends its wooden-looking legs, and makes a move undecidedly.

"What are you doing, werewolf!" is the exclamation Iona hears from the dark mass moving to and fro, as soon as they have started.

"Where the devil are you going? To the r-r-right!"

"You do not know how to drive. Keep to the right!" calls the officer angrily.

A coachman from a private carriage swears at him; a passerby, who has run across the road and rubbed his shoulder against the horse's nose, looks at him furiously as he sweeps the snow from his sleeve. Iona shifts about on his seat as if he were on needles, moves his elbows as if he were trying to keep his equilibrium, and gapes about like someone suffocating, who does not understand why and wherefore he is there.

"What scoundrels they all are!" jokes the officer; "one would think they had all entered into an agreement to jostle you or fall under your horse."

Iona looks round at the officer, and moves his lips. He evidently wants to say something, but the only sound that issues is a snuffle.

"What?" asks the officer.

Iona twists his mouth into a smile, and with an effort says hoarsely:

"My son, *Barin*, died this week."

"Hm! What did he die of?"

Iona turns with his whole body toward his fare, and says:

"And who knows! They say high fever. He was three days in the hospital, and then died . . . God's will be done."

"Turn round! The devil!" sounds from the darkness. "Have you popped off, old doggie, eh? Use your eyes!"

"Go on, go on," says the officer, "otherwise we shall not get there by tomorrow. Hurry up a bit!"

The cabdriver again stretches his neck, sits up, and with a bad grace, brandishes his whip. Several times again he turns to look at his fare, but the latter has closed his eyes, and apparently is not disposed to listen. Having deposited the officer in Viborg, he stops by the tavern, doubles himself up on his seat, and again remains motionless, while the snow once more begins to cover him and his horse. An hour, and another . . . Then, along the footpath, with a squeak of galoshes, and quarreling, come three young men, two of them tall and lanky, the third one short and humpbacked.

"Cabby, to the Police Bridge!" in a cracked voice calls the humpback. "The three of us for two *griveniks!*"

Iona picks up his reins, and smacks his lips. Two *griveniks* is not a fair price, but he does not mind whether it is a *rouble* or five *kopeks*—to him it is all the same now, so long as they are fares. The young men, jostling each other and using bad language, approach the sleigh, and all three at once try to get onto the seat; then begins a discussion as to which two shall sit and who shall be the one to stand. After wrangling, abusing each other, and much petulance, it is at last decided that the humpback shall stand, as he is the smallest.

"Now then, hurry up!" says the humpback in a twanging

voice, as he takes his place and breathes in Iona's neck. "Old furry! Here, mate, what a cap you have! There is not a worse one to be found in all Petersburg! . . ."

"He-he!—he-he!" giggles Iona. "Such a . . ."

"No you, 'such a,' hurry up, are you going the whole way at this pace? Are you? . . . Do you want it in the neck?"

"My head feels like bursting," says one of the lanky ones. "Last night at the Donkmasovs, Vaska and I drank the whole of four bottles of cognac."

"I don't understand what you lie for," says the other lanky one angrily; "you lie like a brute."

"God strike me, it's the truth!"

"It's as much the truth as that a louse coughs!"

"He, he," grins Iona, "what gay young gentlemen!"

"Pshaw, go to the devil!" says the humpback indignantly.

"Are you going to get on or not, you old pest? Is that the way to drive! Use the whip a bit! Go on, devil, go on, give it to him well!"

Iona feels at his back the little man wriggling, and the tremble in his voice. He listens to the insults hurled at him, sees the people, and little by little the feeling of loneliness leaves him. The humpback goes on swearing until he gets mixed up in some elaborate six-foot oath, or chokes with coughing. The lankies begin to talk about a certain Nadejda Petrovna. Iona looks round at them several times; he waits for a temporary silence, then, turning round again, he murmurs:

"My son . . . died this week."

"We must all die," sighs the humpback, wiping his lips after an attack of coughing. "Now, hurry up, hurry up! Gentlemen, I really cannot go any farther like this! When will he get us there?"

"Well, just you stimulate him a little in the neck!"

"You old pest, do you hear, I'll bone your neck for you! If one treated the like of you with ceremony one would have to go on foot! Do you hear, old serpent Gorinytch! Or do you not care a spit?"

Iona hears rather than feels the blows they deal him.

"He, he," he laughs, "They are gay young gentlemen, God bless 'em!"

"Cabby, are you married?" asks a lanky one.

"I? He, he, gay young gentlemen! Now I have only a wife and the moist ground . . . he, ho, ho . . . that is to say, the grave. My son has died, and I am alive . . . A wonderful thing, death mistook the door . . . instead of coming to me, it went to my son . . ."

Iona turns round to tell them how his son died, but at this moment, the humpback, giving a little sigh, announces, "Thank God, we have at last reached our destination," and Iona watches them disappear through the dark entrance. Once more he is alone, and again surrounded by silence . . . His grief, which has abated for a short while, returns and rends his heart with greater force. With an anxious and hurried look, he searches among the crowds passing on either side of the street to find whether there may be just one person who will listen to him. But the crowds hurry by without noticing him or his trouble. Yet it is such an immense, illimitable grief. Should his heart break and the grief pour out, it would flow over the whole earth, so it seems, and yet no one sees it. It has managed to conceal itself in such an insignificant shell that no one can see it even by day and with a light.

Iona sees a hall porter with some sacking, and decides to talk to him.

"Friend, what sort of time is it?" he asks.

"Past nine. What are you standing here for? Move on."

Iona moves on a few steps, doubles himself up, and abandons himself to his grief. He sees it is useless to turn to people for help. In less than five minutes he straightens himself, holds up his head as if he felt some sharp pain, and gives a tug at the reins; he can bear it no longer. "The stables," he thinks, and the little horse, as if it understands, starts off at a trot.

About an hour and a half later Iona is seated by a large dirty stove. Around the stove, on the floor, on the benches, people are snoring; the air is thick and suffocatingly hot. Iona looks at the sleepers, scratches himself, and regrets having returned so early.

"I have not even earned my fodder," he thinks. "That's what's my trouble. A man who knows his job, who has had enough to eat, and his horse too, can always sleep peacefully."

A young cabdriver in one of the corners half gets up, grunts sleepily, and stretches towards a bucket of water.

"Do you want a drink?" Iona asks him.

"Don't I want a drink?"

"That's so? Your good health! But listen, mate—you know, my son is dead . . . Did you hear? This week, in the hospital . . . It's a long story."

Iona looks to see what effect his words have, but sees none—the young man has hidden his face and is fast asleep again. The old man sighs, and scratches his head. Just as much as the young one wants to drink, the old man wants to talk. It will soon be a week since his son died, and he has not been able to speak about it properly to anyone. One must tell it slowly and carefully; how his son fell ill, how he suffered, what he said before he died, how he died. One must describe every detail of the funeral, and the journey to the hospital to fetch the dead son's clothes. His daughter Anissia has remained in the village —one must talk about her too. Is it nothing he has to tell? Surely the listener would gasp and sigh, and sympathize with him? It is better, too, to talk to women; although they are stupid, two words are enough to make them sob.

"I'll go and look after my horse," thinks Iona; "there's always time to sleep. No fear of that!"

He puts on his coat, and goes to the stables to his horse; he thinks of the corn, the hay, the weather. When he is alone, he dares not think of his son; he can speak about him to anyone, but to think of him, and picture him to himself, is unbearably painful.

"Are you tucking in?" Iona asks his horse, looking at its bright eyes; "go on, tuck in, though we've not earned our corn, we can eat hay. Yes! I am too old to drive—my son could have, not I. He was a first-rate cabdriver. If only he had lived!"

Iona is silent for a moment, then continues:

"That's how it is, my old horse. There's no more Kuzma Ionitch. He has left us to live, and he went off pop. Now let's say, you had a foal, you were the foal's mother, and suddenly, let's say, that foal went and left you to live after him. It would be sad, wouldn't it?"

The little horse munches, listens, and breathes over its master's hand . . .

Iona's feelings are too much for him, and he tells the little horse the whole story.

THE FEAR

Robert Frost (1875–   )

A lantern light from deeper in the barn
Shone on a man and woman in the door
And threw their lurching shadows on a house
Near by, all dark in every glossy window.
A horse's hoof pawed once the hollow floor,
And the back of the gig they stood beside
Moved in a little. The man grasped a wheel,
The woman spoke out sharply, "Whoa, stand still!
I saw it just as plain as a white plate,"
She said, "as the light on the dashboard ran
Along the bushes at the roadside—a man's face.
You *must* have seen it too."

                         "I didn't see it.
Are you sure—"

             "Yes, I'm sure!"

                        "—it was a face?"
"Joel, I'll have to look, I can't go in,
I can't, and leave a thing like that unsettled.
Doors locked and curtains drawn will make no difference.
I always have felt strange when we came home
To the dark house after so long an absence,
And the key rattled loudly into place
Seemed to warn someone to be getting out
At one door as we entered at another.
What if I'm right, and someone all the time—
Don't hold my arm!"

"You speak as if this were a travelled road.
You forget where we are. What is beyond
That he'd be going to or coming from
At such an hour of night, and on foot too?
What was he standing still for in the bushes?"

"It's not so very late—it's only dark.
There's more in it than you're inclined to say.
Did he look like—?"

                  "He looked like anyone.

I'll never rest to-night unless I know.
Give me the lantern."
                              "You don't want the lantern."
She pushed past him and got it for herself.
"You're not to come," she said. "This is my business
If the time's come to face it, I'm the one
To put it the right way. He'd never dare—
Listen! He kicked a stone. Hear that, hear that!
He's coming towards us. Joel, go in—please.
Hark!—I don't hear him now. But please go in."

"In the first place you can't make me believe it's—"

"It is—or someone else he's sent to watch.
And now's the time to have it out with him
While we know definitely where he is.
Let him get off and he'll be everywhere
Around us, looking out of trees and bushes
Till I sha'n't dare to set a foot outdoors.
And I can't stand it. Joel, let me go!"

"But it's nonsense to think he'd care enough."

"You mean you couldn't understand his caring.
Oh, but you see he hadn't had enough—
Joel, I won't—I won't—I promise you.
We mustn't say hard things. You mustn't either."

"I'll be the one, if anybody goes!
But you give him the advantage with this light.
What couldn't he do to us standing here!
And if to see was what he wanted, why
He has seen all there was to see and gone."

He appeared to forget to keep his hold,
But advanced with her as she crossed the grass.

"What do you want?" she cried to all the dark.
She stretched up tall to overlook the light
That hung in both hands hot against her skirt.

"There's no one; so you're wrong," he said.

                             "There is.—
What do you want?" she cried, and then herself
Was startled when an answer really came.

"Nothing." It came from well along the road.

She reached a hand to Joel for support:
The smell of scorching woollen made her faint.

"What are you doing round this house at night?"

"Nothing." A pause: there seemed no more to say.
And then the voice again: "You seem afraid.
I saw by the way you whipped up the horse.
I'll just come forward in the lantern light
And let you see."
                  "Yes, do.—Joel, go back!"
She stood her ground against the noisy steps
That came on, but her body rocked a little.
"You see," the voice said.

                       "Oh." She looked and looked.
"You don't see—I've a child here by the hand.
A robber wouldn't have his family with him."

"What's a child doing at this time of night—?"

"Out walking. Every child should have the memory
Of at least one long-after-bedtime walk.
What, son?"

"Then I should think you'd try to find
Somewhere to walk—"

                      "The highway, as it happens—
We're stopping for the fortnight down at Dean's."

"But if that's all—Joel—you realize—
You won't think anything. You understand?
You understand that we have to be careful.
This is a very, very lonely place.
Joel!" She spoke as if she couldn't turn.
The swinging lantern lengthened to the ground,
It touched, it struck, it clattered and went out.

LA BELLE DAME SANS MERCI

John Keats (1795–1821)

O what can ail thee, knight-at-arms,
    Alone and palely loitering?
The sedge has wither'd from the lake,
    And no birds sing.

O what can ail thee, knight-at-arms,
    So haggard and so woe-begone?
The squirrel's granary is full,
    And the harvest's done.

I see a lily on thy brow
    With anguish moist and fever dew,
And on thy cheeks a fading rose
    Fast withereth too.

'I met a lady in the meads,
    Full beautiful—a faery's child;
Her hair was long, her foot was light,
    And her eyes were wild.

'I made a garland for her head,
    And bracelets too, and fragrant zone;
She look'd at me as she did love,
    And made sweet moan.

'I set her on my pacing steed,
    And nothing else saw all day long,
For sideways she would lean, and sing
    A faery's song.

'She found me roots of relish sweet,
    And honey wild, and manna-dew,
And sure in language strange she said—
    "I love thee true!"

'She took me to her elfin grot,
    And there she wept and sigh'd full sore,
And there I shut her wild, wild eyes
    With kisses four.

'And there she lulled me asleep,
    And there I dream'd—ah! woe betide!
The latest dream I ever dream'd
    On the cold hill's side.

'I saw pale kings and princes too,
    Pale warriors, death-pale were they all;
They cried—"La Belle Dame sans Merci
    Hath thee in thrall!"

'I saw their starved lips in the gloom,
    With horrid warning gaped wide;
And I awoke, and found me here
    On the cold hill's side.

'And this is why I sojourn here,
    Alone and palely loitering,
Though the sedge is wither'd from the lake,
    And no birds sing.'

THE APOSTATE

George Milburn (1906–   )

Harry, you been jacking me up about how I been neglecting
Rotary here lately, so I'm just going to break down and tell
you something. Now I don't want you to take this personal,
Harry, because it's not meant personal at all. No siree! Not
a-tall! But, just between you and I, Harry, I'm not going to be
coming out to Rotary lunches any more. I mean I'm quitting
Rotary! . . .

Now whoa there! Whoa! Whoa just a minute and let me
get in a word edgeways. Just let me finish my little say.

Don't you never take it into your head that I haven't been
wrestling with this thing plenty. I mean I've argued it all out
with myself. Now I'm going to tell you the whyfor and the
whereof and the howcome about this, Harry, but kindly don't
let what I say go no further. Please keep it strictly on the Q.T.
Because I guess the rest of the boys would suspicion that I was
turning highbrow on them. But you've always been a buddy to

me, Harry, you mangy old son of a hoss thief, you, so what I'm telling you is the straight dope.

Harry, like you no doubt remember, up till a few months ago Rotary was about "the most fondest thing I is of," as the nigger says. There wasn't nothing that stood higher for me than Rotary.

Well, here, about a year ago last fall I took a trip down to the university. Yes, sir, that boy is getting a college education. I mean, I'm all for the youth having a college education.

Of course I think that there is such a thing as too much education working a detriment. Take, for instance, some of these longhairs running around knocking the country right now. But what I mean is, a good, sound, substantial college education. I don't mean a string of letters a yard long for a man to write after his John Henry. I just mean that I want my boy to have his sheepskin, they call it, before he starts out in the world. Like the fellow says, I want him to get his A.B. degree, and then he can go out and get his J.O.B.

Now, Harry, I always felt like a father has got certain responsibilities to his son. That's just good Rotary. That's all that is. You know that that's just good Rotary yourself, Harry. Well, I always wanted Hubert to think about me just like I was a pal to him, or say an older brother, maybe. Hubert always knew that all he had to do was come to me, and I would act like a big buddy to him, irregardless.

Well, like I was telling you, Harry, I started Hubert in to the university two years ago, and after he had been there about two months, I thought I would run down and see how he was getting along and go to a football game. So I and Mrs. T. drove over one Friday. We didn't know the town very well, so we stopped at a filling-station, and I give Hubert a ring, and he come right on down to where we was to show us the way. Just as soon as he come up, I could see right then that he had something on his mind bothering him.

He called me aside and took me into the filling-station restroom, and says: "For the love of God, Dad, take that Rotary button out of your coat lapel," he says to me.

Harry, that come as a big surprise to me, and I don't mind telling you that it just about took the wind out of my sails. But I wasn't going to let on to him, so I rared back on my dignity, and says, "Why, what do you mean, take that Rotary button out of my lapel, young man?" I says to him.

"Dad," Hubert says to me, serious, "any frat house has always got a few cynics in it. If you was to wear that Rotary button in your lapel out to the frat house, just as soon as you got out of sight, some of those boys at the house would razz the life out of me," he says.

"Hubert," I says, "There's not a thing that this lapel badge represents that any decent, moral person could afford to make fun of. If that's the kind of Reds you got out at your fraternity, the kind that would razz a what you might call sacred thing—yes sir, a sacred thing—like Rotary, well I and your mamma can just go somewheres else and put up. I don't guess the hotels have quit running," I says to him.

By now I was on my high horse right, see?

"Now, Dad," Hubert says, "it's not that. I mean, person'ly I'm awful proud of you. It's just that I haven't been pledged to this fraternity long, see, and when some of those older members found out you was a Rotarian they would deal me a lot of misery, and I couldn't say nothing. Person'ly I think Rotary is all right," he says to me.

"Well, you better, son," I says, "or I'm going to begin to think that you're sick in the head."

The way he explained it, though, Harry, that made it a horse of a different tail, as the saying goes, so I give in and took off my Rotary button right there. Stuck it in my pocket, see? So we went on out and visited at Hubert's fraternity house, and do you know that those boys just got around there and treated we folks like we was princes of the blood. I mean you would of thought that I was an old ex-graduate of that university. And we saw the big pigskin tussle the next day, fourteen to aught, favor us, and we had such a scrumptious time all around I forgot all about what Hubert had said.

Ever'thing would of been all right, except for what happened later. I guess some of those older boys at the frat house begin using their form of psychology on Hubert. I mean they finely got his mind set against Rotary, because when he come home for the summer vacation that was about the size of things.

I mean all last summer, I thought Hubert would never let

up. He just kept it up, making sarcastic remarks about Rotary, see? Even when we was on our vacation trip. You know we drove out to California and back last summer, Harry. Come back with the same air in the tires we started out with. Well, I thought it would be kind of nice to drop in and eat with the Hollywood Rotary—you know, just to be able to say I had. Well, do you know that that boy Hubert made so much fun of the idea I just had to give it up? That was the way it was the whole trip. He got his mother around on his side, too. Just to be frank with you, I never got so sick and tired of anything in all my born days.

Well, Harry, I had my dander up there for a while, and all the bickering in the world couldn't of shook me from my stand. But finely Hubert went back to college in September, and I thought I would have a little peace. Then I just got to thinking about it, and it all come over me. "Look here, Mister Man," I says to myself, "your faith and loyalty to Rotary may be a fine thing, and all that, but it's just costing you the fellowship of your own son." Now a man can't practice Rotary in the higher sense, and yet at the same time be letting his own son's fellowship get loose from him. So there it was. Blood's thicker than water, Harry. You'll have to admit that.

Right along in there, Harry, was the first time I begin to attending meetings irregular. I'll tell you—you might not think so—but it was a pretty tough struggle for me. I remember one Monday noon, Rotary-meeting day, I happened to walk past the Hotel Beckman just at lunchtime. The windows of the Venetian Room was open, and I could hear you boys singing a Rotary song. You know that one we sing set to the tune of "Last Night on the Back Porch." It goes:

> I love the Lions in the morning,
> The Exchange Club at night,
> I love the Y's men in the evening,
> And Kiwanis are all right . . .

Well, I couldn't carry a tune if I had it in a sack, but anyway that's the way it goes. So I just stopped in my tracks and stood there listening to that song coming out of the Hotel Beckman dining room. And when the boys come to the last verse,

> I love the Optimists in the springtime,
>   The Ad Club in the fall,
> But each day—and in every way—
>   I love Rotary best of all . . .

I tell you, Harry, that just got me. I had a lump in my throat big enough to choke a cow. The tears begin coming up in my eyes, and it might sound ridiculous to hear me tell it now, but I could of broke down and bawled right there on the street. I got a grip on myself and walked on off, but right then I says to myself, "The hell with Hubert and his highbrow college-fraternity ideas; I'm going back to Rotary next week."

Well, I did go back the next week, and what happened decided me on taking the step I decided on. Here's what decided me. You know, I never got very well acquainted with Gay Harrison, the new secretary. I mean, of course, I know him all right, but he hasn't been in Rotary only but about a year. Well, on that particular day, I just happened to let my tongue slip and called him Mister Harrison, instead of by his nickname. Well, of course, the boys slapped a dollar fine on me right then and there. I haven't got no kick to make about that, but the point is, I had a letter from Hubert in my pocket right then, telling me that he had run short of money. So I just couldn't help but be struck by the idea "I wish I was giving Hubert this dollar." So that's what decided me on devoting my time and finances to another kind of fellowship, Harry.

I get down to the university to see Hubert more frequent now. I make it a point to. And the boys come to me, and I been helping them a little on their frat building fund. There's a fine spirit of fellowship in an organization like that. Some boys from the best families of the State are members, too. You might think from what I said that they'd be uppish, but they're not. No siree. Not a bit of it. I been down there enough for them to know me, now, and they all pound me on the back and call me H.T., just like I was one of them. And I do them, too. And I notice that when they sit down to a meal, they have some songs they sing just as lively and jolly as any we had at Rotary. Of course, like Hubert said, a few of them might have some wild-haired ideas about Rotary, but they're young yet.

And as far as I can see there's not a knocker nor a sourbelly among them. Absolutely democratic.

It puts me in mind of a little incidence that happened last month when the frat threw a big Dad's Day banquet for us down there. All the fathers of the boys from all over the state was there. Well, to promote the spirit of fellowship between dad and son, the fraternity boys all agreed to call their dads by their first name, just treating the dads like big buddies. So at the table Hubert happened to forget for a minute, and says to me "Dad" something. Well sir, the president of the frat flashed right out, "All right, Hubie, we heard you call H.T. 'Dad'. So that'll just cost you a dollar for the icecream fund." Ever'body had a good laugh at Hubert getting caught like that, but do you know, that boy of mine just forked right over without making a kick. That shows the stuff, don't it, Harry? Nothing wrong with a boy like that.

And the whole bunch is like that, ever' one of them. I'll tell you, Harry, the boys at the frat of Hubert's are the builders in the coming generation. Any man of vision can see that.

Well, that's that. Now what was you going to say?

THE FIRST DEATH OF HER LIFE

Elizabeth Taylor (1912–   )

Suddenly, tears poured from Lucy's eyes. She rested her forehead against her mother's hand and let the tears soak into the counterpane.

Dear Mr. Wilcox, she began, for her mind was always composing letters, I shall not be at the shop for the next four days, as my mother has passed away and I shall not be available until after the funeral. My mother passed away very peacefully . . .

The nurse came in. She took her patient's wrist for a moment, replaced it on the bed, removed a jar of white lilac from the table, as if this were no longer necessary, and went out again.

The girl kneeling by the bed had looked up, but Dear Mr. Wilcox, she resumed, her eyes returning to the counterpane,

My mother has died. I shall come back to work the day after tomorrow. Yours, sincerely, Lucy Mayhew.

Her father was late. She imagined him hurrying from work, bicycling through the darkening streets, dogged, hunched up, slush thrown up by his wheels. Her mother did not move. Lucy stroked her mother's hand, with its loose gold ring, the calloused palm, the fine, long fingers. Then she stood up stiffly, her knees bruised from the waxed floor, and went to the window.

Snowflakes turned idly, drifting down over the hospital gardens. It was four o'clock in the afternoon and already the day seemed over. So few sounds came from this muffled and discolored world. In the hospital itself, there was a deep silence.

Her thoughts came to her in words, as if her mind spoke them first, understood them later. She tried to think of her childhood—little scenes she selected to prove how she and her mother had loved one another. Other scenes, especially last week's quarrel, she chose to forget, not knowing that in this moment she sent them away forever. Only loving-kindness remained. But, all the same, intolerable pictures broke through—her mother at the sink; her mother ironing; her mother standing between the lace curtains, staring out at the dreary street with a wounded look in her eyes; her mother tying the same lace curtains with yellow ribbons; attempts at lightness, gaiety, which came to nothing; her mother gathering her huge black cat to her, burying her face in its fur while a great, shivering sigh—of despair, of boredom—escaped her.

Her mother no longer sighed. She lay very still and sometimes took a little sip of air. Her arms were neatly at her side. Her eyes, which all day long had been turned to the white lilac, were closed. Her cheekbones rose sharply from her bruised, exhausted face. She smelled faintly of wine. A small lilac flower floated on a glass of champagne, now discarded on the table at her side.

The champagne, with which they hoped to stretch out the thread of her life minute by minute, the lilac, the room of her own, all came to her at the end of a life of drabness and denial, just as, all along the mean street of the small English town where they lived, the dying and the dead were able to claim a lifetime's savings from the bereaved.

She is no longer there, Lucy thought, standing beside the bed. All day, her mother had stared at the white lilac; now she had sunk away. Outside, beyond the hospital gardens, mist settled over the town, blurred the street lamps.

The nurse returned with the matron. Lucy tautened, ready to be on her best behavior. In her heart, she trusted her mother to die without frightening her, and when the matron, deftly drawing Lucy's head to rest on her own shoulder, said in her calm voice, "She has gone," Lucy felt she had met this happening halfway.

A little bustle began, quick footsteps along the empty passages, and for a moment she was left alone with her dead mother. She laid her hand timidly on the soft, dark hair, so often touched, played with, when she was a child, standing on a stool behind her mother's chair while she sewed.

There was still the smell of wine and the hospital smell. It was growing dark in the room. She went to the dressing table and took her mother's handbag, very worn and shiny, and a book, a library book that she had chosen carefully, believing her mother would read it. Then she had a quick sip from the glass on the table, a mouthful of champagne, which she had never tasted before, and looking wounded and aloof, walked down the middle of the corridor, feeling nurses falling away to left and right. Opening the glass doors onto the snowy gardens, she thought that it was like the end of a film. But no music rose up and engulfed her. Instead, there was her father turning in at the gates. He propped his bicycle against the wall and began to run clumsily across the wet gravel.

THE BALLAD OF MOLL MAGEE

William Butler Yeats (1865–1939)

Come round me, little childer;
There, don't fling stones at me
Because I mutter as I go;
But pity Moll Magee.

My man was a poor fisher
With shore lines in the say;

My work was saltin' herrings
The whole of the long day.

And sometimes from the saltin' shed
I scarce could drag my feet,
Under the blessed moonlight,
Along the pebbly street.

I'd always been but weakly,
And my baby was just born;
A neighbour minded her by day,
I minded her till morn.

I lay upon my baby;
Ye little childer dear,
I looked on my cold baby
When the morn grew frosty and clear.

A weary woman sleeps so hard!
My man grew red and pale,
And gave me money, and bade me go
To my own place, Kinsale.

He drove me out and shut the door,
And gave his curse to me;
I went away in silence,
No neighbour could I see.

The windows and the doors were shut,
One star shone faint and green,
The little straws were turnin' round
Across the bare boreen.

I went away in silence:
Beyond old Martin's byre
I saw a kindly neighbour
Blowin' her mornin' fire.

She drew from me my story—
My money's all used up,
And still, with pityin', scornin' eye,
She gives me bite and sup.

She says my man will surely come,
And fetch me home agin;
But always, as I'm movin' round,
Without doors or within,

Pilin' the wood or pilin' the turf,
Or goin' to the well,
I'm thinkin' of my baby
And keenin' to mysel'.

And sometimes I am sure she knows
When, openin' wide His door,
God lights the stars, His candles,
And looks upon the poor.

So now, ye little childer,
Ye won't fling stones at me;
But gather with your shinin' looks
And pity Moll Magee.

7

Drama

A play exists to create emotional response in an audience. ∽
GEORGE PIERCE BAKER

The poet, the novelist, the actor, appeal to the heart by indirect means; the effect produced depends upon the extent to which the heart is open to receive impressions. ∽ DENIS DIDEROT

As WE HAVE SAID,[1] the traditional parts of narrative reappear in dramatic forms, though somewhat altered. The concentration, organization, and momentum of the drama combine to furnish the interpreter and his audience with highly satisfying moments. Yet it would be unfair not to point out that the peculiar nature of drama renders it a hazardous as well as a rewarding experience in interpretation. By its immediate visual presentation, its action in the present tense, drama conveys a sense of the fullness of life. Furthermore, the *action* of the play entails *interaction* among the persons of the play. It becomes imperative for the interpreter to retain the action and interaction which are the heart of drama, but his method is to substitute concentrated energy and emotional depth for the visual cues of the fully mounted play.

---

[1] See Chapters 2 and 6.

In Chapter 8 there are a number of exercises planned to illustrate the difference between the response of interpreter and actor. In the last section of this chapter, entitled "The Interpreter's Response," as well as in Chapters 11 and 12, there is further discussion of the interpreter's techniques in presenting dramatic literature. In particular, the interpreter's relation to his audience, described in connection with the continuum of the open-closed situation, must be clearly established. Because the interpreter "shows" the play to his audience, without a supporting cast, but with only himself to rely upon, his style is bound to contain elements of narration; that is, although he strives for the omniscient point of view, the interpreter can never be overlooked. He is *there*. Through him, as through the narrator of *Our Town, I Remember Mama,* or *The Glass Menagerie,* the action of the play unfolds. Although plays in which a narrator is part of the playwright's design are thus seen to be readily adaptable to the art of interpretation, they are so few in number that the interpreter cannot stop with them. He must look further for plays exemplifying the standards of good literature, and especially the standards of good drama. Such plays will possess one or more of the following characteristics: clear structure, with credible plot development and well-marked crises or climaxes; thematic or symbolic interest; powerful or appealing characters; purposeful dialogue.

The Member of the Wedding, by Carson McCullers, fulfills these requirements for interpretation. On the whole, the structure is well-knit, with clearly-marked climaxes; theme and symbols combine to increase the depth of the action; the characters, especially the two main characters, have strength and life. The last scene of Act I, portions of Act II dealing with Frankie's reactions to the wedding, and the first scene of Act III constitute a readable sequence. The scene from Act III, reproduced below, is climactic so far as the main plot is concerned and contains preparation for the two scenes which conclude the play. The scene is emotionally and intellectually satisfying, provided the interpreter has supplied sufficient exposition and background in introducing it.

Just as the narrator whose part is written into the play sets the stage, describes characters, and provides linkages, so the interpreter gives background materials, introduces characters, and describes action which must be omitted but is essential for understanding of the scenes being read. The interpreter will ordinarily want to leave his audience with a sense of completion or fulfillment, possible only when the play as a whole is suggested, if not presented. The choice of a scene from the first act of a play leaves the interpreter with less summarizing to do, because a first act is likely to be filled with exposition, but such an early scene leaves many unanswered questions. Answering them in his own words, the interpreter runs the risk of ending on a low level of excitement and interest. A scene past the mid-point of action is often more satisfying, but demands, as does this one from *The Member of the Wedding*, skillful preparation.

Much of the discussion on programing in Chapter 12 is applicable to the introduction of dramatic material—in fact, to the introduction of any form of literature—and need not be presented here. Yet let us go so far as to say that an interpreter, whether or not his audience has a printed program, often needs to use an introduction to develop rapport and provide the appropriate atmosphere or mood, as well as to give factual information. The introduction of dramatic material must often substitute for the printed cast of characters and synopsis expected in the theater; and it must always establish the mood of the play under consideration. Students who manage other introductory comments with skill often complain that the introduction of a play is the most demanding of all. The critic-teacher can be helpful to these students and can often suggest methods for achieving the following goals for an introduction to a play:

1. Immediate interest in action and characters.
2. Economical wording, with no overload.
3. Orderly narration of necessary facts and events.
4. Distinguishing mark or tag for each character to be presented.
5. Focus on main plot and characters, with quick dismissal of lesser elements.
6. Evidence throughout that the introduction is a part of the aesthetic whole and not a hasty makeshift.
7. Physical and vocal attunement to the spirit of the play itself.
8. Effective transition (through words, posture, and intonation) to dialogue of the play. (No hesitation, sneaks, or slides, but dramatic passage!)

Yet the attainment of these goals in the introduction must never dwarf the importance of the play itself. The interpreter must apportion his time so that the play itself occupies let us say nine-tenths of the whole, and the other tenth may be used for introductions and transitions.

Obviously, the first thing to do in preparation for the interpretation of drama is to read carefully the entire play to be presented, not a synopsis, not a critical essay about it, but the play itself. If the playwright has written other plays, read as many of them as you can, but read the one you have chosen with special care and thoroughness, even though you have seen it produced. We provide here only a portion of *The Member of the Wedding*, but if you are to interpret this scene effectively, you will need to fit it into your own concept of the whole.

THE MEMBER OF THE WEDDING

(*Carson McCullers, 1917–*)

Act III. Scene I. The scene is the same: the kitchen. It is the day of the wedding. When the curtain rises Berenice, in her apron, and T. T. Williams in a white coat have just finished preparations for the wedding refreshments. Berenice has been watching the ceremony through the half-open door leading into the hall. There are sounds of congratulations offstage, the wedding ceremony having just finished.

BERENICE (*to T. T. Williams*).   Can't see much from this door. But I can see Frankie. And her face is a study. And John Henry's chewing away at the bubble gum that Jarvis bought him. Well, sounds like it's all over. They crowding in now to kiss the bride. We better take this cloth off the sandwiches. Frankie said she would help you serve.

T. T.   From the way she's acting, I don't think we can count much on her.

BERENICE.   I wish Honey was here. I'm so worried about him since what you told me. It's going to storm. It's a mercy they didn't decide to have the wedding in the back yard like they first planned.

T. T.   I thought I'd better not minch the matter. Honey was in a bad way when I saw him this morning.

BERENICE.   Honey Camden don't have too large a share of judgment as it is, but when he gets high on them reefers, he's got no more judgment than a four-year-old child. Remember that time he swung at the police and nearly got his eyes beat out?

T. T.   Not to mention six months on the road.

BERENICE.   I haven't been so anxious in all my life. I've got two people scouring Sugarville to find him. (*in a fervent voice*) God, you took Ludie but please watch over my Honey Camden. He's all the family I got.

T. T.   And Frankie behaving this way about the wedding. Poor little critter.

BERENICE.   And the sorry part is that she's perfectly serious about all this foolishness. (*Frankie enters the kitchen through the hall door.*) Is it all over? (*T. T. crosses to the icebox with sandwiches.*)

FRANKIE.   Yes. And it was such a pretty wedding I wanted to cry.

BERENICE.   You told them yet?

FRANKIE.   About my plans—no, I haven't yet told them.

(*John Henry comes in and goes out.*)

BERENICE.   Well, you better hurry up and do it, for they going to leave the house right after the refreshments.

FRANKIE.   Oh, I know it. But something just seems to happen to my throat; every time I tried to tell them different words came out.

BERENICE.   What words?

FRANKIE.   I asked Janice how come she didn't marry with a veil. (*with feeling*) Oh, I'm so embarrassed. Here I am all dressed up in this tacky evening dress. Oh, why didn't I listen to you! I'm so ashamed.

(*T. T. goes out with a platter of sandwiches.*)

BERENICE.   Don't take everything so strenuous like.

FRANKIE.   I'm going in there and tell them now! (*She goes.*)

JOHN HENRY (*coming out of the interior bedroom, carrying several costumes*). Frankie sure gave me a lot of presents when she was packing the suitcase. Berenice, she gave me all the beautiful show costumes.

BERENICE.   Don't set so much store by all those presents. Come tomorrow morning and she'll be demanding them back again.

JOHN HENRY.   And she even gave me the shell from the Bay. (*He puts the shell to his ear and listens.*)

BERENICE.   I wonder what's going on up there. *(She goes to the door and opens it and looks through.)*

T. T. *(returning to the kitchen)*. They all complimenting the wedding cake. And drinking the wine punch.

BERENICE.   What's Frankie doing? When she left the kitchen a minute ago she was going to tell them. I wonder how they'll take this total surprise. I have a feeling like you get just before a big thunder storm.

(Frankie enters, holding a punch cup.)

BERENICE.   You told them yet?

FRANKIE.   There are all the family around and I can't seem to tell them. I wish I had written it down on the typewriter beforehand. I try to tell them and the words just—die.

BERENICE.   The words just die because the very idea is so silly.

FRANKIE.   I love the two of them so much. Janice put her arms around me and said she had always wanted a little sister. And she kissed me. She asked me again what grade I was in in school. That's the third time she's asked me. In fact, that's the main question I've been asked at the wedding.

(John Henry comes in, wearing a fairy costume, and goes out. Berenice notices Frankie's punch and takes it from her.)

FRANKIE.   And Jarvis was out in the street seeing about this car he borrowed for the wedding. And I followed him out and tried to tell him. But while I was trying to reach the point, he suddenly grabbed me by the elbows and lifted me up and sort of swung me. He said: "Frankie, the lankie, the alaga fankie, the tee-legged, toe-legged, bow-legged Frankie." And he gave me a dollar bill.

BERENICE.   That's nice.

FRANKIE.   I just don't know what to do. I have to tell them and yet I don't know how to.

BERENICE.   Maybe when they're settled, they will invite you to come and visit with them.

FRANKIE.   Oh no! I'm going *with* them.

(Frankie goes back into the house. There are louder sounds of voices from the interior. John Henry comes in again.)

JOHN HENRY.   The bride and the groom are leaving. Uncle Royal is taking their suitcases out to the car.

(Frankie runs to the interior room and returns with her suitcase. She kisses Berenice.)

FRANKIE.   Good-bye, Berenice. Good-bye, John Henry. (She stands a moment and looks around the kitchen.) Farewell, old ugly kitchen. (She runs out.)

(There are sounds of good-byes as the wedding party and the family guests move out of the house to the sidewalk. The voices get fainter in the distance. Then, from the front sidewalk there is the sound of disturbance. Frankie's voice is heard, diminished by distance, although she is speaking loudly.)

FRANKIE'S VOICE.   That's what I am telling you. (Indistinct protesting voices are heard.)

MR. ADDAMS' VOICE   (indistinctly). Now be reasonable, Frankie.

FRANKIE'S VOICE   (screaming). I have to go. Take me! Take me!

JOHN HENRY   (entering excitedly). Frankie is in the wedding car and they can't get her out. (He runs out but soon returns.) Uncle Royal and my Daddy are having to haul and drag old Frankie. She's holding onto the steering wheel.

MR. ADDAMS' VOICE.   You march right along here. What in the world has come into you? (He comes into the kitchen with Frankie who is sobbing.) I have never heard of such an exhibition in my life. Berenice, you take charge of her.

(Frankie flings herself on the kitchen chair and sobs with her head in her arms on the kitchen table.)

JOHN HENRY.   They put old Frankie out of the wedding. They hauled her out of the wedding car.

MR. ADDAMS   (clearing his throat). That's sufficient, John Henry. Leave Frankie alone. (He puts a caressing hand on Frankie's head.) What makes you want to leave your old papa like this? You've got Janice and Jarvis all upset on their wedding day.

FRANKIE.   I love them so!

BERENICE   (looking down the hall). Here they come. Now please be reasonable, Sugar.

(The bride and groom come in. Frankie keeps her face buried in *her arms and does not look up. The bride wears a blue suit with a white flower corsage pinned at the shoulder.)*

JARVIS.   Frankie, we came to tell you good-bye. I'm sorry you're taking it like this.

JANICE.   Darling, when we are settled we want you to come for a nice visit with us. But we don't yet have any place to live. *(She goes to Frankie and caresses her head. Frankie jerks.)* Won't you tell us good-bye now?

FRANKIE   *(with passion).* We! When you say *we*, you only mean you and Jarvis. And I am not included. *(She buries her head in her arms again and sobs.)*

JANICE.   Please, darling, don't make us unhappy on our wedding day. You know we love you.

FRANKIE.   See! *We*—when you say we, I am not included. It's not fair.

JANICE.   When you come visit us you must write beautiful plays, and we'll all act in them. Come, Frankie, don't hide your sweet face from us. Sit up. *(Frankie raises her head slowly and stares with a look of wonder and misery.)* Good-bye, Frankie, darling.

JARVIS.   So long, now, kiddo.

(They go out and Frankie still stares at them as they go down the hall. She rises, crosses towards the door and falls on her knees.)

FRANKIE.   Take me! Take me!

(Berenice puts Frankie back on her chair.)

JOHN HENRY.   They put Frankie out of the wedding. They hauled her out of the wedding car.

BERENICE.   Don't tease your cousin, John Henry.

FRANKIE.   It was a frame-up all around.

BERENICE.   Well, don't bother no more about it. It's over now. Now cheer up.

FRANKIE.   I wish the whole world would die.

BERENICE.   School will begin now in only three more weeks and you'll find another bosom friend like Evelyn Owen you so wild about.

JOHN HENRY (seated below the sewing machine). I'm sick, Berenice. My head hurts.

BERENICE. No you're not. Be quiet, I don't have the patience to fool with you.

FRANKIE (hugging her hunched shoulders). Oh, my heart feels so cheap!

BERENICE. Soon as you get started in school and have a chance to make these here friends, I think it would be a good idea to have a party.

FRANKIE. Those baby promises rasp on my nerves.

BERENICE. You could call up the society editor of the Evening Journal and have the party written up in the paper. And that would make the fourth time your name has been published in the paper.

FRANKIE (with a trace of interest). When my bike ran into that automobile, the paper called me Fankie Addams, F-A-N-K-I-E. (She puts her head down again.)

JOHN HENRY. Frankie, don't cry. This evening we can put up the teepee and have a good time.

FRANKIE. Oh, hush up your mouth.

BERENICE. Listen to me. Tell me what you would like and I will try to do it if it is in my power.

FRANKIE. All I wish in the world, is for no human being ever to speak to me as long as I live.

BERENICE. Bawl, then, misery.

(Mr. Addams enters the kitchen, carrying Frankie's suitcase, which he sets in the middle of the kitchen floor. He cracks his finger joints. Frankie stares at him resentfully, then fastens her gaze on the suitcase.)

MR. ADDAMS. Well, it looks like the show is over and the monkey's dead.

FRANKIE. You think it's over, but it's not.

MR. ADDAMS. You want to come down and help me at the store tomorrow? Or polish some silver with the shammy rag? You can even play with those old watch springs.

FRANKIE *(still looking at her suitcase).* That's my suitcase I packed. If you think it's all over, that only shows how little you know. *(T. T. comes in.)* If I can't go with the bride and my brother as I was meant to leave this town, I'm going anyway. Somehow, anyhow, I'm leaving town. *(Frankie raises up in her chair.)* I can't stand this existence—this kitchen—this town—any longer! I will hop a train and go to New York. Or hitch rides to Hollywood, and get a job there. If worse comes to worse, I can act in comedies. *(She rises.)* Or I could dress up like a boy and join the Merchant Marines and run away to sea. Somehow, anyhow, I'm running away.

BERENICE. Now quiet down—

FRANKIE *(grabbing the suitcase and running into the hall).* Please, Papa, don't try to capture me.

(Outside the wind starts to blow.)

JOHN HENRY *(from the doorway).* Uncle Royal, Frankie's got your pistol in her suitcase.

(There is the sound of running footsteps and of the screen door slamming.)

BERENICE. Run catch her.

(T. T. and Mr. Addams rush into the hall, followed by John Henry.)

MR. ADDAMS' VOICE. Frankie! Frankie! Frankie!

(Berenice is left alone in the kitchen. Outside the wind is higher and the hall door is blown shut. There is a rumble of thunder, then a loud clap. Thunder and flashes of lightning continue. Berenice is seated in her chair, when John Henry comes in.)

JOHN HENRY. Uncle Royal is going with my Daddy, and they are chasing her in our car. *(There is a thunder clap.)* The thunder scares me, Berenice.

BERENICE *(taking him in her lap).* Ain't nothing going to hurt you.

JOHN HENRY. You think they're going to catch her?

BERENICE *(putting her hand to her head).* Certainly. They'll be bringing her home directly. I've got such a headache. Maybe my eye socket and all these troubles.

JOHN HENRY *(with his arms around Berenice).* I've got a headache, too. I'm sick, Berenice.

BERENICE.   No you ain't. Run along, Candy. I ain't got the patience to fool with you now.

   (Suddenly the lights go out in the kitchen, plunging it in gloom. The sound of wind and storm continues and the yard is a dark storm-green.)

JOHN HENRY.   Berenice!

BERENICE.   Ain't nothing. Just the lights went out.

JOHN HENRY.   I'm scared.

BERENICE.   Stand still, I'll just light a candle. *(muttering)* I always keep one around, for such like emergencies. *(She opens a drawer.)*

JOHN HENRY.   What makes the lights go out so scarey like this?

BERENICE.   Just one of them things, Candy.

JOHN HENRY.   I'm scared. Where's Honey?

BERENICE.   Jesus knows. I'm scared, too. With Honey snow-crazy and loose like this—and Frankie run off with a suitcase and her Papa's pistol. I feel like every nerve been picked out of me.

JOHN HENRY   *(holding out his seashell and stroking Berenice).* You want to listen to the ocean?

   (The curtain falls.)

The Situation

There are several conventions in connection with the theater which are of little consequence for the interpreter, but the convention we have called the *closed situation* is of primary importance to him. It is understood that there is no apparent communication between players and audience, despite the fact that everything players do and say is directed to the audience and has been planned solely for the audience. During the course of a play, the audience observes (while being unobserved) the private lives of individuals who are immersed in crisis and conflict and are totally unaware of being observed. The interpreter cannot follow this dramatic convention to the letter, for he is obliged first to appear as himself and then alternately to "show" the play to his audience and bridge gaps in action with exposition directed openly to his audience. But so far as he possibly can, the interpreter sustains an omniscient point of view which permits him

to move from one character to another and to convey a sense of interaction among characters. Practical considerations, the rhythmical
movement of the play, and the intensity of the emotion in drama all
combine to create *closure* in the dramatic situation, a more complete
closure than exists for any other interpretative situation. It is conceivable that this scene from *The Member of the Wedding* could
continue without explanation involving direct communication. Certainly it demands hair-trigger responses from the interpreter who must
through emotional intensity and revelation of characters arrive at the
rhythmical exchange and development of dramatic action.

The action of *The Member of the Wedding* unfolds in a few days
of August, 1945, in a small town in the southern United States. Carson
McCullers, a native of Georgia, works in familiar territory, but it is
probable that *artistic* reasons prompted her to select a southern town
for the action of *The Member of the Wedding*. Berenice, Mr. Addams,
and Honey are more convincing and acceptable in the southern setting.
Recollection that numerous army camps were located in the South
during World War II makes much of the action plausible, for the
proximity of the troops and the excitement of much coming and
going could not help affecting the lives of southern citizens and, in
particular, the lives of impressionable adolescents.

The action of the play is confined to the kitchen of the Addams
home, and this unchanging background contributes to the unity, and
consequently to the tension, of the play. The centrally located kitchen
and the cook who dominates it are convincingly realistic, but what
is more significant, they are symbolic as well. In addition, the scene
holds implications of the cultural and economic status of the Addams
family and a flavor of life in the South. It is described as follows: "A
part of a Southern back yard and kitchen. At stage left there is a
scuppernong arbor. A sheet, used as a stage curtain, hangs raggedly
at one side of the arbor. There is an elm tree in the yard. The kitchen
has in the center a table with chairs. The walls are drawn with child
drawings. There is a stove to the right and a small coal heating stove
with coal scuttle in rear center of kitchen. The kitchen opens on the
left into the yard. At the interior right a door leads to a small inner
room. Another door leads into the front hall."

The possibilities for action are apparent at once. Whether coming
to the Addams house or coming from another room in the house, the
persons involved find the kitchen a natural center.

Assimilation of Content

The characters [2] in the play are:

Berenice Sadie Brown, the cook, a stout motherly Negro woman with an air of great capability and devoted protection. She is about forty-five years old. She has a quiet, flat face and one of her eyes is made of blue glass. Sometimes, when her socket bothers her, she dispenses with the false eye and wears a black patch. When we first see her, she is wearing the patch and is dressed in a simple print work dress and apron.

Frankie, a gangling girl of twelve with blonde hair cut like a boy's, . . . a dreamy, restless girl, with periods of energetic activity alternated with a rapt attention to her inward world of fantasy. She is thin and awkward and very much aware of being too tall.

John Henry, Frankie's small cousin, aged seven, picks and eats any scuppernongs he can reach. He is a delicate, active boy and wears gold-rimmed spectacles which give him an oddly judicious look. He is blond and sunburned and when we first see him he is wearing a sun-suit and is barefooted.

Jarvis, a good-looking boy of twenty-one, wearing an army uniform.

Janice, a young, pretty, fresh-looking girl of eighteen or nineteen, is charming but rather ordinary, with brown hair done up in a small knot.

Mr. Addams, Frankie's father, is a deliberate and absent-minded man of about forty-five. A widower of many years, he has become set in his habits. He is dressed conservatively, and there is about him an old-fashioned look and manner.

Helen Fletcher and *Doris*, two girls about Frankie's age.

Mrs. West, John Henry's mother, a vivacious, blonde woman, about thirty-three. She is dressed in sleazy, rather dowdy summer clothes.

T. T. Williams is a large and pompous-looking Negro man of about fifty. He is dressed like a church deacon, and his manner is timid and overpolite.

Honey Camden Brown is a slender, limber Negro boy of about twenty. He is quite light in color and he wears loud-colored, snappy clothes. He is brusque and there is about him an odd mixture of hostility and playfulness. He is very high-strung and volatile.

Sis Laura is an ancient Negro woman, the vegetable lady. Said to be about ninety.

Barney MacKean, a boy of thirteen.

Frankie Addams is a motherless adolescent girl, with a busy father, who, she says, never sees her. Sensitive, imaginative, she is mothered by the Negro cook, Berenice Sadie Brown. When her older brother

---

2 See pp. 1–2 of the play (New York: New Directions, 1951). Descriptions adapted by permission of New Directions.

brings his fiancée home just before their wedding, Frankie is captivated by their happiness and impressed by their belonging together. Childishly she believes that she can be a part of their love if only she can go away with them after the wedding ceremony. She thinks of herself as a lonely "I" and of the lovers as a companionable pair who can speak of themselves as "We." She wants to be part of their companionship and thinks that since they belong to each other, if she belongs to them, she too will be a "We."

Berenice, whose own search for love has brought her four husbands, sets out to convince Frankie that her plan of joining the wedding pair is not the normal way of finding happiness, but her arguments go unheeded. Frankie, shopping for a dress to wear at the wedding, tells everyone in town of her plans. Mingled with her desire for love is her desire for excitement and change beyond what is likely to occur in the small town in which she lives. Part of her longing comes from her feelings of rejection, brought on by the treatment she has received from boys and girls her own age, who have been shocked by her fearlessness and restless imagination and by her daring way with words. Secretly yearning to be part of their activities, she openly and loudly ridicules their activities and calls them names. She feels superior to John Henry, but is forced to spend a good share of her time in his company or feel utterly alone.

Immediately after the wedding ceremony, Frankie, who has been afraid to tell her brother Jarvis and his bride of her plans, makes a scene and is unceremoniously yanked out of the wedding car when she tries to carry out her intentions. In her humiliation and anger, she runs away. John Henry, who has been complaining of a headache without getting attention or sympathy, becomes ill with meningitis, and soon after Frankie comes home, he dies. Berenice's foster-brother, Honey Camden Brown, has disappeared just before the wedding in order to avoid arrest for drawing a razor on a white man. In the final scene of the play, we learn that Honey has hanged himself in jail. In this scene, too, we see a metamorphosis in Frankie, who has become a bosom friend of the girl next door and of Barney, the boy she formerly scorned. She and her father are moving out of the neighborhood to share a new house with Uncle Eustace and Aunt Pet, John Henry's parents. She still looks forward to travel, but now it will be with the new friend Mary, and they will only stop for a brief visit with Jarvis and Janice, who are in Germany with the Occupation

Forces. Berenice says she could never work for Mrs. West, and sits alone in the kitchen as Frankie skips away.

The first scene of Act III carries the plot only to Frankie's running away.

The theme which the action carries is simply that the individual is utterly isolated, that nothing can dispel for long the loneliness which is his birthright. Frankie epitomizes this isolation, and during the play each character has his own peculiar brand of loneliness. Honey, for instance, is isolated by the whites; the old vegetable woman, by her extreme age. The more normal one is, the less lonely he is, and thus Berenice achieves a kind of balance after enduring much sorrow and violence in her life. Yet she shivers at signs of abnormality, and dislikes the sideshow freaks of the circus who fascinate Frankie. At the end of the play, Berenice is alone while Frankie has lost her loneliness, but somehow this change in outlook appears to be transient and changing, too.

The impact of symbols in the play is heavy. The wedding represents the "we-ness" that Frankie yearns for; Mama's picture is love, the pistol is death; the kitchen suggests the world, the food the source of well-being, Berenice, the spirit of sanity and normality, without which life is unbearable. Symbols for vision appear: Berenice has a glass eye so she sees with only one eye; John Henry wears spectacles, but Frankie tells him he sees as well without them as with them and therefore he doesn't need them; John Henry tells Frankie that her "gray eyes is glass." Honey's horn, with its interrupted music, symbolizes his broken, short life, or possibly the interrupted, frustrated possibilities of the Negro race. Old age, adolescence, childhood, even middle age, as exemplified in the play, have each their special brand of isolation. The question raised in the first act becomes more than a question of plot. It is not only "Will Frankie go away as she plans with Jarvis and Janice?" but "Will Frankie overcome her loneliness and achieve the 'we-ness' for which she yearns?" The second question, "What will Honey's pride and high temper lead him to?" causes a counter-movement to occur, for Honey's life darkens and ends tragically, while Frankie's takes a lighter turn. The two plots merge in Berenice, the mainstay of each rebel, although she can do little to change the course of action in either case.

The emphasis is upon Frankie in scene 1, Act III, but Honey's affairs are matter for discussion. Short as the structural scene is, there are twenty-three basic units or scenes,[3] which we may indicate as follows:

(1) T. T. and Berenice	Preparation for wedding refreshments: a storm is brewing; Berenice worries over Honey's absence.
(2) T. T., Berenice, and Frankie	Frankie has not told her plans.
(3) T. T., Berenice, and Frankie	John Henry hurries in and out.
(4) T. T., Berenice, and Frankie	Frankie is ashamed of her dress.
(5) Berenice and Frankie	Frankie resolves to tell of her plans.
(6) Berenice and John Henry	John Henry exults over things Frankie gave him while packing her suitcase.
(7) Berenice	Enigmatic remark about what's going on.
(8) Berenice and T. T.	Premonitory feelings.
(9) Berenice, T. T., and Frankie	She hasn't told her plans.
(10) Berenice, T. T., Frankie, and John Henry	John Henry enters in fairy costume and goes out without speaking.
(11) Berenice, T. T., and Frankie	Frankie says Jarvis gave her a dollar bill.
(12) Berenice, T. T., and John Henry	John Henry reports that the bride and groom are leaving, getting into car.
(13) Berenice, T. T., John Henry, and Frankie	Frankie flies in with suitcase and bids them and ugly old kitchen good-bye.
(14) Berenice and T. T.	Voices off.
(15) Berenice, T. T., and John Henry	John Henry reports struggle with Frankie.
(16) Berenice and T. T.	
(17) Berenice, T. T., Frankie, John Henry, Mr. Addams	They all try to pacify Frankie.
(18) Berenice, T. T., Frankie, John Henry, Mr. Addams, Jarvis, Janice	Bride and groom kiss Frankie, tell her she is to visit them as soon as they are settled.

[3] See glossary at the end of this chapter for distinctions in the use of the term "scene."

216   *Chapter Seven*

(19)	Berenice, T. T., Frankie, John Henry	Frankie falls on her knees at the door, beseeching Jarvis and Janice to take her with them.
(20)	Berenice, T. T., Frankie, John Henry, Mr. Addams	Frankie will not be reasonable.
(21)	Berenice, T. T., John Henry, Mr. Addams	Frankie grabs suitcase and runs out screaming that they must not "capture" her.
(22)	Berenice	Mr. Addams calling off, "Frankie!"
(23)	Berenice and John Henry	John Henry, afraid of thunder, has a headache. Berenice takes him in her lap. She, too, has fear.

The climactic action of the scene is composed of swift changes and strong emotion. With the exception of a few speeches regarding Honey, there is no exposition, but there is careful preparation for the denouement: the storm suggests conflict and violence, and John Henry's headache can no longer be dismissed. He has mentioned it too often.

Achievement of Artistic Form

In our discussion earlier we suggested that each division is part of a carefully wrought whole and that knowledge of the entire play is fundamental to interpreting any of its parts. Such knowledge makes it possible for the interpreter to select a portion of the play and present it in such a way that it suggests the fullness and "ongoingness" of the life implicit in the whole work. To do so, we shall need to discern the composition of two characteristics of form, *rhythm* and *tone*.

Three important ingredients contributing to rhythm and tone are *purposeful movement, relationships among characters,* and *a sense of reality.* Perhaps movement is the most dominant of these ingredients of drama. In *The Member of the Wedding,* short scenes and much coming and going impart a sense of movement, or liveliness. Within the longer scenes the attainment of peaks of feeling sustains the forward movement. The scenes we have numbered seventeen, eighteen, and nineteen, totaling thirty-one speeches, contain the climactic action not only of this unit of Act III, but of the entire play. Scene nineteen, in which Frankie's fortunes reach their lowest ebb, is the longest of the three we have mentioned, but its length passes unnoticed because of the depth of Frankie's mood and the sharpness of her conflict with Berenice. The abrupt change in her mood, from despair to defiance, adds speed to the action and culminates in her running away in scene twenty.

Purposeful movement is not merely a matter of speed; it also depends to some extent upon unity. Berenice's presence on the stage in all the scenes helps to unify the action. It is interesting that throughout the play, Berenice, typifying the normal, welds pieces of action together and, at the same time, brings symbolic meaning to the action. The action is rounded out further by the device of ending each act, no matter how stormy, with only a few persons on stage—Frankie and John Henry at the close of Act I, Berenice with Frankie and John Henry at the close of Act II, Berenice alone at the end of the play. Scene 1 of Act III closes with Berenice and John Henry together, in a poignant scene in which feeling deepens as action decreases and the number of characters on the stage is diminished.

Certain traits consistently displayed by the characters emphasize the theme and thus increase our sense of purposeful, unified action. Frankie, as protagonist, refuses to listen to Berenice, who, nevertheless, persists in her reminders and arguments. Berenice never abandons the comfortable "middle" view, so comfortless to Frankie. John Henry symbolizes childhood and persists in his disaffectedness, serving as a modern chorus and in this way binding scenes together. Patterns of individual behavior become more significant when seen in relation to the symbolic references of the play: Berenice is lonely because of her relative invulnerability; Mr. Addams is lonely because he lacks understanding; John Henry is alone, while not comprehending fully the meaning of human loneliness; the bride and groom, having taken life's major move toward dispelling loneliness, feel most content, but Frankie, having struggled to overcome her "I-ness" and to take on their "we-ness," now defeated, feels least loved and most forlorn.

Frankie's reaction to the bridal pair and the interactions of other characters propel the play forward. We find Frankie excitedly happy in Act I, tender toward the bride and groom in Act III just before she tries to get into their car. When they disappoint her, she is angry and accusing. The sympathy Frankie gets (from everyone but John Henry) and her adolescent reaction to it accentuate her isolation: she is unable to make the human contact she wants and needs. When she is distraught, Mr. Addams treats her affectionately and yearningly and

Berenice remains kind, practical, and dependable in all her relationships.

The characters partake of life as we know it. Among the speeches and actions contributing to our sense of reality are these: Frankie reports that Janice has asked her three times what grade she is in in school; Jarvis grabs Frankie in his exuberance and swings her around and gives her a dollar bill; the bride and groom are distressed and ineffective in pacifying Frankie; John Henry teases when everyone else is seriously perplexed or disturbed; Frankie shows herself susceptible to small comforts, like getting her party written up in the *Evening Journal*; when Frankie is obdurate in her grief, Berenice retorts, "Bawl, then, misery." The dialogue is appropriate, too, to the age and essence of each character. John Henry, though somewhat precocious, talks like a child; Berenice has an adequate, but down-to-earth vocabulary, Frankie uses an incongruous mixture of adult and little girl vocabulary and attitudes. Dialect is unobtrusive, but the colloquialisms are colorful. Although the reminiscences of Berenice in Act II tend to deepen the reflective tone of the play, there is never a time when localisms and realization of characters detract from our sense of purposeful direction or slow the action noticeably.

The factors contributing to rhythmic and tonal effects in dramatic writing are seen to be directed movement toward a conclusion, interactions among characters according to the essence of each character, and a kind of trueness to life in character and action. To be aware of these contributions to total effect and to communicate his awareness to his audience is the declared purpose of the interpreter.

The Interpreter's Response

The steps taken in preparation for the interpretation of *The Member of the Wedding* are similar to those taken in the preparation of other forms of poetic art. Although there are useful techniques for externalizing dramatic action, such techniques depend upon thorough preparation and familiarity with the purpose, movement, and theme of the play. If the interpreter gains understanding, it will dominate the performance, giving it purpose and form; if he fails to gain understanding, techniques are shallow mannerisms.

We have said that the interpreter's strength lies not in costume, scenery, or supporting cast, but in emotional depth and controlled energy conveying a sense of full action. Since the action of a play is realized through its characters, the interpreter must study character traits, reactions, and rhythms for insight into the style his interpretation will have. After studying speeches and responses for content and their bearing upon other characters, the interpreter attempts to deliver the speeches and scenes in such a way that the illusion of life and the suggestion of dramatic action occur. Whatever his body and voice express will be taken as a sign of total assimilation, and his adjustment and flexibility are his only means of creating rhythm and, indirectly, the *tone*, or pervasive feeling, of the work under consideration. Sometimes one arrives at new or greater understanding of a character through listening to his own voice or having an evaluation of his vocal adjustment to the character. Although we cannot *arrive at* a good reading by adjusting loudness, inflection, or rate, we can often *improve* a good reading by attention to these technical aspects of vocal production.

Physical attitudes are of the utmost importance in suggesting sex, age, and, of course, the feelings of a character. The interpreter does not move about the stage as though he were taking all the parts. Instead, he stands with book in hand or at a lectern and keeps overt action at a minimum. But his body is responsive in its alternation of tension and relaxation and with economy of movement reveals not only the dominant traits, but the specific reactions of each character speaking. Frankie at all times requires angularity, some awkwardness, and tension adequate to convey the nervous energy which permeates her. In contrast to Frankie, John Henry appears placid and unruffled, yet inquisitive and alert. Berenice is dominant and must have firm stance to suggest her bulk as well as her temperament. More reserved than Berenice, Mr. Addams is in every way less dominant. T. T. is dignified, heavy, and slow in comparison with Berenice, who is capable of quick mental and physical action. Mr. Addams, Berenice, and T. T. are approximately the same age, but Mr. Addams is more authoritative than T. T. and has less vitality than Berenice. Janice and Jarvis (since Honey does not appear) represent the next generation, but are more adult than Frankie, who in turn, is more grown up than John Henry.

The quality of voice for each character in *The Member of the Wedding* seems peculiarly important. Berenice's personality requires vocal depth, resonance, and deliberateness. Mr. Addams will have a tired voice, perhaps prim diction, but, under the stimulation of the wedding, his voice (within the limits of his personality) ought to have a more vibrant quality and probably a faster rate. Frankie and

John Henry, with lighter, younger voices, contrast noticeably with Berenice and Mr. Addams, but Frankie's voice must have considerable range. Jarvis and Janice will not participate in the mounting tension of the scene, but will be enjoying their imagined future and consequently will speak brightly, somewhat quickly.

One question that each interpreter of this play must solve for himself is, "How much Southern dialect is appropriate?" "Shall it be used sparingly for Berenice and T. T., and not at all for the others?" "Shall there be a suggestion of dialect for all?" "Shall there be none whatsoever?" Doubtless a softening of consonants, a drawl, and the omission of r (except when it links final and initial vowels) ought to be uniform practice for the speeches of all the characters. Whether the interpreter is skilled in dialect or finds himself unequal to the task is a factor in his decision. Better to use no dialect than to use it badly and run the risk of distracting his audience. The universal qualities of the play do not depend upon dialect or locale. Voices of male readers need not take wide swings upward for female characters, nor should the voices of female readers affect the bass tone of male characters. If the voice reflects the changing mood of the play, lightness or heaviness of quality and stress will go a long way toward suggesting femininity or masculinity.

The function of each character in the scene, his contribution to the action, is of paramount importance and helps to identify him. With knowledge of the function of each character, the interpreter who expresses sympathy and liveliness is on his way to success in achieving response. It would be a mistake for him to feel rigidly enclosed in a given pitch range or pattern of movement for a given character. His consistent use of angles of address, however, assists the audience in following the action. Suggested for narration, this external differentiation is a platform convention, closely allied with the physical appearance and movement of the characters. While character angles alone are insufficient to distinguish among characters, their use helps to keep characters distinct. In the part of the scene where Mr. Addams brings Frankie in from the wedding car and Jarvis and Janice follow, it might be convenient to have Frankie speak center, Berenice toward the left, T. T. toward the left, but at a wider angle than Berenice, Mr. Addams toward the right, Janice and Jarvis toward the right at a wider angle than Mr. Addams. John Henry would speak center.

Allied with the assigning of angles of address is the custom of setting the scene out beyond the audience.[4] Such placement allows for widening or narrowing horizons and prospects and helps the audience to forget that the stage is not filled with performers and furnishings: it gives listeners the impression that they are being addressed; and by encouraging the uplifted chin, it promotes clarity of utterance.

The interpreter of dramatic literature meets his greatest challenge in attempting to suggest the flow of action and the interaction of the characters. Interaction is a good deal more than keeping characters "straight." It is above all focusing attention upon each speaker in turn, and by skillful transitions, projecting to his audience the feeling of observing an interchange. Within speeches themselves there will be small shifts and contrasts, for every speech will advance action and provide a shift in feeling. The process seems to include complete response to whatever an individual speech contains and to interlocking words and inferences which indicate relationships. The movement of idea and feeling which contains all the characters in a given scene also controls the relationship between and among scenes. An entrance signals change of scene. Noting that a new person enters the scene, the interpreter will manage emphasis in such a way that the new arrival receives the attention he deserves, shifting from him only when someone else deserves to be in focus. Sometimes in moments of great conflict and intensity, two figures will be equally prominent, but when the tension subsides, one of the two will remain in focus, while the other will be out of the scene or subdued. Occasionally, as in scene seventeen, the one in focus says nothing. Here Frankie is sobbing and all the speeches are directed to her. In scene nineteen Berenice brushes John Henry away to give her attention to Frankie, only to find herself in conflict with Frankie. Awareness of the movement of each scene comes from the simple device of asking "Who dominated the opening of the scene? The close?"

Without making any part of his responses mechanical, the interpreter must be exceedingly familiar with the sequence of events and his use of angles must be automatic. A halting reading results when each character sounds as though he is alone, but an effect that is equally distressing is the breathless one of character hurled upon character and incident upon incident without transition or motivation. The interpreter must listen for the speech he utters before he responds to it. He must show that he is responding by his physical adjustment

---

[4] See Chapter 8.

before he says a word. Or, if he feels that he must jump in with a word or phrase, he should pause as soon as he can justify doing so and signify the relationship to the preceding speech. For instance, after Berenice says to T. T., "Frankie said she would help you serve," the interpreter will very likely indicate T. T.'s response by a shake of the head or some negative gesture before saying, "From the way she's been acting." When Berenice changes the subject from Frankie to Honey in the ensuing speech, there is need for motivation, and again, the response would be physical rather than a quick, vocal pick-up. Later on, after Frankie enters and Berenice asks, "You told them yet?" we have an example of a quick pick-up of the cue, but a pause is in order after the first phrase, as Frankie answers, "About my plans —no, I haven't yet told them."

The interpreter introduces his play with brief descriptions of character and scene. He may give the audience the playwright's exact descriptions, but usually it is preferable to meet the audience with one's own extemporaneous remarks. After launching the play or scene in this way, the interpreter of drama has little opportunity for direct contact with his audience. Only when he summarizes to telescope scenes, gives stage directions, or indicates the entrance of new characters does he have a chance again to meet his listeners in the open situation. Some interpreters communicate much more through bodily adjustments than do others and will need to summarize very little. All of us, nevertheless, will occasionally need to indicate a change of setting or passage of time. If, after reading Scene 1 of Act III, you were to continue with the last scene, you would need to explain that several weeks had elapsed since the wedding. Some interpreters prefer to adhere for these scene changes, as well as for character descriptions, to words of the playwright. At least, if one gives the playwright's own version, he is assured of accuracy, and reasonable brevity. The danger is that the delivery of such portions will be too bookish and matter-of-fact. All interpolations must be in keeping with the action at the point where they take place; that is, the interpreter's vocabulary and utterance ought to take on the coloring of the scene at hand. Only in this way can mood and unbroken action be sustained.

Ideally, there would be no omissions and abbreviations; practically, the interpreter finds it necessary to meet time limits. He is also faced with the realities of his situation: he is one individual, but he must suggest the presence of several characters, and he must work without properties, usually without lighting effects, and certainly without theatrical make-up and costume. It is therefore often advantageous for him to omit minor characters and to summarize, or deftly and quickly refer to subordinate plots. Sometimes when a minor character accompanies a major character, his speeches only reinforce the latter and can be cut completely or incorporated into the speech of the stronger character. Only thorough understanding of the plot, theme, and characters can make such editing successful. For instance, if one were to assume that John Henry's echoes were unnecessary, the symbolic overtones of *The Member of the Wedding* would be fatally diminished.

Certain plays seem more readily adapted to interpretation than others.[5] *The Member of the Wedding*, with its rewarding characters and symbolism, seems suitable for most audiences. If the interpreter selects materials wisely and prepares painstakingly, he and his audience will find the dramatic mode absorbing and rewarding.

Glossary of Terms[6]

ACT: Episode made up of a series of connected scenes or basic units. May or may not be composed of more than one structural unit.

ACTION: The sum-total of physical movements carried out on the stage. (The plot is the whole story including exposition, but action is confined to brief succession of incidents which occur in the course of the play.)

CHARACTERS: Revealed through action. Speech of self or others. Presented in moment of crisis or tension. Traits selected carefully in relation to theme and plot.

DIALOGUE: The play depends upon dialogue. All scene descriptions and directions are secondary. In the dialogue are clues to action, character, and theme.

EXPOSITION: Recounting of past events up to opening of play. Functional in good plays. Opening of play loaded with exposition.

PLOT: The articulated skeleton of events. Exposition, development, turning point, and major climax; second development and denouement.

---

[5] See Chapters 2 and 12.

[6] In compiling these definitions we have drawn upon various sources, but when in doubt, have relied heavily upon Alan Downer, ed., *The Art of the Play* (New York: Henry Holt & Company, Inc., 1955), and upon Fred Benjamin Millett, *Reading Drama* (New York: Harper & Brothers, 1950).

POINT OF VIEW: The third person. The playwright speaks through his characters and seems, like the audience, to see the characters while himself unobserved.

PREPARATION: Hint of what is to come; the raising of questions to be answered. Logical reason for each climax.

SCENE: Used to indicate small segment of action during which there are no exits or entrances. Basic unit. Used also to indicate unchanged setting. Structural unit.

SETTING: Time and place. Except in nonrepresentational plays, described carefully.

Selections for Interpretation

KING RICHARD II

William Shakespeare (1564–1616)

King Richard returns from Ireland to find that many subjects have joined Bolingbroke, who now leads rebel forces. With Richard in this scene are the Bishop of Carlisle, Aumerle, and soldiers. Scroop has just entered and greeted his king.

K. RICH.   Mine ear is open and my heart prepar'd.
The worst is worldly loss thou canst unfold.
Say, is my kingdom lost? Why, 'twas my care;
And what loss is it to be rid of care?
Strives Bolingbroke to be as great as we?
Greater he shall not be; if he serve God,
We'll serve Him too and be his fellow so.
Revolt our subjects? That we cannot mend;
They break their faith to God as well as us.
Cry woe, destruction, ruin, and decay:
The worst is death, and death will have his day.

SCROOP.   Glad am I that your Highness is so arm'd
To bear the tidings of calamity.
Like an unseasonable stormy day
Which makes the silver rivers drown their shores
As if the world were all dissolv'd to tears,
So high above his limits swells the rage

Of Bolingbroke, covering your fearful land
With hard bright steel and hearts harder than steel.
White-beards have arm'd their thin and hairless scalps
Against thy majesty; boys, with women's voices,
Strive to speak big, and clap their female joints
In stiff unwieldy arms against thy crown;
Thy very beadsmen learn to bend their bows
Of double-fatal yew against thy state;
Yea, distaff-women manage rusty bills
Against thy seat: both young and old rebel,
And all goes worse than I have power to tell.

K. RICH.   Too well, too well thou tell'st a tale so ill.
Where is the Earl of Wiltshire? Where is Bagot?
What is become of Bushy? Where is Green?
That they have let the dangerous enemy
Measure our confines with such peaceful steps?
If we prevail, their heads shall pay for it.
I warrant they have made peace with Bolingbroke.

SCROOP.   Peace have they made with him indeed, my lord.

K. RICH.   O villains, vipers, damn'd without redemption!
Dogs, easily won to fawn on any man!
Snakes, in my heart-blood warm'd, that sting my heart!
Three Judases, each one thrice worse than Judas!
Would they make peace? Terrible hell make war
Upon their spotted souls for this offence!

SCROOP.   Sweet love, I see, changing his property,
Turns to the sourest and most deadly hate.
Again uncurse their souls; their peace is made
With heads, and not with hands. Those whom you curse
Have felt the worst of death's destroying wound
And lie full low, grav'd in the hollow ground.

AUMERLE.   Is Bushy, Green, and the Earl of Wiltshire dead?

SCROOP.   Ay, all of them at Bristol lost their heads.

AUMERLE.   Where is the Duke my father with his power?

K. RICH.   No matter where; of comfort no man speak.
Let's talk of graves, of worms, and epitaphs;
Make dust our paper and with rainy eyes
Write sorrow on the bosom of the earth.

Let's choose executors and talk of wills;
And yet not so; for what can we bequeath
Save our deposed bodies to the ground?
Our lands, our lives, and all are Bolingbroke's,
And nothing can we call our own but death,
And that small model of the barren earth
Which serves as paste and cover to our bones.
For God's sake, let us sit up on the ground
And tell sad stories of the death of kings!
How some have been depos'd; some slain in war;
Some haunted by the ghosts they have depos'd;
Some poison'd by their wives; some sleeping kill'd;
All murdered: for within the hollow crown
That rounds the mortal temples of a king
Keeps Death his court, and there the antic sits,
Scoffing his state and grinning at his pomp,
Allowing him a breath, a little scene,
To monarchize, be fear'd, and kill with looks,
Infusing him with self and vain conceit,
As if this flesh which walls about our life
Were brass impregnable; and humour'd thus
Comes at the last and with a little pin
Bores through his castle wall, and—farewell king:
Cover you heads, and mock not flesh and blood
With solemn reverence. Throw away respect,
Tradition, form, and ceremonious duty;
For you have but mistook me all this while.
I live with bread like you, feel want,
Taste grief, need friends: subjected thus,
How can you say to me I am a king?

CARLISLE.   My lord, wise men ne'er sit and wail their woes,
But presently prevent the ways to wail.
To fear the foe, since fear oppresseth strength,
Gives in your weakness strength unto your foe,
And so your follies fight against yourself.
Fear, and be slain; no worse can come to fight;
And fight and die is death destroying death,
Where fearing dying pays death servile breath.

AUMERLE.　My father hath a power; inquire of him,
　　　　And learn to make a body of a limb.

K. RICH.　Thou chid'st me well. Proud Bolingbroke, I come
　　　　To change blows with thee for our day of doom.
　　　　This ague fit of fear is over-blown;
　　　　And easy task it is to win our own.
　　　　Say, Scroop, where lies our uncle with his power?
　　　　Speak sweetly, man, although thy looks be sour.

SCROOP.　Men judge by the complexion of the sky
　　　　The state and inclination of the day;
　　　　So may you by my dull and heavy eye,
　　　　My tongue hath but a heavier tale to say.
　　　　I play the torturer by small and small
　　　　To lengthen out the worst that must be spoken.
　　　　Your uncle York is join'd with Bolingbroke,
　　　　And all your northern castles yielded up,
　　　　And all your southern gentlemen in arms
　　　　Upon his party.

K. RICH.　　　　　　　Thou hast said enough.
　　　　Beshrew thee, cousin, which didst lead me forth
　　　　Of that sweet way I was in to despair!
　　　　What say you now? What comfort have we now?
　　　　By heaven, I'll hate him everlastingly
　　　　That bids me be of comfort any more.
　　　　Go to Flint castle; there I'll pine away;
　　　　A king, woe's slave, shall kingly woe obey.
　　　　That power I have, discharge; and let them go
　　　　To ear the land that hath some hope to grow,
　　　　For I have none. Let no man speak again
　　　　To alter this, for counsel is but vain.

AUMERLE.　My liege, one word.

K. RICH.　　　　　　　He does me double wrong
　　　　That wounds me with the flatteries of his tongue.
　　　　Discharge my followers; let them hence away,
　　　　From Richard's night to Bolingbroke's fair day.
　　　　　　　　　　　　III. ii. 93-218

ANDROCLES AND THE LION

George Bernard Shaw (1856–1950)

PROLOGUE

Overture: forest sounds, roaring of lions, Christian hymn faintly.

A jungle path. A lion's roar, a melancholy suffering roar, comes from the jungle. It is repeated nearer. The lion limps from the jungle on three legs, holding up his right forepaw, in which a huge thorn sticks. He sits down and contemplates it. He licks it. He shakes it. He tries to extract it by scraping it along the ground, and hurts himself worse. He roars piteously. He licks it again. Tears drop from his eyes. He limps painfully off the path and lies down under the trees, exhausted with pain. Heaving a long sigh, like wind in a trombone, he goes to sleep.

Androcles and his wife Megaera come along the path. He is a small, thin, ridiculous little man who might be any age from thirty to fifty-five. He has sandy hair, watery compassionate blue eyes, sensitive nostrils, and a very presentable forehead; but his good points go no further: his arms and legs and back, though wiry of their kind, look shrivelled and starved. He carries a big bundle, is very poorly clad, and seems tired and hungry.

His wife is a rather handsome pampered slattern, well fed and in the prime of life. She has nothing to carry, and has a stout stick to help her along.

MEGAERA *(suddenly throwing down her stick)*. I wont go another step.

ANDROCLES *(pleading wearily)*. Oh, not again, dear. Whats the good of stopping every two miles and saying you wont go another step? We must get on to the next village before night. There are wild beasts in this wood: lions, they say.

MEGAERA. I dont believe a word of it. You are always threatening me with wild beasts to make me walk the very soul out of my body when I can hardly drag one foot before another. We havnt seen a single lion yet.

ANDROCLES. Well, dear, do you want to see one?

MEGAERA *(tearing the bundle from his back)*. You cruel brute, you dont care how tired I am, or what becomes of me *(she throws the bundle on the ground)*: always thinking of yourself. Self! self! self! always yourself! *(She sits down on the bundle.)*

Drama 229

ANDROCLES (*sitting down sadly on the ground with his elbows on his knees and his head in his hands*). We all have to think of ourselves occasionally, dear.

MEGAERA. A man ought to think of his wife sometimes.

ANDROCLES. He cant always help it, dear. You make me think of you a good deal. Not that I blame you.

MEGAERA. Blame me! I should think not indeed. Is it my fault that I'm married to you?

ANDROCLES. No, dear: that is my fault.

MEGAERA. Thats a nice thing to say to me. Arnt you happy with me?

ANDROCLES. I dont complain, my love.

MEGAERA. You ought to be ashamed of yourself.

ANDROCLES. I am, my dear.

MEGAERA. Youre not: you glory in it.

ANDROCLES. In what, darling?

MEGAERA. In everything. In making me a slave, and making yourself a laughing-stock. It's not fair. You get me the name of being a shrew with your meek ways, always talking as if butter wouldnt melt in your mouth. And just because I look a big strong woman, and because I'm goodhearted and a bit hasty, and because youre always driving me to do things I'm sorry for afterwards, people say "Poor man: what a life his wife leads him!" Oh, if they only knew! And you think I dont know. But I do, I do, (*screaming*) I do.

ANDROCLES. Yes, my dear: I know you do.

MEGAERA. Then why dont you treat me properly and be a good husband to me?

ANDROCLES. What can I do, my dear?

MEGAERA. What can you do! You can return to your duty, and come back to your home and your friends, and sacrifice to the gods as all respectable people do, instead of having us hunted out of house and home for being dirty disreputable blaspheming atheists.

ANDROCLES. I'm not an atheist, dear: I am a Christian.

MEGAERA. Well, isnt that the same thing, only ten times worse? Everybody knows that the Christians are the very lowest of the low.

ANDROCLES. Just like us, dear.

MEGAERA. Speak for yourself. Dont you dare to compare me to common people. My father owned his own public-house; and sorrowful was the day for me when you first came drinking in our bar.

ANDROCLES. I confess I was addicted to it, dear. But I gave it up when I became a Christian.

MEGAERA. Youd much better have remained a drunkard. I can forgive a man being addicted to drink: It's only natural; and I dont deny I like a drop myself sometimes. What I cant stand is your being addicted to Christianity. And whats worse again, your being addicted to animals. How is any woman to keep her house clean when you bring in every stray cat and lost cur and lame duck in the whole countryside? You took the bread out of my mouth to feed them: you know you did: dont attempt to deny it.

ANDROCLES. Only when they were hungry and you were getting too stout, dearie.

MEGAERA. Yes: insult me, do. (*Rising*) Oh! I wont bear it another moment. You used to sit and talk to those dumb brute beasts for hours, when you hadnt a word for me.

ANDROCLES. They never answered back, darling. (*He rises and again shoulders the bundle.*)

MEGAERA. Well, if youre fonder of animals than of your own wife, you can live with them here in the jungle. Ive had enough of them and enough of you. I'm going back. I'm going home.

ANDROCLES (*barring the way back*). No, dearie: dont take on like that. We cant go back. Weve sold everything: we should starve; and I should be sent to Rome and thrown to the lions—

MEGAERA. Serve you right! I wish the lions joy of you. (*Screaming*) Are you going to get out of my way and let me go home?

ANDROCLES. No, dear—

MEGAERA.   Then I'll make my way through the forest; and when I'm eaten by the wild beasts youll know what a wife youve lost. (*She dashes into the jungle and nearly falls over the sleeping lion.*) Oh! Oh! Andy! Andy! (*She totters back and collapses into the arms of Androcles, who, crushed by her weight, falls on his bundle.*)

ANDROCLES   (*extracting himself from beneath her and slapping her hands in great anxiety*). What is it, my precious, my pet? Whats the matter? (*He raises her head. Speechless with terror, she points in the direction of the sleeping lion. He steals cautiously towards the spot indicated by Megaera. She rises with an effort and totters after him.*)

MEGAERA.   No, Andy: youll be killed. Come back.

(*The lion utters a long snoring sigh. Androcles sees the lion, and recoils fainting into the arms of Megaera, who falls back on the bundle. They roll apart and lie staring in terror at one another. The lion is heard groaning heavily in the jungle.*)

ANDROCLES   (*whispering*). Did you see? A lion.

MEGAERA   (*despairing*). The gods have sent him to punish us because youre a Christian. Take me away, Andy. Save me.

ANDROCLES   (*rising*). Meggy: theres one chance for you. Itll take him pretty nigh twenty minutes to eat me (I'm rather stringy and tough) and you can escape in less time than that.

MEGAERA.   Oh, dont talk about eating. (*The lion rises with a great groan and limps toward them.*) Oh! (*She faints.*)

ANDROCLES   (*quaking, but keeping between the lion and Megaera*). Dont you come near my wife, do you hear? (*The lion groans. Androcles can hardly stand for trembling.*) Meggy: run. Run for your life. If I take my eye off him, it's all up. (*The lion holds up his wounded paw and flaps it piteously before Androcles.*) Oh, he's lame, poor old chap! He's got a thorn in his paw. A frightfully big thorn. (*Full of sympathy*) Oh, poor old man! Did um get an awful thorn into um's tootsums wootsums? Has it made um too sick to eat a nice little Christian man for um's breakfast? Oh, a nice little Christian man will get um's thorn out for um; and then um shall eat the nice Christian man and the nice Christian man's nice big tender wifey pifey. (*The lion responds by moans of self-pity.*) Yes, yes, yes, yes, yes. Now, now (*taking the paw in his hand*), um is not to bite and not to scratch, not even if it hurts a very very little. Now make velvet paws. Thats right. (*He pulls gingerly at the thorn. The lion, with an angry yell of pain, jerks back his paw so abruptly that Androcles is thrown on his back.*) Steadeee! Oh, did the nasty cruel little Christian man hurt the sore paw? (*The lion moans assentingly but apologetically.*) Well, one more little pull and it will be all over. Just one little, little, leetle pull; and then um will live happily ever after. (*He gives the thorn another pull. The lion roars and snaps his jaws with a terrifying clash.*) Oh, mustnt frighten um's good kind doctor, um's affectionate nursey. That didnt hurt at all: not a bit. Just one more. Just to shew how the brave big lion can bear pain, not like the little crybaby Christian man. Oopsh! (*The thorn comes out. The lion yells with pain, and shakes his paw wildly.*) Thats it! (*Holding up the thorn.*) Now it's out. Now lick um's paw to take away the nasty inflammation. See? (*He licks his own hand. The lion nods intelligently and licks his paw industriously.*) Clever little liony-piony! Understands um's dear old friend Andy Wandy. (*The lion licks his face.*) Yes, kissums Andy Wandy. (*The lion, wagging his tail violently, rises on his hind legs, and embraces Androcles, who makes a wry face and cries*) Velvet paws! Velvet paws! (*The lion draws in his claws.*) Thats right. (*He embraces the lion, who finally takes the end of his tail in one paw, places that tight round Androcles' waist, resting it on his hip. Androcles takes the other paw in his hand, stretches out his arm, and the two waltz rapturously round and round and finally away through the jungle.*)

MEGAERA (*who has revived during the waltz*). Oh, you coward, you havnt danced with me for years; and now you go off dancing with a great brute beast that you havnt known for ten minutes and that wants to eat your own wife. Coward! Coward! Coward! (*She rushes off after them into the jungle.*)

Richard Brinsley Sheridan (1751–1816)

Act III. Scene III. Mrs. Malaprop's Lodgings. Mrs. Malaprop, with a letter in her hand, and Captain Absolute.

MRS. MALAPROP. Your being Sir Anthony's son, captain, would it-self be a sufficient accommodation; but from the ingenuity of your appearance, I am convinced you deserve the character here given of you.

ABSOLUTE. Permit me to say, madam, that as I never yet have had the pleasure of seeing Miss Languish, my principal inducement in this affair at present is the honour of being allied to Mrs. Mal-aprop; of whose intellectual accomplishments, elegant man-ners, and unaffected learning, no tongue is silent.

MRS. MALAPROP. Sir, you do me infinite honour! I beg, captain, you'll be seated. —(*They sit.*) Ah! few gentlemen, now-a-days, know how to value the ineffectual qualities in a woman! Few think how a little knowledge becomes a gentlewoman! —Men have no sense now but for the worthless flower of beauty!

ABSOLUTE. It is but too true, indeed, ma'am; —yet I fear our ladies should share the blame—they think our admiration of beauty so great, that knowledge in them would be superfluous. Thus, like garden-trees, they seldom show fruit, till time has robbed them of the more specious blossom. —Few, like Mrs. Malaprop and the orange tree, are rich in both at once.

MRS. MALAPROP. Sir, you overpower me with goodbreeding. —He is the very pine-apple of politeness! —You are not ignorant, cap-tain, that this giddy girl has somehow contrived to fix her affections on a beggarly, strolling, eaves-dropping ensign, whom none of us have seen, and nobody knows anything of.

ABSOLUTE. Oh, I have heard the silly affair before. —I'm not at all prejudiced against her on that account.

MRS. MALAPROP. You are very good and very considerate, captain. I am sure I have done everything in my power since I exploded the affair; long ago I laid my positive conjunctions on her, never to think on the fellow again;—I have since laid Sir An-thony's preposition before her; but, I am sorry to say, she seems resolved to decline every particle that I enjoin her.

ABSOLUTE. Oh, the devil! my last note. (*Aside.*)

MRS. MALAPROP. Ay, here it is.

ABSOLUTE. Ay, my note indeed! O the little traitress Lucy. (*Aside.*)

MRS. MALAPROP. There, perhaps you may know the writing. (*Gives him the letter.*)

ABSOLUTE. I think I have seen the hand before—yes, I certainly must have seen this hand before—

MRS. MALAPROP. Nay, but read it, captain.

ABSOLUTE. (*Reads.*) "My soul's idol, my adored Lydia!" —Very tender indeed!

MRS. MALAPROP. Tender! ay, and profane too, o' my conscience.

ABSOLUTE. (*Reads.*) "I am excessively alarmed at the intelligence you send me, the more so as my new rival——"

MRS. MALAPROP. That's you, sir.

ABSOLUTE. (*Reads.*) "Has universally the character of being an accomplished gentleman and a man of honour." Well, that's handsome enough.

MRS. MALAPROP. Oh, the fellow has some design in writing so.

ABSOLUTE. That he had, I'll answer for him, ma'am.

MRS. MALAPROP. But go on, sir—you'll see presently.

ABSOLUTE. (*Reads.*) "As for the old weather-beaten she-dragon who guards you—" Who can he mean by that?

MRS. MALAPROP. Me, sir! —me! —he means me! —There—what do you think now? —but go on a little further.

ABSOLUTE. Impudent scoundrel! —(*Reads.*) "it shall go hard but I will elude her vigilance, as I am told that the same ridiculous vanity, which makes her dress up her coarse features, and deck her dull chat with hard words which she don't understand——"

MRS. MALAPROP. There, sire, an attack upon my language! what do you think of that? —an aspersion upon my parts of speech! was ever such a brute! Sure, if I reprehend any thing in this world, it is the use of my oracular tongue, and a nice derangement of epitaphs!

ABSOLUTE. He deserves to be hanged and quartered! let me see— (*Reads.*) "same ridiculous vanity——"

MRS. MALAPROP. You need not read it again, sir.

ABSOLUTE. I beg pardon, ma'am. —(*Reads.*) "does also lay her open to the grossest deceptions from flattery and pretended admira- tion—" an impudent coxcomb! "—so that I have a scheme to see you shortly with the old harridan's consent, and even to make her a go-between in our interview." —Was ever such assurance!

MRS. MALAPROP. Did you ever hear anything like it? —he'll elude my vigilance, will he—yes, yes! ha! ha! he's very likely to enter these doors; we'll try who can plot best!

ABSOLUTE. So we will, ma'am—so we will! Ha! ha! ha! a conceited puppy, ha! ha! ha! Well, but, Mrs. Malaprop, as the girl seems so infatuated by this fellow, suppose you were to wink at her corresponding with him for a little time—let her even plot an elopement with him—then do you connive at her escape— while I, just in the nick, will have the fellow laid by the heels, and fairly contrive to carry her off in his stead.

MRS. MALAPROP. I am delighted with the scheme; never was anything better perpetrated!

ABSOLUTE. But, pray, could not I see the lady for a few minutes now? —I should like to try her temper a little.

MRS. MALAPROP. Why, I don't know—I doubt she is not prepared for a visit of this kind. There is a decorum in these matters.

ABSOLUTE. O Lord! she won't mind me—only tell her Beverley——

MRS. MALAPROP. Sir!

ABSOLUTE. Gently, good tongue.   (*Aside.*)

MRS. MALAPROP. What did you say of Beverley?

ABSOLUTE. Oh, I was going to propose that you should tell her, by way of jest, that it was Beverley who was below; she'd come down fast enough then—ha! ha! ha!

MRS. MALAPROP. 'Twould be a trick she well deserves; besides, you know the fellow tells her he'll get my consent to see her—ha! ha! Let him if he can, I say again. Lydia, come down here!

—(*Calling.*) He'll make me a go-between in their interviews! —ha! ha! ha! Come down, I say, Lydia! I don't wonder at your laughing, ha! ha! ha! his impudence is truly ridiculous.

ABSOLUTE. 'Tis very ridiculous, upon my soul, ma'am—ha! ha! ha!

MRS. MALAPROP. The little hussy won't hear. Well, I'll go and tell her at once who it is—she shall know that Captain Absolute is come to wait on her. And I'll make her behave as becomes a young woman.

ABSOLUTE. As you please, ma'am.

MRS. MALAPROP. For the present, captain, your servant. Ah! you've not done laughing yet, I see—elude my vigilance; yes, yes; ha! ha! ha!

ABSOLUTE. Ha! ha! ha! one would think now that I might throw off all disguise at once, and seize my prize with security; but such is Lydia's caprice, that to undeceive were probably to lose her. I'll see whether she knows me.

(*Walks aside, and seems engaged in looking at the pictures.*)

Enter LYDIA

LYDIA. What a scene am I now to go through! Surely nothing can be more dreadful than to be obliged to listen to the loathsome addresses of a stranger to one's heart. I have heard of girls persecuted as I am, who have appealed in behalf of their favoured lover to the generosity of his rival; suppose I were to try it—there stands the hated rival—an officer too! —but oh, how unlike my Beverley! I wonder he don't begin—truly he seems a very negligent wooer! —quite at his ease, upon my word! —I'll speak first—Mr. Absolute.

ABSOLUTE. Ma'am. (*Turns around.*)

LYDIA. O heavens! Beverley!

ABSOLUTE. Hush! —hush, my life! softly! be not surprised!

LYDIA. I am so astonished! and so terrified! and so overjoyed! —for Heaven's sake! how came you here?

ABSOLUTE. Briefly, I have deceived your aunt—I was informed that my new rival was to visit here this evening, and contriving to have him kept away, have passed myself on her for Captain Absolute.

LYDIA.   O charming! And she really takes you for young Absolute!

ABSOLUTE.   Oh, she is convinced of it.

LYDIA.   Ha! ha! ha! I can't forbear laughing to think how her sagacity is overreached!

ABSOLUTE.   But we trifle with our precious moments—such another opportunity may not occur; then let me now conjure my kind, my condescending angel, to fix the time when I may rescue her from undeserving persecution, and with a licensed warmth plead for my reward.

LYDIA.   Will you then, Beverley, consent to forfeit that portion of my paltry wealth? —that burden on the wings of love?

ABSOLUTE.   Oh, come to me—rich only thus—in loveliness! Bring no portion to me, but thy love—'twill be generous in you, Lydia— for well you know, it is the only dower your poor Beverley can repay.

LYDIA.   How persuasive are his words! —how charming will poverty be with him!   (*Aside.*)

ABSOLUTE.   Ah! my soul, what a life will we then live! Love shall be our idol and support! we will worship him with a monastic strictness; abjuring all worldly toys, to centre every thought and action there. Proud of calamity, we will enjoy the wreck of wealth; while the surrounding gloom of adversity shall make the flame of our pure love show doubly bright. By Heavens! I would fling all goods of fortune from me with a prodigal hand, to enjoy the scene where I might clasp my Lydia to my bosom, and say, the world affords no smile to me but here—(*Embracing her.*) If she holds out now, the devil is in it!   (*Aside.*)

LYDIA.   Now could I fly with him to the antipodes! but my persecution is not yet come to a crisis.   (*Aside.*)

Re-enter MRS. MALAPROP, listening

MRS. MALAPROP.   I am impatient to know how the little hussy deports herself.   (*Aside.*)

ABSOLUTE.   So pensive, Lydia! —is then your warmth abated?

MRS. MALAPROP.   Warmth abated! —so! —she has been in a passion, I suppose.   (*Aside.*)

LYDIA.   No—nor ever can while I have life.

MRS. MALAPROP.   An ill-tempered little devil! She'll be in a passion all her life—will she?   (*Aside.*)

LYDIA.   Think not the idle threats of my ridiculous aunt can ever have any weight with me.

MRS. MALAPROP.   Very dutiful, upon my word!   (*Aside.*)

LYDIA.   Let her choice be Captain Absolute, but Beverley is mine.

MRS. MALAPROP.   I am astonished at her assurance! —to his face—this is to his face!

ABSOLUTE.   Thus then let me enforce my suit.   (*Kneeling.*)

MRS. MALAPROP.   (*Aside.*) Ay, poor young man! —down on his knees entreating for pity! —I can contain no longer. —(*Coming forward.*) Why, thou vixen! —I have overheard you.

ABSOLUTE.   Oh, confound her vigilance!   (*Aside.*)

MRS. MALAPROP.   Captain Absolute, I know not how to apologize for her shocking rudeness.

ABSOLUTE.   (*Aside.*) So all's sage, I find. —(*Aloud.*) I have hopes, madam, that time will bring the young lady——

MRS. MALAPROP.   Oh, there's nothing to be hoped for from her! she's as headstrong as an allegory on the banks of the Nile.

LYDIA.   Nay, madam, what do you charge me with now?

MRS. MALAPROP.   Why, thou unblushing rebel—didn't you tell this gentleman to his face that you loved another better? —didn't you say you never would be his?

LYDIA.   No, madam —I did not.

MRS. MALAPROP.   Good heavens! what assurance! —Lydia, Lydia, you ought to know that lying don't become a young woman! —— Didn't you boast that Beverley, that stroller Beverley, possessed your heart? —Tell me that, I say.

LYDIA.   'Tis true, ma'am, and none but Beverley——

MRS. MALAPROP.   Hold! —hold, Assurance! —you should not be so rude.

ABSOLUTE.   Nay, pray, Mrs. Malaprop, don't stop the young lady's speech; she's very welcome to talk thus—it does not hurt me in the least, I assure you.

MRS. MALAPROP. You are too good, captain—too amiably patient—but come with me, miss. —Let us see you again soon, captain—remember what we have fixed.

ABSOLUTE. I shall, ma'am.

MRS. MALAPROP. Come, take a graceful leave of the gentleman.

LYDIA. May every blessing wait on my Beverley, My loved Bev——

MRS. MALAPROP. Hussy! I'll choke the word in your throat! —come along—come along.

(*Exeunt severally;* CAPTAIN ABSOLUTE *kissing his hand to* LYDIA—MRS. MALAPROP *stopping her from speaking.*)

ANTIGONE

Sophocles (c. 496–c. 406 B.C.)

(*Enter, from the palace, Eurydice.*)

CHORUS
Eurydice is with us now, I see.
Creon's poor wife. She may have come by chance.
She may have heard something about her son.

EURYDICE
I heard your talk as I was coming out
to greet the goddess Pallas with my prayer.
And as I moved the bolts that held the door
I heard of my own sorrow.
I fell back fainting in my women's arms.
But say again just what the news you bring.
I, whom you speak to, have known grief before.

MESSENGER
Dear lady, I was there, and I shall tell,
leaving out nothing of the true account.
Why should I make it soft for you with tales
to prove myself a liar? Truth is right.
I followed your husband to the plain's far edge,
where Polyneices' corpse was lying still
unpitied. The dogs had torn him all apart.

We prayed the goddess of all journeyings,
and Pluto, that they turn their wrath to kindness,
we gave the final purifying bath,
then burned the poor remains on new-cut boughs,
and heaped a high mound of his native earth.
Then turned we to the maiden's rocky bed,
death's hollow marriage-chamber.
But, still far off, one of us heard a voice
in keen lament by that unblest abode.
He ran and told the master. As Creon came
he heard confusion crying. He groaned and spoke:
"Am I a prophet now, and do I tread
the saddest of all roads I ever trod?
My son's voice crying! Servants, run up close,
stand by the tomb and look, push through the crevice
where we built the pile of rock, right to the entry.
Find out if that is Haemon's voice I hear
or if the gods are tricking me indeed."
We obeyed the order of our mournful master.
In the far corner of the tomb we saw
her, hanging by the neck, caught in a noose
of her own linen veiling.
Haemon embraced her as she hung, and mourned
his bride's destruction, dead and gone below,
his father's actions, the unfated marriage.
When Creon saw him, he groaned terribly,
and went toward him, and called him with lament:
"What have you done, what plan have you caught up,
what sort of suffering is killing you?
Come out, my child, I do beseech you, come!"
The boy looked at him with his angry eyes,
spat in his face and spoke no further word.
He drew his sword, but as his father ran,
he missed his aim. Then the unhappy boy,
in anger at himself, leant on the blade.
It entered, half its length, into his side.
While he was conscious he embraced the maiden,
holding her gently. Last, he gasped out blood,
red blood on her white cheek.

Corpse on a corpse he lies. He found his marriage.
Its celebration in the halls of Hades.
So he has made it very clear to men
that to reject good counsel is a crime.

(*Eurydice returns to the house.*)

Part Three

Part Three

The Interpreter's Use
of His Body

Suit the action to the word, the word to the action. ᔛ
WILLIAM SHAKESPEARE

*For action is either a certaine visible eloquence, or an eloquence of
the bodie, or a comely grace in deliuering conceits, or an externall
image of an internall mind, or a shaddow of affections, or three
springs which flow from one fountaine, called,* vox, vultus, vita,
*voice, countenance, life. . . . Action then vniuersally is a na-
turall or artificiall moderation, qualification, modification, or composition of the voice, countenance, and gesture of the bodie, proceeding from some passion, and apt to stir vp the like.* ᔛ
THOMAS WRIGHT

Join not Esau's Hands, with Jacob's Voyce. ᔛ JOHN BULWER

THE STORY IS OFTEN TOLD that Demosthenes, when asked what was
the chief part of an orator, replied, "Action," and, when asked what
was second and what third, replied again, "Action." To him, of course,
the word *action* denoted the entire matter of rhetorical delivery, both
body and voice skills, but the quotation is worth remembering for its
recognition that delivery can mar or enhance the finest of composi-

tions. Limiting his remarks to the right management of the voice, Aristotle too recognized the importance of delivery, though he deplored that men, being as they are, are so much affected by it. Through the years later rhetoricians have regarded bodily and vocal behavior as one of the traditional divisions of their subject.

A Point of View

Obviously, before we listen to a speaker we look at him. The eye is indeed quicker than the ear; light waves travel far faster than do sound waves. When we go to the theater or to a lecture and find a husky football player or a lady's picture hat blocking our view, we look for another seat. Television screens are rapidly replacing radio sets, and we anticipate that before long our home telephones will be so equipped that we can watch the stockbroker to whom we give a buy or sell order, the girl or boy whom we would date, or the parent who wonders why we are out of money. We feel that our communication will be more effective if the listener can see our faces and if we, as speakers, can respond to the facial expressions and bodily actions of our listeners. There truly seems to be general agreement that "actions speak louder than words" and that "things seen are mightier than things heard."

Despite this agreement, however, opinion has grown in some quarters that the interpreter uses only his voice in communicating with the audience. Occasionally it is said that an interpreter should never use gesture, shift his weight, or make a move on the platform. Such a notion arose possibly as protest against the poses and mechanical, artificial gestures of some elocutionists who held the platform in the late nineteenth and early twentieth centuries. In our day of casual dress and manners and of prevailing realism in art, it is to be expected that we object to studied and stylized gesture. Also, the familiar, informal mode of the radio speaker or actor, whose delivery is adapted to the listener's living room, seems to have affected all speaking in public, until we have developed a "stand-in-one-spot-and-mumble" school. Yet the interpreter never leaves his body at home, and so long as he is in view of the audience, his posture, stance, bearing, facial expression, and gesture will either help make his words vivid and meaningful or they will blur, detract from, and interfere with the ideas and feelings, which, we have said, it is his function to share with the audience. Moreover, there is ample laboratory evidence that a person's voice control is conditioned in large part by his total body control. Voice production, after all, is a matter of neuromuscular coordination, and vocal shortcomings, granted normal intelligence and a normal structure of the voice and hearing mechanism, arise from excess tension or excess flaccidity of muscle. Another way of saying the same thing is that from a lively, alert, expressive body will come a varied and flexible voice, while from a monotonous body will come a monotonous voice.

Today there is growing belief among linguists and anthropologists that language is action. Tools are sometimes said to be an extension of man's hands; similarly, it could be said that words are an extension of man's actions. This means that there is an action basis for whatever man says. The speaker, the interpreter, and the actor who perceive this action basis, and suggest it as they utter words, will stimulate the listeners as others never do. Revealing the action basis of the words lends clarity and vividness to utterance. To find the means of such revelation the interpreter will need to understand general principles of bodily expression and to develop habits of free, purposive response.

There are some obstacles to this study. Like music and the dance, the speech arts, including the art of the interpreter, cease to exist when the performance is ended. One can return to a painting again and again to observe, analyze, and study it, but there is no return to the actor's or speaker's production. True, some semblance of it can be preserved in recordings, and moving pictures might be made, though for the student this would usually not be practicable. Still pictures are of little value, because the speaker, like the dancer, uses movement which is dynamic, having meaning only in relation to what has preceded and to what follows.

Another obstacle is the infinite possible variety in form of gesture and movement. For literally hundreds of years men have explored the question of the universality of patterns of expressive action. In 1644 John Bulwer, an English physician, published *Chirologia* and *Chironomia*, treatises stressing the role of the body in speech. He ascribed sixty-four natural and universal signs to the hands and described each of them. What he wrote had tremendous influence, appearing in whole or in part in other books on the subject even in the late nineteenth century. Through the years rules for gesture were sought and elaborate descriptions were written to guide the actor and speaker in the expression of emotions. This example, quoted from John Burgh's *The Art of Speaking* (London, 1761), amuses us today:

The Interpreter's Use of His Body 247

Despair, as in a condemned criminal, or one, who has lost all hope of salvation, bends the eyebrows downward, *clouds* the forehead, *rolls* the *eyes* around frightfully; *opens* the *mouth* toward the ear, *bites* the *lips*; *widens* the *nostrils*; *gnashes* the *teeth*, like a fierce wild beast. The *heart* is too much *hardened* to suffer *tears* to flow; yet the *eyeballs* will be *red* and *inflamed* like those of an animal in a rabid state. The *head* is *hung* down upon the breast. The *arms* are *bended* at the elbows; the *fists clenched* hard; the *veins* and *muscles swelled*; the *skin livid*; and the whole *body strained* and violently agitated; *groans*, expressive of inward torture, more frequently uttered than *words*. If any words, they are *few*, and expressed with a *sullen, eager bitterness*; the tone of the voice often *loud* and *furious*. As it often drives people to distraction, and self-murder, it can hardly be over acted by one who would represent it.

Burgh's descriptions of the expressive behavior suitable in the expression of seventy-six emotions also were copied in whole and in part by writers both in England and America. Yet even these men who laid down rules asserted that nature was their guide and that a speaker should never use a gesture or movement without purpose. In the nineteenth century Charles Darwin wrote his important inquiry, *The Expression of the Emotions in Man and Animal*, and during the present century psychologists have carried on investigations to determine whether there are ways all men behave in given states of emotion and what the relationships are between body and thought, and body and feeling.[1] Today, the matter attracts the attention of anthropologists who examine and compare the nonverbal aspects of human communication in various societies.

Modern laboratory experiments reveal individual differences in emotional expression, but they also indicate that as the intensity of the emotion increases the degree of similarity in its expression becomes greater.[2] Studies have been made of the reliability of judgments in interpreting bodily responses of others, and, although Asch believes that "Certain expressions occur universally in response to particular emotional experiences," [3] there seems to be agreement that we *assume*

---

[1] See Gordon W. Allport, *Personality, A Psychological Interpretation* (New York: Henry Holt and Company, Inc., 1937), p. 71 f and 465 f; Solomon E. Asch, *Social Psychology* (Englewood Cliffs, N. J.: Prentice-Hall, Inc., 1952), p. 185 f; Daniel Katz and Richard L. Schanck, *Social Psychology* (New York: John Wiley and Sons, Inc., 1938), p. 331 f; Frederick Hansen Lund, *Emotions, Their Psychological, Physiological, and Educative Implications* (New York: The Ronald Press Company, 1939), p. 15 f.

[2] Allport, p. 71.

[3] Asch, p. 203.

conventional or standard expressions and that we *learn* various social masks which are meaningful to others within our society.[4] Indeed, it seems that from days of infancy we become increasingly aware of the social role both of our own and of others' expressive movement. Man's most basic language appears to be expressive movement, and one theory of the origin of speech is that it developed from bodily expression and gesture. Life itself is found to be activity of two types, bodily and mental, the two overlapping and intermingling in an inseparable fashion. Thinking consists largely of motor adjustments or beginnings of motor responses, often imperceptible. Recall is a mental duplication of actual behavior or of fragments of past responses. Feelings and emotions are inextricably linked with body behavior, some of it hidden, some of it easily perceived by an observer. Consider, for example, these lines from *Henry the Eighth*, when Norfolk, speaking of Cardinal Wolsey, says:

> My lord, we have
> Stood here observing him. Some strange commotion
> Is in his brain; he bites his lip, and starts;
> Stops on a sudden, looks upon the ground,
> Then lays his finger on his temple; straight
> Springs out into fast gait; then stops again,
> Strikes his breast hard, and anon he casts
> His eye against the moon. In most strange postures
> We have seen him set himself.

And the King answers:

> It may well be;
> There is a mutiny in's mind.

In connection with this relationship between emotion and body responses, it is interesting to note affective metaphors such as:

cold feet	stiff-necked opposition
hair stood on end	a bitter pill
inner butterflies	in bad taste
red with anger	sweet disposition
white with fear	losing one's grip

---

[4] See Allport, p. 471 f; Asch, p. 195 f; Katz and Schanck, p. 340 f.

hot under the collar	on your toes
frozen with terror	a faint heart
an upstanding man	a heart of ice
a cold shoulder	an aching heart
look down your nose	an itching palm
a bosom friend	no stomach for it
torn with grief	racked with sorrow

These metaphors are evidence of the fact that emotional states and attitudes are experienced in terms of body and that they are accompanied by changes in posture, gesture, facial expression, and general body tonicity, as well as by those in heartbeat, rate of respiration, and glandular activity. Our awareness of these changes, interpreted in relation to the situation or the context, constitutes the emotion.

The psychological mechanism by which we interpret the expressive movements of others is known as *empathy*. As we duplicate or start to duplicate the kinesthetic movements of those whom we observe and to whom we listen, we apprehend and understand their thoughts and emotions, share their attitudes, and find communication enriched. In Chapter 10 we shall treat empathy more fully.[5]

At this point, let us observe that a rich mental and emotional life in an individual involves great activity of the response-mechanism and that the speaker's bodily responses will not only enrich meanings for him but also will stimulate the audience to full response.

General Behavior Tendencies

From the amoeba to man there appear two basic behavior tendencies: those of approach and those of withdrawal, corresponding, respectively, to pleasure and pain. When the stimulus is pleasant the organism approaches, and from an unpleasant stimulus it seeks escape. Man flees from or attacks and destroys stimuli which give him pain; he nurtures and caresses those which give him pleasure. The body expands and opens with pleasure; it contracts with pain. A combination of withdrawing and rejecting evidences struggle, a combination also seen in the primary emotion of disgust. Other primary emotions are fear, anger, and amusement. From them, as basic ingredients, man builds a large repertoire of emotions and attitudes: scorn, admiration, reproach, envy, joy, anxiety, wonder, and *many* more.

---

[5] See p. 306 f.

Love, for example, is part of gratitude, grief, pity, and sorrow; anger gives rise to resentment, jealousy, envy, and hatred; fear contributes to awe, surprise, wonder, suspicion, bashfulness, and loathing.

For the expression of any one of these there will not be a single, set pattern of response, but there are general ways in which the body can and does move to serve man in communicating his thoughts and feelings. A listener responds not to the inner, but to the outer physical changes of those to whom he attends. The interpreter's problem becomes one of selecting, magnifying, emphasizing, or distorting expressive movement in such a way that what the listener sees will strengthen and vivify the meaning of the words he hears. The goal is harmony between words spoken and body expression. To this end the interpreter must develop a condition of aliveness and of keen sensory response, a free, coordinated use of the entire body, and a rich, varied vocabulary of responsive movement.

Expressive Agents of the Body

Expressive movement reduces itself to posturing and gesturing, and from those the interpreter must eliminate all details that do not contribute to the listener's understanding, appreciation, and enjoyment of the piece of literature at hand.

The Body as a Whole

Attention should first be paid to posture. It expresses not only the physical states of strength or its opposite, but also manifests attitude and emotion. Posture is the alignment of the bodily parts: legs, torso, arms, and head. In moments of confidence, poise, determination, and happiness, man asserts himself against the pull of gravity; in those of discouragement, fatigue, indifference, and grief, he tends to give in to its pull. In the former attitudes he stands erect; in the latter, he slumps. Expansion and contraction are revealed primarily in the torso —the lift of the chest and the degree of tension in the back muscles. In recognition of the visceral changes taking place within the torso during the experiencing of any emotional state, the torso has been called "the emotion-box." It manifests primary movements of approach and withdrawal; it can bend, stretch, twist, and turn. The largest nerve center of the body is located just under the breast bone, at "the pit of the stomach." This spot should be thought of as the center of the body, expressive movement, not only of the torso but also of the entire body, emanating from that point. From here comes the impulse for handling the various parts of the body. From this "center" the body opens and the head lifts, or it closes and the head sinks. David Belasco once said that man acts with his backbone, and Stanislavski suggested that a performer think of a bolt at the base of the spine which can be tightened or loosened, adding or subtracting strength in posture.

Characterized by slightly more expansion than contraction, the interpreter's posture should normally manifest interest in the audience, faith in himself, and authority in the situation. Stage presence is largely established by posture. When we say a performer has "good" stage presence, what do we mean? Probably we sense a heightened tonicity of muscle, an increased degree of energy, and an "aliveness" assuring us our attention will be challenged and held. A performer with "good" stage presence stands to his full height; his weight is balanced, his joints are free, and he shows a readiness to move when need arises. In short, the bodily parts are under control, and the man is not like the hero of the nonsense novel who "flung himself upon his horse and rode madly off in all directions."

In carrying us through space toward that which attracts and away from that which repels, the legs also enable us to manifest the primary responses of approach and withdrawal. Many an interpreter seems dull because he lets his weight settle on his heels and keeps it there without change; we conclude from his apparent withdrawal that he has no interest in his audience and no awareness of any shifts in the thought of what he reads. Movement, the psychologists tell us, is a primary factor of attention. In many life situations man cannot afford to disregard what moves: for the hiker the moving object may be a rattler; for the driver, a child in his path; for the skin-diver, a shark among the seaweed. The interpreter will find that both shifts of weight and actual steps will serve to renew the listener's attention and to manifest progression within the essay, lyric, narrative, or drama. Transitions in thought can be indicated by movement in space.

The Body and Its Parts

The arms and hands likewise indicate approach or rejection. Indeed, man's whole mental life is thought to have developed with his use of his hands, and their potentiality as expressive agents has been appreciated since ancient days. Quintilian, who lived in the first century A.D., wrote of more than ninety things the hands could say. Bulwer, of whom we have already spoken, wrote at length about what the hands can express, and there have been many other manuals of gesture. With the hands we point out, we make, and we describe. With them we offer, invite, grasp, stop, push away, soothe, pat, strike, scratch, caress, emphasize, and protect. In pain we clench them, in grief we wring them, and in fatigue we say we "cannot lift them." Nor is this all; you can make many additions to what we have stated the hands say. The interpreter's goal must be not to allow the hands to make little speeches of their own as he reads the author's words, but to let all they do make the words more vivid. He must neither overuse them nor let the very monotony of their position call attention to them. They must not get in the way, but their being kept on the reading stand or behind the back does not keep them out of the way. Absence of motion can be as meaningful as motion. Whatever position the hands or any other mobile part of the body takes will be an expressive one, and what they express needs to be in harmony with what is being said. Also, movements of the hand must issue from a larger movement initiated in the upper torso and flowing through shoulder and arm.

Like other bodily parts, the head manifests the general impulses of approach and withdrawal. It can move as a whole from side to side and up and down. But its chief use as an expressive agent lies in the truly wonderful possibilities of facial expression, principally in changes around the mouth and eyes, as is illustrated by this paragraph about a Hollywood actress:

> Her face, which she can work like a rubber mask, turns from sunny to sad, from Harlequin to Columbine, with imperceptible art. Her lips can tremble like a child's on the verge of tears or curl with three-martini irony; her blue eyes can blink in puppy-dog innocence or wink in complicity with all the world. Perhaps her most typical expression is that of a pixy hooked on happy pills, but she can also look like a small kitten that has just swallowed a very large canary, a waif who has lost her bus ticket home, a country girl trying to act like a vamp despite her wholesome apple cheeks.[6]

---

[6] *Time*, LXXIII (June 22, 1959), p. 66. Courtesy TIME; copyright Time Inc., 1959.

A child tends to be fully expressive from toes to head, but as we grow older we are inclined to confine expression to limited areas. Thus the face and hands are often called the most expressive parts of the body. Like posture, facial expression is not usually voluntarily controlled, and for this reason we feel that it indeed is "a mirror of the soul." The two fundamental types of expressions of the face are the pleasant and the unpleasant; there are twenty-four pairs of facial muscles, only eight of which are said to give pleasant expressions! There is indication that people judge a smiling face to be more intelligent than one continually serious and that a smile arouses a favorable attitude in an observer.[7] This does not mean that an interpreter should smile all the time; it does suggest that a smile as one first faces the audience will help establish good rapport between speaker and hearer. When we meet a friend, our faces light up and then we speak words of greeting. The same order of events is suitable when one faces an audience.

In the face we see the aliveness of man's chief sensory responses: sight, hearing, taste, and smell. Writers, we learned in an earlier chapter, make frequent references to sensory experience.[8] In vivid delivery words of this sort are preceded by an externalized bodily response. The interpreter recalls sights, sounds, tastes, smells, and facial expression gives evidence of the memory. There is not the full response there would be if the situation depicted in the words were present and actual. If, for example, we say, "The glaring sun blinded him," or, "He smacked his lips with pleasure," or, "The odor of fresh-cut hay assailed his nostrils," we do not narrow our eyes to the extent we would at the moment light does blind us, noisily bring our lips together, or sniff as we might in the other case, were the stimulus present in actuality. But there *is* vestigial movement. We are told that all expressive movement is the beginning of bodily action biologically serviceable in the real life situation. Earlier we found the difference between literature and life to be a quantitative, not a qualitative one. So are physical responses in interpretation different only in quantity or extent. We could say that expressive movement reveals the inclination or the disposition toward a mode of conduct which would be biologically useful to the individual. Small movements of face, hands, and head, and slight changes of posture reveal the impulse for large movement which, under other circumstances, the individual would make. By movement,

---

[7] Allport, p. 484.
[8] See p. 41 f.

gesture, and facial expression the action basis of the words spoken is implied, not demonstrated or completely re-enacted. The expressive behavior becomes a symbol, not a sign of meaning.

At this point it may be helpful to speak of degrees of bodily activity permissible in interpretation as compared with acting. There is no Grand Canyon between these two forms, but the conventions for the two arts *do* differ in degree, if *not* in kind. Just as the difference between literature and life is quantitative, so is the difference between interpretation and acting. The principles so far presented in this chapter apply to any speaker—debater, interpreter, and actor. Every speaker needs a well-coordinated, expressive body and purposive use of it. The actor, however, employs complete, literal, representative movement and gesture. He asks the members of the audience to look *at* him and to see the action *on* the stage; his actions may, indeed, take the place of words. The interpreter, on the other hand, asks the audience to join with him in *imagining* the action of words and envisioning it in the mind. He *suggests* attitudes, feelings, emotions, sensory responses, and acts. You might say he begins the gesture, and the audience completes it imaginatively. Perhaps a few examples will clarify:

1. Suppose the line is: "Give me that apple! I *will* have it—it's mine." (The *actor* will literally appropriate the apple. The *interpreter* will carry out no full pantomime of grabbing an object, but he will need to show determination, assertion, and attack through posture and body expansion.)

2. Or: "Let me help you up from that chair." (The *actor* will take hold of the other person and literally aid him to rise. The *interpreter* will, in posture, or even by a step forward, suggest approach and he might slightly extend his hand in offer of assistance. He will not act out the business of raising another from a chair, but through a lift in the torso he will suggest such action.)

3. Or: "Brush this dust off me . . ." (The *actor* will indicate the exact spot on his person where the dust actually is and do some brushing. The *interpreter* will indicate an attitude of rejection and might, by a slight movement, suggest the action of brushing, but the spot to be brushed will be imagined, as is the dust.)

4. Or: "Wert thou not my brother, I would not take this hand from thy throat till this other had pull'd out thy tongue for saying so . . ." (The *actor*, playing Orlando, at this point or a moment before, will literally grab Oliver by the throat with one hand and with the other will suggest the action of pulling out the tongue. The *interpreter*, reading Orlando's lines, will reveal by facial expression, posture, and hand tension the attitude of

The Interpreter's Use of His Body 255

anger and aggression, but he will give no literal pantomime of holding another by the throat.)

5. Or: "Unhand me, villain." (The *actor* will use the literal pantomime of breaking away from a present antagonist. The *interpreter* will need to suggest the effort of breaking another's hold, the antagonist, however, being visualized in the realm of the audience, not thought of as "on stage" in flesh and blood.)

6. Or: "I sprang to the stirrup . . ." (A literal re-enactment of mounting a horse would be as ludicrous for the *actor* as for the *interpreter*.)

We suggest that the interpreter will find the basis for action which *is* suitable by carrying out the full movement in his early practice and then, in his reading to an audience, keeping only the residue necessary to lend vividness to his words and stimulate the imaginations of his hearers.

Relation of Parts to Whole

In speaking of the parts of the body separately we have run the risk of implying that they act in isolation from one another. This is far from true. The body speaks as a whole, and the parts are not independently activated. When the body as a whole is responsive, the posture is controlled, the gestures are sufficiently plentiful and free, and the face is alive. Man reacts as an entire organism, and the totality is greater than the sum of the parts. In a study using full-length photographs of an actor in several emotional poses, it was found that observers give the most accurate judgments when "the whole body including the face is visible; next in value is the whole body excluding the face; then the torso including arms and hands; then the feet, knees, legs and hips (the entire lower portion of the body): least valuable are the head and shoulders with the face blocked out." [9] The study did not include judgments of the face alone. A later study limited to facial expressions of emotion indicated that observers make correct identifications more reliably from the full face than from the eye or mouth region alone.[10]

There is reason to believe that the most meaningful movement of

---

[9] Allport, p. 484.

[10] James C. Coleman, "Facial Expressions of Emotions," *Psychological Monographs*, Volume 63, Number 1, 1949, 1–36. Also see Werner Wolff, *The Expression of Personality* (New York: Harper & Brothers, 1943), pp. 18–42.

all is change in the general body tonicity, in the diffused and over-all degree of tension and relaxation. As emotional intensity increases, muscles contract in proportion to the heightening of the emotion. Subliminally, if not consciously, a listener perceives the changes in tension and imitates them. Indeed, when the meaning of the words and the *feel* of the muscles do not agree, the speaker seems not to *mean* what he says, and a listener is inclined to believe what the muscles say. This can be illustrated in a variety of ways. Try to say, "I just saw a frightful accident," and to smile and look happy as you utter the words. The effect is comedy! Or try saying some simple sentence, such as, "I am glad to see you," first with a dour face and slump of the body, then with as inexpressive a face and as wooden a body as you can muster, and then with a smile and a light in your eyes and a movement forward (as, unless you are hampered by life-long habits of inexpressiveness, you would do "naturally").

An interpreter will find that much of the time slight changes in general tonicity without change of base or overt use of hands will be adequate expressive movement. Let the body speak as a whole, let the face reflect idea and attitude, and there will probably be live delivery and projection of the meaning of the author's words. To gain freedom of response, however, we say again that in practice the movements should be large and full, no matter how small and subtle they may be before an audience. In final performance restraint is a virtue, but restraint cannot operate in the absence of something to be controlled. The beginner will do well to use exaggerated, large movement in his practice. When he comes to the interpretation event, he will then have a memory of movement to serve as the basis for *suggesting* the action of words.

Criteria for Effectiveness

Strength in posture and gesture is the first requisite of expressive action. Equating the action and the word, we should apportion the energy of the movement to the thought and the feeling. Changing the energy or the dynamics of an action changes the feeling for ourselves and for observers. Duration of the action, degree of force in the re-lease of the energy, and over-all rate of movement vary and convey nuances of meaning. To *express*, in its word roots, means literally to *press out*; to secure an externalization of the response, strength is

The Interpreter's Use of His Body 257

needed in this pressing out. The interpreter must have a desire to communicate as well as to express, and this desire will give added strength and energy to his expressive movement.

Such a desire will also add dimension to his action. Dimension is related to *form and purpose,* our next, inseparable requisites. Recognizing that all movement has meaning, the interpreter will select his actions. Random, formless activity indicates a man's insecurity and does not enliven the reading. This does not say that there should be a set compositional pattern or that gesture is to be studied, systematized, mechanical, or self-conscious. Let us admit, however, that many, if not most, "natural" gestures may be aimless, indefinite, and incomplete. Also, let us remember that there are some recognized conventions or stereotypes of action in our society. A movement of the head, for example, from side to side, we conventionally accept as negation, not affirmation. Like the dancer, the interpreter needs to become "linewise." Horizontal lines, generally speaking, denote feelings of repose, extent of time and space, breadth of ideas; vertical lines denote dignity, power, and exaltation. The reader will determine whether the words he is uttering are made vivid by a lift of the hand or by a dangling, inert hand; he will not stand rigid with hands clenched when he says, "An aching weariness filled his body"; he will seek a fusion of inner and outer experience. The form of expressive action needs to become significant of the thoughts and feelings to be shared with the hearers. Just as words become meaningful by arrangement within context, so do actions relate to what precedes and what follows. There are phrases of action as well as of language. It is all too easy to carry over from a preceding sentence or paragraph a posture and facial expression which, appropriate in the first, are inappropriate in what follows.

Furthermore, the reader should relate the form of his movement to his sensitivity to space; his action must *fill* the room, not be lost before it reaches an auditor five feet away, when there are also listeners twenty feet distant. This feeling of "out-thereness," as it has been called, is the essence of the whole matter of projection, which we shall mention again in Chapter 11.

Ease is another requisite. It is evidenced by spontaneous, free response and also by control of action. To achieve ease the interpreter will work for adequate relaxation, promoted by feelings of "inner calm," and for a balance between activity and tension. There will be economy, rhythm, and grace in his movement, and his technique and his expression will become one and the same thing, there being nothing "detected so quickly as the resolution to be expressive and to appear emotional." Gestures, after practice and training, become habitualized so that they occur without conscious direction and never interfere with the focus of attention upon ideas and emotions the interpreter wishes to convey. A speaker suddenly aware of a hand in mid-air will express little but that awareness, and the meaning of the words will be lost both to him and his hearers.

Finally, an appreciation of the potentialities of expressive action, sensory aliveness, a high degree of physical coordination, a readiness to respond, and a lively desire to share the experience of the literature will result in making the interpreter's body a meaningful and expressive instrument.

Summary

In this chapter we have indicated that, from both philosophical and psychological points of view, the body mirrors the life of the mind. Indeed the two cannot be separated. Large and small movements of the body and its parts will reveal the interpreter's understanding and appreciation of the literary object and also his attitudes toward his listeners.

More than do words, facial expression and general body tonicity convey emotion and attitude. The interpreter will seek not one pattern of bodily response, to be adopted by any person reading the lines, but an appropriate response which, not calling attention to itself, strengthens and vivifies the cognitive and affective elements of the literary object. Basic behavior tendencies are those of approach and those of withdrawal. Not only does the posture of the individual manifest these tendencies, but so can any bodily part. When the words and the physical responses of a speaker are not harmonious, we are inclined to believe what we see and not what we hear.

Exhibitionism in expressive behavior is deplorable. The opposite extreme—that of a lifeless, inexpressive, unchanging body—is equally so. The interpretative artist recognizes that his art employs two media, the body and the voice, and that both must serve the writer and the audience.

Criteria for effectiveness in use of the body include energy, form, purpose, and ease.

Practice Materials

Here are a number of short selections or passages which require and should stimulate varying degrees of muscle tension, gesture, and movement. (Similar passages with a clear action basis abound in other selections throughout this book.) Some of them call particularly for changes in posture, in degree of expansion or contraction, or in approach or withdrawal. Others require keen awareness and recall of sensory experience; many offer opportunities for visualization. In all, response to kinesthetic imagery and revelation of attitude will be important. Read them aloud, making them as meaningful and persuasive as you can, noting what kind of behavior seems appropriate and observing how your bodily responses strengthen the ideas for yourself:

1

There was a little preliminary cough, a shuffle, a backward glance over his shoulder at nothing, a straightening of the absurd hat, tie, coat; a jerk at the coat lapel, a hunch of the shoulders, a setting of his features—all affording relief for strained nerves. Click! He was on, walking with that little exaggeration of the Negro shuffle, his arms hanging limp and loose and long, his eyes rolling tragically.[11]

2

LAURA. You *do* like trains, don't you?

EUGENE. Mama took us on one to St. Louis to the Fair, when I was only five. Have you ever touched one?

LAURA. What?

EUGENE. A locomotive. Have you put your hand on one? You have to feel things to fully understand them.

LAURA. Aren't they rather hot?

EUGENE. Even a cold one, standing in a station yard. You know what you feel? You feel the shining steel rails under it . . . and the rails send a message right into your hand—a message of all the mountains that engine ever passed—all the flowing rivers, the forests, the towns, all the houses, the people; the

---

[11] Edna Ferber, *Mother Knows Best* (Garden City, New York: Doubleday, Page and Company), Copyright 1927 by Edna Ferber, Copyright © renewed 1955 by Edna Ferber, p. 22.

washlines flapping in the fresh cool breeze—the beauty of the people in the way they live and the way they work—a farmer waving from his field, a kid from the school yard—the faraway places it roars through at night, places you don't even know, can hardly imagine. Do you believe it? You feel the rhythm of a whole life, a whole country clicking through your hand.[12]

3

So the next night, after midnight, four men crossed Miss Emily's lawn and slunk about the house like burglars, sniffing along the base of the brickwork and at the cellar openings while one of them performed a regular sowing motion with his hand out of a sack slung from his shoulder. They broke open the cellar door and sprinkled lime there, and in all the outbuildings. As they recrossed the lawn, a window that had been dark was lighted and Miss Emily sat in it, the light behind her, and her upright torso motionless as that of an idol. They crept quietly across the lawn and into the shadow of the locusts that lined the street. After a week or two the smell went away.[13]

4

High on the shore sat the great god Pan,
While turbidly flowed the river;
And hacked and hewed as a great god can,
With his hard bleak steel at the patient reed,
Till there was not a sign of a leaf indeed
To prove it fresh from the river.

He cut it short did the great god Pan,
(How tall it stood in the river!)
Then drew the pith, like the heart of a man,
Steadily from the outside ring,
And notched the poor dry empty thing
In holes, as he sat by the river.

12 Ketti Frings, *Look Homeward, Angel* (New York: Charles Scribner's Sons, 1958). Reprinted by permission of the Estate of Thomas Wolfe, Pincus Berner, Administrator.
13 From "A Rose for Emily" by William Faulkner, *These Thirteen* (New York: Random House, Inc., 1931). Reprinted by permission of the publisher.

The Interpreter's Use of His Body 261

"This is the way," laughed the great god Pan,
(Laughed as he sat by the river,)
"The only way since gods began
To make sweet music, they could succeed!"
Then, dropping his mouth to a hole in the reed,
He blew in power by the river.[14]

5

The scene of the following lines is Alexandria, a room in the palace. Because of Fulvia's death Antony has been called back to Rome, and a lonely Cleopatra says:

Give me some music; music, moody food
Of us that trade in love . . . .
Give me mine angle; we'll to th' river: there—
My music playing far off—I will betray
Tawny-finn'd fishes; my bended hook shall pierce
Their slimy jaws; and, as I draw them up,
I'll think them every one an Antony,
And say, "Ah, ha! you're caught."
CHARMIAN.   'Twas merry when
You wagered on your angling; when your diver
Did hand a salt-fish on his hook, which he
With fervency drew up.
CLEOPATRA.   That time—O times!—
I laughed him out of patience; and that night
I laughed him into patience . . .
                    (Enter a Messenger)
                O! from Italy!
Ram thou thy tidings in mine ears,
That long time have been barren.
MESSENGER.   Madam, madam,—
CLEOPATRA. Antonio's dead! —if thou say so, villain,
Thou kill'st thy mistress, but well and free,
If thou so yield him, there is gold, and here
My bluest veins to kiss; a hand that kings
Have lipp'd, and trembled kissing.
MESSENGER. First, madam, he is well.

---

[14] From "A Musical Instrument" by Elizabeth Barrett Browning.

262   *Chapter Eight*

CLEOPATRA.   Why, there's more gold.
  But, sirrah, mark, we use
  To say the dead are well. Bring it to that,
  The gold I give thee will I melt, and pour
  Down thy ill-uttering throat.
    · · · · ·
  Yet, if thou say Antony lives, is well
  Or friends with Caesar, or not captive to him,
  I'll set thee in a shower of gold, and hail
  Rich pearls upon thee.
MESSENGER.   Madam, he's well . . . .
  Caesar and he are greater friends than ever . . . .
  Madam, he's married to Octavia.
CLEOPATRA. The most infectious pestilence upon thee!
  (*Strikes him down*). . . . Hence,
  Horrible villain! or I'll spurn thine eyes
  Like balls before me; I'll unhair thy head.
  Thou shalt be whipp'd with wire, and stew'd in brine,
  Smarting in lingering pickle.
    · · · · ·
  Rogue, thou hast liv'd too long.
    (*Draws a knife*) [15]

6

  The two points of candlelight at Maria Rosa's head fluttered uneasily; the shadows shifted and dodged on the stained darkened walls. To Maria Concepción everything in the smoldering enclosing room shared an evil restlessness. The watchful faces of those called as witnesses, the faces of old friends, were made alien by the look of speculation in their eyes. The ridges of the rose-colored rebozo thrown over the body varied continually, as though the thing it covered was not perfectly in repose. Her eyes swerved over the body in the open painted coffin, from the candle tips at the head to the feet, jutting up thinly, the small scarred soles protruding, freshly washed, a mass of crooked, half-healed wounds, thorn-pricks and cuts of sharp stones. Her gaze went back to the candle flame, to Juan's eyes warning her, to the gendarmes talking among themselves. Her eyes would not be controlled.

---

[15] From *Antony and Cleopatra* by William Shakespeare.

With a leap that shook her her gaze settled upon the face of Maria Rosa. Instantly her blood ran smoothly again; there was nothing to fear. Even the restless light could not give a look of life to that fixed countenance. She was dead. Maria Concepción felt her muscles give way softly; her heart began beating steadily without effort. She knew no more rancor against that pitiable thing, lying indifferently in its blue coffin under the fine silk rebozo.[16]

7

Groping along the tunnel, step by step,
He winked his prying torch with patching glare
From side to side, and sniffed the unwholesome air.
Tins, boxes, bottles, shapes too vague to know,
A mirror smashed, the mattress from a bed;
And he, exploring fifty feet below
The rosy gloom of battle overhead.
Tripping, he grabbed the wall; saw someone lie
Humped at his feet, half-hidden by a rug,
And stooped to give the sleeper's arm a tug.
"I'm looking for headquarters." No reply.
"God blast your neck!" (For days he'd had no sleep.)
"Get up and guide me through this stinking place."
Savage, he kicked a soft, unanswering heap,
And flashed his beam across the livid face
Terribly glaring up, whose eyes yet wore
Agony dying hard ten days before;
And fists of fingers clutched a blackening wound.
Alone he staggered on until he found
Dawn's ghost that filtered down a shafted stair
To the dazed, muttering creatures underground
Who hear the boom of shells in muffled sound.
At last, with sweat of horror in his hair,
He climbed through darkness to the twilight air,
Unloading hell behind him step by step.[17]

---

[16] From *Flowering Judas and Other Stories*, copyright, 1930, 1935, 1938, by Katherine Anne Porter. Reprinted by permission of Harcourt, Brace and Company, Inc.

[17] Siegfried Sassoon, "The Rear-Guard." From *Counter Attack*. Published by E. P. Dutton & Co., Inc. Copyright, 1940, by Siegfried Sassoon. Reprinted by permission of Brandt & Brandt.

8

He held the line tight in his right hand and then pushed his thigh against his right hand as he leaned all his weight against the wood of the bow. Then he passed the line a little lower on his shoulders and braced his left hand on it.

My right hand can hold it as long as it is braced, he thought. If it relaxes in sleep my left hand will wake me as the line goes out. It is hard on the right hand. But he is used to punishment. Even if I sleep twenty minutes or a half an hour it is good. He lay forward cramping himself against the line with all of his body, putting all his weight onto his right hand, and he was asleep.

· · · · · ·

He woke with the jerk of his right fist coming up against his face and the line burning out through his right hand. He had no feeling of his left hand but he braked all he could with his right and the line rushed out. Finally his left hand found the line and he leaned back against the line and now it burned his back and his left hand, and his left hand was taking all the strain and cutting badly. He looked back at the coils of line and they were feeding smoothly. Just then the fish jumped making a great bursting of the ocean and then a heavy fall. Then he jumped again and again and the boat was going fast although line was still racing out and the old man was raising the strain to breaking point and raising it to breaking point again and again. He had been pulled down tight onto the bow and his face was in the cut slice of dolphin and he could not move.[18]

9

Darling trotted back, smiling, breathing deeply but easily, feeling wonderful, not tired, though this was the tail end of practice and he'd run eighty yards. The sweat poured off his face and soaked his jersey and he liked the feeling, the warm moistness lubricating his skin like oil. Off in a corner of the field some players were punting and the smack of leather

[18] From *The Old Man and the Sea* by Ernest Hemingway (New York: Charles Scribner's Sons, 1953).

The Interpreter's Use of His Body 265

against the ball came pleasantly through the afternoon air. The freshmen were running signals on the next field and the quarterback's sharp voice, the pound of eleven pairs of cleats, the "Dig, now, dig!" of the coaches, the laughter of the players all somehow made him feel happy as he trotted back to midfield, listening to the applause and shouts of the students along the sidelines, knowing that after that run the coach would have to start him Saturday against Illinois.[19]

10

Although it was so brilliantly fine—the blue sky powdered with gold and great spots of light like white wine splashed over the Jardins Publiques—Miss Brill was glad that she had decided on her fur. The air was motionless, but when you opened your mouth there was just a faint chill, like a chill from a glass of iced water before you sip, and now and again a leaf came drifting—from nowhere, from the sky. Miss Brill put up her hand and touched her fur. Dear little thing! It was nice to feel it again. She had taken it out of its box that afternoon, shaken out the moth-powder, given it a good brush, and rubbed the life back into the dim little eyes. "What has been happening to me?" said the little sad eyes. Oh, how sweet it was to see them snap at her again from the red eiderdown!
. . . But the nose, which was of some black composition, wasn't at all firm. It must have had a knock, somehow. Never mind—a little dab of black sealing-wax when the time came— when it was absolutely necessary. . . . Little rogue! Yes, she really felt like that about it. Little rogue biting its tail just by her left ear. She could have taken it off and laid it on her lap and stroked it. She felt a tingling in her hands and arms, but that came from walking, she supposed. And when she breathed, something light and sad—no, not sad, exactly— something gentle seemed to move in her bosom.[20]

---

[19] Irwin Shaw, "The Eighty Yard Run," *Welcome to the City* (New York: Random House, Inc., 1942). Reprinted by permission of the publisher.

[20] Katherine Mansfield, "Miss Brill," from *The Short Stories of Katherine Mansfield* (New York: Alfred A. Knopf, 1937). Copyright 1922, 1937 by Alfred A. Knopf, Inc. Reprinted by permission of Alfred A. Knopf, Inc., and The Society of Authors as the literary representative of the estate of the late Katherine Mansfield.

The Interpreter's Use
of His Voice

O what is it in me that makes me tremble so at voices?
Surely whoever speaks to me in the right voice, him or her I
    shall follow,
As the water follows the moon, silently, with fluid steps, anywhere
    around the globe. ∽ WALT WHITMAN

It is the object of the science and art of reading, to realize as fully
as possible the imperfectly realized instincts of the voice. ∽
HIRAM CORSON

IF IN SOME QUARTERS *bodily* expression receives the hit-or-miss treatment accorded a stepchild, quite the reverse is true of *vocal* expression, which has long been the "favorite" of theorists and practitioners
in speech. The truth is that full expression of the meaning in literature calls upon all the forces of the interpretative artist, just as living
a full life requires the utilization of all the faculties. We have already
spoken of the interaction of body and voice [1] and of another kind of
interaction, that between outward expression and the complex in-

---

[1] In Chapter 8.

ternal activity we know as mind. It is our task as interpreters to function in such a way that the visible and audible signals conveyed to our listeners are reliable indicators of the mental relationships resulting from our individual responses to the literature. We know that the meaning conveyed to an audience is the result of a series of intricate, coordinated responses to ideational and attitudinal factors in whatever material is under consideration, but we also know that sometimes individual responses are properly made and then lost in the process of communication. Why does this loss occur? Sometimes, as we said earlier, physical inertia or personality factors, such as shyness or fear, get in the way; sometimes, poor reading habits or vocabulary. Sometimes—and this is our immediate interest—the voice is the focus of difficulty.

A Point of View

It was T. S. Eliot who once remarked, "A study of anatomy will not teach you how to make a hen lay eggs." [2] Without applying this bit of homely wisdom too seriously, and without underestimating the value of physiological information about how the voice works, we shall limit our treatment of voice rather sharply. Numerous texts on the nature and production of voice give current approaches to its study and improvement, and the sizable contributions of researchers in anthropology, physiology, psychology, linguistics, and acoustics make whatever brief treatment we might offer redundant. We shall attempt to deal only with matters of vocal usage bearing closely upon interpretation. The question is simply: How can the interpreter utilize the vocal means of expression to accomplish his purpose?

We shall not repeat here the admonitions given elsewhere in the book that effortlessness and smoothness in performance come only with mastery of meaning. An impressive voice and delivery can never compensate for inadequate preparation, nor can faulty pronunciation and phrasing often be looked upon only as vocal problems. At all times it must be understood that the voice is affected by the style of the literature, the expectations of the audience, and the adjustment of the interpreter to the foregoing and to himself. It might be well to

---

[2] From the essay "The Music of Poetry," from On Poetry and Poets by T. S. Eliot, copyright 1943, 1957 by T. S. Eliot, p. 19. Used by permission of the publishers, Farrar, Straus and Cudahy, Inc., and Faber and Faber, Ltd.

note here, too, that although the study of literature and interpretation provides motivations for continuing vocal improvement and developing vocal effectiveness to the utmost, we are not thinking primarily of using literature for the purpose of vocal exercise. We are assuming that the serious student of interpretation has what we call a "normal" voice, one without physiological or functional peculiarities sufficient to attract attention. If he has not, we assume that steps will be taken to remove existing defects.

Frequently the possessor of a "normal" voice encounters troublesome sequences and combinations of sound. The ability to take words off the page and make them sound like our own is a test of motor coordination in conjunction with thought processes, a matter of total control, as we have said. Unfortunately, many of us have vocal limitations without being aware of them. We are inclined to look upon the well-trained voice as an actor's trademark, but not a necessity for everyday living. This attitude, coupled with tendencies in popular writing to oversimplify, renders some of us almost helpless in formal audience situations or in the handling of elevated styles and literature from earlier periods. Yet often only after disconcerting experiences do we discover that vocal flexibility, responsiveness, and strength are not gifts or accidents, but the fruits of training.

Training means practice periods as well as numerous experiences in testing one's skill before different audiences in varied situations. For practice, it is advantageous to work with materials different from those intended for an audience. Similar in form, equal in difficulty to audience materials, the selections for practice will serve us best if they are clear examples of the problems to be encountered in the selection to be communicated, but are short enough to be repeated without causing fatigue. As we grow in vocal skill and total interpretative skill, the separation of practice and audience material becomes less important, but at first it helps us to retain spontaneity and enthusiasm for whatever we select for the audience event.

The method is like that of the pianist or vocal soloist who uses scales and practice exercises before turning to the concentrated practice of his concert program. And like the musician, the interpreter who has made thorough preparation in technique *before* he faces his audience need not be concerned about the technical matters of presentation, but is free to concentrate on achieving the synthesis of material and technique characteristic of an aesthetic whole. In this respect, vocal usage resembles table manners, which are easy if one practices them daily, but cannot be learned at the dinner party. And further, if one has to think about table service, he is not likely to succeed in making a pleasant total impression as dinner companion.

Dr. Hugh Blair, speaking about giving attention to the "how" of communication at the time of communication, had this to say:

> If one has naturally any gross defects in his voice or gestures, he begins at the wrong end if he attempts at reforming them only when he is to speak in public . . . For when a speaker is engaged in a public discourse, he should not then be employing his attention about his manner or thinking of his tones and his gestures.[3]

A recent statement of opinion is all the more striking because it comes from a text devoted to voice improvement:

> To be sure, all vocal changes depend upon the muscular manipulation of the structures used in breathing, phonation, resonation, and articulation. Yet once you are using these structures skillfully, you achieve variations in timing, loudness, melody, quality, and articulation not so much by planning muscular movements as by responding emotionally and physically to the idea and feeling you wish to express. Under the stimulation of this response, *integration* of the vocal skills is achieved.[4]

An invaluable aid in voice improvement is the tape recorder, or some other recording device. Objective listening to our own recordings, with subsequent evaluation from an observant teacher, gives us a basis for working out a program of improvement. Combined with listening to the voices of our associates and to records (or tape recordings) of professional speakers, actors, interpreters, and poets, self-recording and listening can be a revealing exercise. Stimulation comes from hearing others a little or a great deal better than ourselves, and without expert examples many of us would waste time and energy. Yet we must not be overwhelmed by the ease, facility, and power of the professionals we admire. Nor should we be swayed toward imitating the style of another. Each of us by preserving his own best traits can develop a characteristic style that will be in keeping with his total personality. Professional examples offer short-cuts, clues to ways of

---

[3] From "Pronunciation or Delivery," *Lectures on Rhetoric and Belles Lettres* (Brooklyn: Thomas Kirk, 1807), II, 134.

[4] Elise Hahn, Donald E. Hargis, Charles W. Lomas, and Daniel Vandraegen, *Basic Voice Training for Speech*, 2nd ed. (New York: McGraw-Hill Book Company, 1957), p. 204. Copyright, 1957. By permission of McGraw-Hill Book Company, Inc.

achieving variety, aesthetic distance, and rhythmic flow, but to copy them would be fatal to development. Not the artist, but his method of work, his degree of concentration, his command of phrasing should be imitated. Sensibly handled, a broad program of critical listening will give dimension and purpose to the effort of voice improvement.

It can be seen that voice improvement is part of a total preparation and discipline for the interpretation of literature. Like other aspects of preparation, voice improvement precedes the audience situation and is not consciously attended to during the actual presentation. Vocal style has its beginning in the literature under consideration, but cannot be worthy of the association if it is marked by awkwardness, affectation, or dullness. In Chapter 3 we named *correctness, clarity, appropriateness,* and *vividness* as the basic characteristics of written style, and these four characteristics are admirably suited to serve as criteria for vocal effectiveness. Since in normal speech a sound rarely appears in isolation, we shall be concerned mainly with the application of the four criteria to the dynamics of utterance, but very briefly, we need to consider the individual sounds, or vocal elements, that make up the speech flow.

The Vocal Elements

When we start to write about the elements of our spoken language, we encounter a "symbolic" difficulty, the age-old problem of finding a symbol for each sound. Modern spelling has moved so far away from representation of spoken sounds that standard dictionaries employ systems of diacritical markings to indicate how each letter *sounds*. With the aid of these markings, key words, and respellings, there is an attempt to offer reliable information about the sound of letters. There are handbooks devoted to pronunciation, among them the *NBC Handbook of Pronunciation*, which uses respelling, and the International Phonetic Alphabet, usually designated as the IPA. The IPA is an attempt to establish a series of written symbols to represent each sound in the living languages of today, and these symbols are of great practical use to the student of speech and language because they are (with some exceptions) negotiable from language to language. Yet even with the IPA, transcribing rapid speech is difficult. Phoneticians, in an effort to represent the subtle features and distinctions heard by the ear, make use of additional marks for stress, pitch tendencies, and quantity and other time values. The result is a "narrow," rather than a "broad," transcription of speech. For our purposes, although we deal with modifications of stress, pitch, and quantity, the symbols of the IPA are adequate.[5]

Whatever your guide, once you ascertain its reliability, you will want to check your utterance of the elements of English speech, your coins of speech exchange, against it. With the help of your teacher of interpretation or another trained critic, you should soon be able to determine how acceptable your utterance is and how extensive your practice of the vowels, consonants, and diphthongs as individual sounds needs to be.

The Elements in Integrated Speech

While it is true that the tune is lost if the notes are wrong, the sounding of single notes, however pure, soon annoys the listener and gets him nowhere. So it is with the notes or sounds of speech which normally occur, not separately, but in a continuous flow of sound from meaningful pause to meaningful pause. A statement from a recent textbook in phonetics illuminates this observation:

. . . the sounds in context are altered in various ways because of their influence on one another and because certain important elements of speech form do not emerge until there is an ongoing flow of meaningful utterance. Speech as we hear it is much more than the sum of its individual sounds. This can be demonstrated in an interesting way in the laboratory. If one were to make separate tape recordings of a sound from each of the phonemes . . . then splice these small lengths of tape together so that they would form meaningful words and sentences, not only would the resulting recording sound most unlike actual speech, but some of it might even be impossible to understand.[6]

Simeon Potter, writing of the dynamic features of spoken language, goes so far as to say that "if you have caught the right rhythms and harmonies, you may use a language agreeably and convincingly, even though your articulation of individual sounds is very far indeed from

---

[5] See A *Pronouncing Dictionary of American English* by John Samuel Kenyon and Thomas Albert Knott (Springfield, Mass.: G. & C. Merriam Company, 1953) for symbols of American English.

[6] James Carrell and William R. Tiffany, *Phonetics; Theory and Application to Speech Improvement* (New York: McGraw-Hill Book Company, 1960), p. 242. Copyright, 1960. By permission of McGraw-Hill Book Company, Inc.

perfect." [7] Without gainsaying the need for excellence in articulating individual sounds, we should like to emphasize the importance of sensing the movement of sound. Understanding a little about what the linguistic scholar means when he refers to the "interrelated configurational features" of language may help us to catch the patterns of language passing our ears.

The interrelated configurational features of the spoken language, which must be approximated in the effective interpretation of literature, are: *stress, pitch,* and *juncture,* or *transition.* These features can in themselves change the meaning of units or formations of spoken language; a change in stress, pitch inflection, or transition, as we shall see later on in the chapter, can alter the meaning of a word or passage. Stress, pitch, and juncture affect each other, too; increased loudness is often accompanied by a rise in pitch, and each juncture employs pitch change and *may* employ stress change.

Stress

Simply enough, stress "refers to the amount of force with which the sound is articulated, or the strength of the movements." [8] There are two aspects of stress in operation in connected utterance, *sense* stress and *syllabic* stress. By using greater force in uttering an entire word, we make it stand out from other words in a sense group (phrase). By applying greater proportionate stress to any one of the words in the sentences below, the effect of stress upon meaning can be seen.

1. But you aren't going to do *that.*
2. But you aren't going to *do* that.
3. But you aren't *going* to do that.
4. But you *aren't* going to do that.
5. But *you* aren't going to do that.
6. *But* you aren't going to do that.

Syllabic stress operates within a single word and is significant in the part of utterance called *pronunciation.* A monosyllable, needless to say, always receives stress when pronounced in *isolation,* but will be affected through association with other words, as can be seen in the sentences above. In connected utterance, a monosyllable may receive

---

[7] Simeon Potter, *Modern Linguistics* (London: Andre Deutsch, Ltd., 1957), p. 59.
[8] Carrell and Tiffany, p. 253.

the first or *primary* degree of stress. Kenyon [9] speaks of *even* stress in describing pronunciation of such combinations as *apple pie, upstairs, fifteen, James Brown,* and others. There is likely to be a slight difference even in these so-called primary stresses, and their pronunciation also, as Kenyon notes, is influenced by meaning.

Second-degree stress, or *secondary* stress, is a lesser but clearly distinguished stress such as occurs in the following words:

/di ,gest (noun)   /in ,sult (noun)   /per ,fect (adjective)
/alter ,nate (verb)   /esti ,mate (verb)   /supple ,ment (verb)
,funda /mental (adjective) ,unin /tentional (adjective)
,reali ˡzation (noun).

A *third* degree of stress, called *tertiary,* is that amount sufficient "to preserve the normal vowel quality without giving it the attention-getting emphasis of a primary or secondary stress." [10] It may be clearly seen in the treatment given the second syllable of "unintentional" above, in other polysyllablic words, and in the second syllable of verb forms such as "calling," "touching," "seeing," "doing," in accepted colloquial speech. The *fourth* degree of stress, or *weak* stress, is best understood as that which falls upon the vowel designated as the "schwa" in the following words:

beret	[bə /rei]
bravado	[brə /va do]
breaker	[/breikɚ]

A thoughtful consideration of pronunciation and phrasing at this stage may reveal the fact that although we often express concern for the accent on syllables, we rarely express equal concern for the non-accent of syllables; and yet, overstress on syllables which properly receive *tertiary* or *weak* stress can destroy the rhythm and distort the meaning of speech. For familiar words and conversation, most of us use sense stress easily and accurately, but when we turn to the writing of others, we are less certain of meaning. The result is that we often sound strained, forced, and a-rhythmical, with serious effects upon total meaning. We shall consider the effect of stress upon communication of meaning again under "Criteria for Effectiveness."

---

[9] *American Pronunciation,* 10th ed. (Ann Arbor, Michigan: George Wahr, 1950), pp. 81–83.
[10] Carrell and Tiffany, p. 255.

Pitch

A psychological term referring to the frequency of the sound wave, pitch is used in reference to the highness or lowness of a sound on the musical scale. Each language has its own peculiar pitch characteristics, and within each language group, individuals have their own recognizable pitch tendencies. The term *pitch level* refers to the central pitch tendency within each individual's range. Other terms needed in a discussion of pitch are *intonation, inflection,* and *step* (or *shift*). *Intonation* refers to a generalized movement in pitch, noticeable when there is continuous listening for a fairly extended period of time; *inflection* is the movement of the voice up or down within one phonation, without a break or pause. A *step* is a change from one pitch to another without the glide characteristic of *inflection.* The melody of a voice comprises all its inflections and movement along the scale. If degrees of pitch from high to low are numbered 4-3-2-1, the pitch pattern of American English may be described as 2-3-1: a rising movement, with a fall at the close of the sentence. Questions, too, may be uttered with a falling inflection, although a second tune or pattern used for questions and incomplete statements rises at the close.

Pitch is often decisive in rendering meaning, even when logical principles or arrangement has been violated in the passage. Added to stress and time factors, it provides countless modifications and subtleties of expression. Pitch undoubtedly is part of our conception of that elusive item called *quality.* Quality is often defined as the attribute of voice which distinguishes it from any other of the same pitch, quantity, and loudness. But the original tone initiated in the vocal folds, which are the determiners of pitch, enters into our judgment of quality. It is likely that the degree of lowness or highness of pitch affects judgment of quality in relation to certain material.

Exercises in Pitch and Stress

1. Read the following lyric with what you consider a high pitch prevailing throughout; then read it again with a low pitch. Try to obtain a judgment of "quality" from a fellow student.

THE NIGHT HAS A THOUSAND EYES

Francis William Bourdillon (1852–1921)

The night has a thousand eyes,
And the day but one;
Yet the light of the bright world dies
With the setting sun.
The mind has a thousand eyes,
And the heart but one;
Yet the light of a whole life dies
When love is done.

2. For information about your intonation patterns, record this or any short passage. Listen to your recording until you are able to note whether your pattern in phrases is 4–3–2–1 or 2–3–1, or an approximation of these two patterns.
3. Listen to your recording again and make a note of the syllables in which you hear (1) upward glide, (2) downward glide, (3) upward step or shift, (4) downward step or shift.
4. Ask the following questions with the traditional question (upward) inflection. Then repeat the question making an effort to let the pitch fall at the close. Which do you think is more effective? Why?

Are you going home tonight?
Who's going home tonight?
What's he doing here?
Charlie's top man?
Did you ask me where I was going?
Can the Ethiopian change his skin, or the leopard his spots?
O generation of vipers, who hath warned you to flee from the wrath to come?
O Paddy dear, an' did ye hear the news that's goin' round?

5. Read the following passage with a gradual increase in force. Have a listener record the shifts in intonation and pitch, if any, that accompany the words receiving greater stress.

The battle, sir, is not to the strong alone; it is to the vigilant, the active, the brave. Besides, sir, we have no election. If we were base enough to desire it, it is now too late to retire from the contest. There is no retreat but in submission and slavery!

Our chains are forged! Their clanking may be heard on the plains of Boston! The war is inevitable—and let it come! I repeat, it, sir, let it come. (Patrick Henry)

6. Some of the following passages require heavy stress, others moderate, and still others light stress for best approximation of meaning. Make your decision about degree of stress and then read the passages to a listener qualified to judge their effectiveness.

> When daisies pied and violets blue,
>   And lady-smocks all silver-white,
> And cuckoo-buds of yellow hue
>   Do paint the meadows with delight,
> The cuckoo then, on every tree,
>   Mocks married men; for thus sings he,
>   Cuckoo;
> Cuckoo, Cuckoo: O word of fear,
>   Unpleasing to a married ear. (William Shakespeare)

> Awake! Awake!
> Ring the alarum bell! Murder and treason!
> Banquo and Donalbain! Malcolm! Awake!
>
> (William Shakespeare)

> Think you, if Laura had been Petrarch's wife,
> He would have written sonnets all his life? (Lord Byron)

TRIAD

Adelaide Crapsey (1878–1914)

> These be
> Three silent things:
> The falling snow . . . the hour
> Before the dawn . . . the mouth of one
> Just dead.[11]

---

[11] From *Verse* (New York: Alfred A. Knopf, Inc., 1915). Reprinted by permission of the publisher.

"LIVE—I AM COMING!"

Oliver Wendell Holmes (1841–1935)

In this symposium my part is only to sit in silence. To express one's feelings as the end draws near is too intimate a task.

But I may mention one thought that comes to me as a listener in. The riders in a race do not stop short when they reach the goal. There is a little finishing canter before coming to a standstill. There is time to hear the kind voices of friends and to say to oneself: The work is done. But just as one says that, the answer comes: "The race is over, but the work never is done while the power to work remains. The canter that brings you to a standstill need not be only coming to rest. It cannot be, while you still live. For to live is to function. That is all there is to living."

And so I end with a line from a Latin poet who uttered the message more than fifteen hundred years ago, "Death plucks my ear and says: Live—I am coming." [12]

Juncture

Juncture refers to the way syllables are joined in connected speech. If a break occurs between the close of one syllable and the initiation of another, the juncture is said to be open: if the syllables flow together without a break, the juncture is normal, or closed. Closed juncture is equated with *blending,* the result of smoothly articulating one sound with another. Properly made junctures are important for distinctness in pronunciation, as we shall see. When a juncture takes place at the end of a phrase or clause, it coincides with meaning and involves pitch change and syllabic duration. We shall therefore speak of *juncture* when discussing the mechanics of utterance, but in referring to the junctures which cut the speech flow into units of meaning, we shall speak of the *pause.*

After repeating each of these phrases, note whether the junctures of your utterance were open or closed:

---

[12] Holmes delivered this selection over the radio on March 7, 1931, on the occasion of his ninetieth birthday.

Break, break, break . . . (Alfred, Lord Tennyson)
She was alone
She was a lone thing.
Lone on the loved hill . . . (William Ellery Leonard) [13]
Now the sun sank and all the ways were darkened. (*The Odyssey* of Homer)

How are meaningful distinctions made in the following?

He was a melancholy, old man.
He was a melancholy old man.
I saw a blue bird yesterday.
I saw a bluebird yesterday.
We have onions today.
We had fun yesterday.
Not at all.
Not atoll.
I want some ice, not some mice.
I scream. Ice cream.

All of us, as has been said, when learning to talk, start applying stress and pitch structures and using junctures by imitating adults around us. We are unlikely to pay attention to these processes unless we study another language or hear someone learning to speak ours—or study the speech process, acting, or interpretation. We soon discover in acting and interpretation that our acquired patterns can work against us, as well as for us. If we violate the patterns our audiences are accustomed to hearing, we are likely to get a negative, uncomprehending, or unfavorable reaction. On the other hand, we should be thankful, if we are nervous or uncertain, that the patterns may for a short time take over for us. When we are handed an editorial to read, or material for audition, for example, our success at sight reading probably depends upon the easy use of these language patterns. In a foreign country, an ear for the tunes of the strange language will, as Potter suggested,[14] prevent misunderstanding, even when the words are incorrect. A tourist in Holland once had this point amusingly demonstrated. She was standing on a corner in Utrecht with map in hand

---

13 From *Two Lives*, p. 108. Copyright 1923 by B. W. Huebsch, 1951 by Charlotte Charlton Leonard. Reprinted by permission of The Viking Press, Inc.
14 See above, pp. 272–273.

when a policeman approached her, lifted his hat, and said, smiling, "Good-bye, Lady, can I help you?" His inflection made it clear that he thought he was saying, "Hello, Lady!"

For the interpreter the implications are plain. The utterance of correct vowels, consonants, and diphthongs, affected by mental and emotional reactions, forms meaningful patterns of sound. The *integration* of the vocal elements is *essential* to the *effective communication* of *literature*.

Exercise in Use of Pitch, Stress, Juncture

Distinguish carefully the relationships in the following passages. Be prepared to defend your use of the configurational elements (pitch, stress, juncture).

1. Hail drums across the South (A newspaper headline)

2. He only died last week.

3. *Laughing Boy* (Oliver La Farge, title of a novel)

4. Dancing school, smoking room, reading room, etc.

5. In his dream Lincoln asked one of the soldiers on guard who was dead. [15]

6. Dead march

7. A College president warned his alumni fund chairman against requesting too much money at one time. "Don't put all your begs in one asking," he said. By the same token, a gangster was supposed to have said at a gangland funeral: "They shouldn't put all those yeggs in one casket." And by still the same token, a Madrid bus driver is reported to have yelled: "I don't want all you Basques in one exit." [16]

8. "Before the Flowers of Friendship Faded Friendship Faded" (Gertrude Stein, title of a poem)

9. My mother bore me in the southern wild,
   And I am black, but O! my soul is white.

---

[15] Ruth Painter Randall, *Mary Lincoln: Biography of a Marriage* (Boston: Little, Brown and Company, 1953), p. 379.

[16] From "Trade Winds," the *Saturday Review* (August 17, 1957), p. 6. Reprinted by permission of Mr. John G. Fuller and the *Saturday Review*.

White as an angel is the English child,
But I am black, as if bereaved of light. (William Blake)

10. To know what the blind man needs, you who can see must imagine what it would be not to see, and you can imagine it more vividly if you remember that before your journey's end you may have to go the dark way yourself. (Helen Keller) [17]

There remains one factor of speech utterance, the time factor. Since all language, whether written or spoken, comes to us in a temporal sequence, the listener's impressions of rate (the time consumed by the utterance) are bound up with total effect. Impressions of rate are *a composite of the actual time consumed* and certain subjective elements, such as *interest* and *immediacy*. Dissatisfaction with rate may well be the effect of weaknesses such as monotony, uncommunicativeness, insufficient loudness. Yet rate cannot be dismissed, for it is part of the structures of stress, pitch, and juncture and controls their interactions. In addition, referring again to the elements, rate in uttering individual sounds (the quantity of a sound) can affect meaning. The length of a vowel, for example, can change its character enough to falsify meaning. We shall speak of rate in considering criteria for effectiveness in relation to the other configurational factors.

Criteria for Effectiveness

In the study of interpretation a constant battle is waged against vagueness, emotionality, and the loose thinking so often associated with appreciation of an art. We fight small skirmishes of that battle when we try to evaluate vocal effectiveness. Such evaluations must be objectified if they are to be useful tools of self-improvement. The first step toward objective evaluation is to isolate the factors contributing to vocal effectiveness, but once isolated, these factors must be fused with the criteria for physical effectiveness and with the discussions throughout the book dealing with total effectiveness, especially with the materials of Chapter 11. As we have said, the four characteristics of *written style* (*correctness*, *clarity*, *appropriateness*, and *vividness*) are suitable criteria for *vocal* usage. Although not always mutually

17 From "A Letter to Mark Twain," in *Out of the Dark* by Helen Keller (Garden City, New York: Doubleday, Page and Company, 1914), p. 209. Copyright 1913 by Doubleday & Company, Inc. Reprinted by permission of the publisher.

exclusive, they are recognizably differentiated from each other. Since we have used them in discussing written style, they help us to keep constantly in mind the literary basis of our endeavors.

Correctness

As you can easily guess, our judgments of correctness center on three items: the shaping of individual phonetic elements, the combination of elements into words, and the linking of sounds and syllables.

The vowels are the sounds that result when, as the vocal folds vibrate, the air passage is relatively unobstructed. Since the vowel is in reality a musical tone, its production directly affects vocal quality. The chief rules for vowel formation are these:

1. The vocal folds vibrate because of the outgoing air from the lungs. Steady, well-supported breathing provides the force for vocal-fold vibration.
2. The shape of the resonators—pharynx and mouth in particular—is important in forming vowel sounds.
3. The movements of the tongue and lips alter the shape of the mouth cavity, and hence, the shape of vowel sounds.
4. The vowel requires no nasal resonance.

Phoneticians describe the vowel as unstable, meaning that vowels vary from one individual to another and that any given individual will tend to vary in his utterance of vowels more than in his utterance of consonants.

Exercise in Vowel Utterance

1. Out, out, brief candle! (William Shakespeare)
2. O wild West Wind, thou breath of Autumn's being.
   (Percy Bysshe Shelley)
3. Now fades the glimmering landscape on the sight,
   And all the air a solemn stillness holds,
   Save where the beetle wheels his droning flight,
   And drowsy tinklings lull the distant folds. (Thomas Gray)
4. The upper air burst into life!
   And a hundred fire-flags sheen,
   To and fro they were hurried about!
   And to and fro, and in and out,
   The wan stars danced between. (Samuel Taylor Coleridge)

5. The lights begin to twinkle from the rocks;
   The long day wanes; the slow moon climbs; the deep
   Moans round with many voices. (Alfred, Lord Tennyson)

Read the passages for vowel utterance in the following ways: rapidly throughout; slowly throughout; then with exaggeration of their essential characteristics.

During these readings note the following: degree of tongue activity; degree of lip activity; variety of tongue and lip action.

Answer *yes* or *no* to the following questions:
Does each vowel retain its characteristic quality? (Is it easily distinguishable from every other vowel sound?)
Does each vowel have sufficient and proper resonance, free of nasal coloring?
Is there any obstruction to the flow of sound?

Check yourself on distinctions by practicing and noting variation in the following sequences:

seat, sit, sate, set, sat; peach, pitch; pin, pen
toot, took; boot, book; loot, look
boat, bought; coat, caught; tote, taught; doter, daughter
ton, tone, town
Make up similar sequences for practice.

Much of what has been said for the vowel applies to the *diphthong*, which differs from the vowel in one respect: the resonance changes within the syllable as it is being produced. You will hear two vowels merging into each other if you listen attentively while shaping the diphthongs in *boy, pie, plow,* and *you.* Practice these and related sounds in sequences such as:

joy, join, spoil, foil, oil, toy, alloy, annoy
sky, lie, eye, aisle, write, rhyme, dime, ice
now, sound, doubt, bought, found, gown, town, down, brown
few, Hugh, human, use, fuse, review, queue, mule

Now turn back to the selections for practicing vowel sounds and pick out the diphthongs present. Using the three questions above, evaluate your utterance of the diphthongs.

The *consonants* are those sounds that depend upon some stoppage of the breath stream for their production and identity. They vary less in and among individuals than do the vowels, and thus are said to be relatively stable. Consonants may be described in relation to the place at which there is stoppage in the breath stream: as voiced or voiceless, depending upon whether they require vocal-fold vibration for their production; and as is usually done, according to the degree of closure that takes place. The headings of this last (and traditional) classification are: stops, fricatives, nasals, laterals, and glides. General principles for the production of consonants are these:

1. Clean production of consonants depends upon quick motor adjustment of the articulators (tongue, lips, jaw, teeth, soft palate, hard palate).
2. Prolonging the consonant unduly can be the source of difficulty, especially such consonants as s, z.
3. Overstressing of consonants is wasteful of energy; economy of production is essential (particularly applicable to the utterance of these sounds: k, g, ʧ, ʤ, as found in *park*, *good*, *church*, *George*).
4. Substitution of one consonant for another is a major fault ("wed" for "red"; "ladder" for "latter").
5. Omission of consonants results in sloppy, inaccurate speech (words that often suffer are: "husban'," "gove'ment," "conduc' ").

Exercise in Consonant Utterance

1. The slender acacia would not shake
   One long milk-bloom on the tree;
   The white lake-blossom fell into the lake
   As the pimpernel dozed on the lea.
   (Alfred, Lord Tennyson)

2. Stone walls do not a prison make,
   Nor iron bars a cage;
   Minds innocent and quiet take
   That for an hermitage. (Richard Lovelace)

3. Moan like an autumn wind high in the lonesome tree-
   tops, moan soft like you wanted somebody terrible,
   cry like a racing car slipping away from a motorcycle
   cop, bang-bang! you jazzmen, bang altogether drums,
   traps, banjos, horns, tin cans—make two people fight
   on the top of a stairway and scratch each other's eyes
   in a clinch tumbling down the stairs. (Carl Sandburg) [18]

---

[18] "Jazz Fantasia," from *Smoke and Steel* (New York: Harcourt, Brace and Company, Inc., 1921), p. 63. Copyright, 1920, by Harcourt, Brace & World, Inc.; renewed, 1948, by Carl Sandburg. Reprinted by permission of the publishers.

4. We are the music-makers,
   And we are the dreamers of dreams,
   Wandering by lone sea-breakers,
   And sitting by desolate streams;
   World-losers and world-forsakers,
   On whom the pale moon gleams;
   Yet we are the movers and shakers
   Of the world for ever, it seems. (Arthur O'Shaughnessy) [19]

5. Put out the light, and then put out the light:
   If I quench thee, thou flaming minister,
   I can again thy former light restore,
   Should I repent me: but once put out thy light,
   Thou cunning'st pattern of excelling nature,
   I know not where is that Promethean heat
   That can thy light relume. (William Shakespeare)

Read the passages for consonant utterance in the following ways: (1) with sharp attack on all initial consonants, (2) with quick release of final consonant, (3) exaggerating attack and release.

Note during these readings: (1) the effect upon adjacent sounds, (2) placement of tongue, (3) amount of movement required for agile adjustment to sounds in succession.

Answer *yes* or *no* to the following questions:
   Does each consonant retain its identifying characteristics?
   Are voiced and voiceless consonants distinguished from each other?
   Is there wastage of breath?
   Are there any unnecessary prolongations?
   Are consonants sharply and cleanly made?
   Are blends properly made?

Check yourself on distinctions by practicing and noting variation in the following sequences:

writing, riding	tread, thread
latter, ladder	trick, thick
bet, bed	thought, taught
rip, rib	myth, miss

[19] From "Ode," in *Poems of Arthur O'Shaughnessy* (New Haven: Yale University Press, 1923), p. 39. Permission to reprint granted by LeRoy P. Percy, Executor, Estate of W. A. Percy.

weal, wheel	racing, razing
den, then	glacier, glazier
bicker, bigger	sheer, jeer
watching, washing	furrow, thorough
chic, cheek	half, have
sir, shirr	wreath, wreathe

Try this for fluency and blending:

"What is this woeful wood?" croaked Littlejack, lost and all alone in another part of the forest. The dark was deep as midnight all around. "Whence comes this humming and this buzzing?" wailed Littlejack. And then he saw the source of the ominous sounds: locusts and hornets and dragonflies, yellowjackets and honeybees. They came in clouds and hosts and squadrons. "Black never thought of *little* things," mourned Littlejack, "when he was issuing edicts." He groped his way slowly into an outlandish grove, but there his way was clogged by a growth of toadstools and mushrooms and monkshood and bloodroot, foxglove, wolfbane and aconite, orchids and opium poppies, and the roots of mandragora. Spanish moss drooped down and Spanish bayonets shot up. "What are these woeful worts?" muttered Littlejack, now up to his ankles and his knees in worts; bloodwort, dragonwort, goutwort, hogwort, holewort, hoodwort, lousewort, moonwort, moorwort, scorpionwort, throatwort, toothwort, and wound-wort." (James Thurber) [20]

In moving through this paragraph of Thurber's fantasy, we make adjustments in rapid succession. The fact that the *worts* are written in alphabetical order fails to make their articulation simple!

Pronunciation

For a long time, correct pronunciation has interested specialist and nonspecialist, and pronunciation drills have been a part of elementary school lessons. It is probably not true that the mispronunciation of a word indicates your incapacity to understand it, but it is very likely

---

[20] From *The Wonderful O* by James Thurber, pp. 55–56. Copyright © 1957 by James Thurber. By permission of publishers, Simon and Schuster, Inc.

that wrong pronunciations are signs of poor preparation and poor listening. Pronunciation errors usually involve one or more of the following:

1. Substitution of incorrect sound for correct one
   naeow, for *now; laig* for *leg, Cheorge* for *George.*
2. Adding or omitting sounds
   grievious for *grievous; pro'ly* for *probably*
3. Misplaced stress
   /i de a for *i /de a*
4. Overassimilation (common in linking words)
   J'eat? for *Did you eat?*

Underassimilation is a type of fussiness. Check yourself on the pronunciation of these words: *literature, picture, temperature.* Is the assimilation easy without being overdone? Other words in daily use are given below. Do you find yourself substituting, adding, or dropping sounds or syllables? Do you place stresses properly and strike the happy mean in assimilating?

> address, athlete, cement, despicable, exquisite, generally, government, introduce, library, medieval, recognize, superintendent

Unfortunately spelling is a poor guide to pronunciation. Here are just a few words for which spelling and pronunciation differ:

> almond, balm, blackguard, often, receipt, sword, Thames, toward, victual, wholly
> bargain, compliment, denote, devote, decide, gentleman, husband, moment, monument, Monday
> breeches, cupboard, draught, hiccough, honey, Greenwich, lover, nation, sieve, slough, Worcester

You will want to add to this list and remind yourself that accepted pronunciation, recorded in *recent* dictionaries, is your standard when approaching unfamiliar words.

Often in performance we compensate for daily casualness regarding pronunciation by being overprecise, with the result that normal *closed* junctures turn into unexpected *open* junctures. Linkages disappear, and an incorrect, unrecognizable series of words meets the ears of listeners. These linkages or blends, in good speech usage, occur as the

The Interpreter's Use of His Voice   287

final syllable of a word joins the first syllable of the following word without a break in phonation. In the phrases and sentences given below, test your ability to make smooth linkages without destroying the form of the words:

> an avoidable error—
> after the ball is over—
> And you know it wasn't his fault.
> The infant was the center of attention.
> 'Way down upon the Swanee River—

Sometimes we run into combinations for which blending is a real task. Try these:

> And no one stopped to help him rise.
> They crashed in a desolate valley amidst storms.
> Donald took Winifred to Dag's Hot Dog Stand.
> The book was a godsend to the scholastic-minded.
> The storm struck with furious strength.

Clarity

Closely allied with correctness is the requirement of clarity, achieved with correctness of utterance and pronunciation and with the use of normal conversational blends and junctures. In addition, the interpreter's purposeful progression toward climax and revelation provides clarity. When stress, pitch changes, and pauses emphasize meaning, clarity is inevitable. The exercises given above for these configurational factors exemplify their role in the achievement of clarity. The *pause* itself takes place as a result of interrelationship within a work and between a performer and his audience. Nothing is more harmful to communication than mechanically placed breathing spots. After the careful analysis which should be made for each selection presented, the interpreter with a normal response to an audience may not need to think of *the pause* as such. If, however, he is working toward a polished performance, he will want to listen carefully to himself with these points in mind:

1. The pause, combined with stress, pitch, and quantity, helps the listener to select essentials of thought and feeling.
2. Shifts of stress, pitch, and quantity take place before and after the meaningful pause.

3. Pauses are of many different lengths, depending upon audience conditions, the personal rhythms of the interpreter, and the significance, difficulty, and weight of emotion in what is read.
4. The matter between pauses—the phrase—may be of any length from one syllable to many words.
5. Punctuation is the printer's attempt to follow the author's lead in organizing for meaning. To follow punctuation without question would very likely result in mechanically placed pauses, fatal to effectiveness.

Practice materials can be found among the selections in the text for the following listening experience:

Divide a passage containing about 150 words into speech phrases by drawing a vertical line at the points where you paused in reading. Evaluate your own and others' handling of these items: the quantity of the syllable preceding the pause; the degree of stress before and after the pause; the direction of inflectional change before and after the pause.

Mark the general intonation direction of the passage by placing a line curving up or down (as you hear your voice move up or down) just above each speech phrase. Then by adding the number of the upswings and the number of the downswings you can ascertain which dominated in your reading. You should also note *where* they came—beginning, middle, or end of passage.

Appropriateness

Appropriateness cannot exist alone. We immediately ask, "Appropriate for what?" Speaking of the voice we may well say, "It is good," but then we may add, "But I don't think it was appropriate to the service," or "Didn't he boom out in that small room?" or "She sounded so unconcerned." These comments indicate that appropriate vocal usage is the product of an adjustment to material, to audience, and, above all, to the self in relation to material and audience. One's sensitivity to a total situation is the basis of appropriate vocal, as well as physical, response. Yet it is conceivable that one could be sensitive and make clumsy or inadequate responses. *Learning to project vocally and physically the inner responses is the whole burden of this book.* The following questions may help you to direct your practice wisely toward *appropriate* vocal usage:

The Interpreter's Use of His Voice   289

1. Is the phrasing appropriate to the material and the situation? (Microphone and auditorium call for different phrasing.)
2. Is the pronunciation appropriate to the situation? (Does it have the correct degree of formality or informality? Is it distinct without being unnatural?)
3. Is the degree of force adapted to the material and to the situation?
4. Does the speed of utterance permit correctness and clarity and allow time for audience reaction?
5. Is the pitch sufficiently varied in shifts and inflections to aid in projecting meaning and arousing interest?
6. Is the voice a true guide to the spirit and intention of the material?
7. Does the quality alter in accordance with changing moods within the work?
8. Is the over-all effect of the voice pleasing?
9. Is the voice appropriate to its user? Is the pitch level appropriate to sex, age, and apparent personality of the interpreter? (Judgments of teacher, classmates, and friends are helpful in finding an answer to this question.)
10. Is there harmony between vocal and bodily tendencies and movements? (It is indeed difficult for most individuals to avoid harmony of body and voice. Try scowling and saying, "What a lovely, warm day!" or hanging your head, dropping your eyes, and saying, "I'm proud of that piece of work, I can tell you!")

An interesting phase of the problem of appropriateness is the conflict that sometimes occurs between audience situation and selection. For instance, can a delicate, personal lyric be appropriate to a large and varied audience? Can an essentially undramatic character like Socrates be projected without damage to his image? How can one reconcile intimacy, intellectual caliber, meditation with public performance? These questions have been answered by John Gielgud in his heading of Shakespearian sonnets, by Laurence Olivier in his film of *Hamlet*, and by Raymond Massey in his portrayal of Lincoln. Do you accept their answers, or do you have reservations?

Vividness

Vividness is the sum-total of interpretative style. It properly exists in the company of correctness, clarity, and appropriateness, but often when it exists, we are willing to excuse its possessor for lacking the other requisites. Simply, it is the life-giving quality, the projection of energy and individuality. It is the opposite of slovenliness, monotony, pedantry, and weakness. We hear, and we want to hear, the vivid voice. Within reason, we do not tire of it. Its ingredients, like the ingredients of beauty, are difficult to abstract. We remember the whole effect. We know that we are being moved and involved in an aesthetic experience.

Individuality, which is practically indefinable, is part of *vividness*. How can you preserve your individuality and communicate it? Perhaps by finding it and making sure what it is. In interpretation, we often find it through discovering an author who speaks for us. Vocally, we are individuals if our voices seem *appropriate* to us. Yet here appears another conflict. You say, "But I am not vivid." Or you say, "That stress seems unnatural to me." Each interpretative experience should leave us with a residue of self, modified and enriched. Vocally, it should have made demands upon us which, in the fulfilling, disclosed resonances, agility, melody heretofore undisclosed.

Liveliness is our most reliable synonym for vividness. (Latin, *vivere*, to live.) We have spoken of *energy*, but a display of vocal energy can be an enervating and not an enjoyable experience. Changing *energy*, expressed in stress variations, change in melody, particularly inflection, sensitivity to time values in vowels and in pauses—all of these under the impetus of meaning contribute to liveliness.

General Exercises

Test your responsiveness to written cues for variations in stress, melody, and time by obtaining a judgment of the vividness you achieve in reading the following passages:

1

When my eyes shall be turned to behold, for the last time, the sun in heaven, may I not see him shining on the broken and dishonored fragments of a once glorious Union; on States dissevered, discordant, belligerent; on a land rent with civil feuds, or drenched, it may be, in fraternal blood! Let their last feeble and lingering glance rather behold the gorgeous ensign of the Republic, now known and honored throughout the earth, still full high advanced, its arms and trophies stream-

The Interpreter's Use of His Voice 291

ing in their original luster, not a stripe erased or polluted, nor a single star obscured, bearing for its motto no such miserable interrogatory as, "What is all this worth?" nor those words of delusion and folly, "Liberty first and union afterwards"; but everywhere, spread all over in characters of living light, blazing on all its ample folds, as they float over the sea and over the land, and in every wind under the whole heavens, that other sentiment, dear to every true American heart—Liberty and Union, now and forever, one and inseparable!

(Daniel Webster)

2

First of all, love is a joint experience between two persons—but the fact that it is a joint experience does not mean that it is a similar experience to the two people involved. There are the lover and the beloved, but these two come from different countries. Often the beloved is only a stimulus for all the stored-up love which has lain quiet within the lover for a long time hitherto. And somehow every lover knows this. He feels in his soul that his love is a solitary thing. He comes to know a new, strange loneliness and it is this knowledge which makes him suffer. So there is only one thing for the lover to do. He must house his love within himself as best he can; he must create for himself a whole new inward world—a world intense and strange, complete in himself. Let it be added here that this lover about whom we speak need not necessarily be a young man saving for a wedding ring—this lover can be man, woman, child, or indeed any human creature on this earth.

Now, the beloved can also be of any description. The most outlandish people can be the stimulus for love. A man may be a doddering great-grandfather and still love only a strange girl he saw in the streets of Cheehaw one afternoon two decades past. The preacher may love a fallen woman. The beloved may be treacherous, greasy-headed, and given to evil habits. Yes, and the lover may see this as clearly as anyone else—but that does not affect the evolution of his love one whit. A most mediocre person can be the object of a love which is wild, extravagant, and beautiful as the poison lilies of the swamp. A good man may be the stimulus for a love both violent and debased, or a jabbering madman may bring

about in the soul of someone a tender and simple idyll. Therefore, the value and quality of any love is determined solely by
the lover himself.

It is for this reason that most of us would rather love than
be loved. Almost everyone wants to be the lover. And the curt
truth is that, in a deep secret way, the state of being beloved
is intolerable to many. The beloved fears and hates the lover,
and with the best of reasons. For the lover is forever trying to
strip bare his beloved. The lover craves any possible relation
with the beloved, even if this experience can cause him only
pain. (Carson McCullers) [21]

3

When Schopenhauer said that reading was merely thinking
with other people's brains, he was right. Reading is even further in that direction. It is becoming someone else for the
time being and running the risk of remaining so. When we
read we do not so much enter into the souls of others; we let
them enter into us. We become Shakespeare or his characters
—Hamlet, Falstaff, Antony, Touchstone. When we read
Schopenhauer we become Schopenhauer, which was probably
what Schopenhauer intended. When we read Whitman we
may become Whitman, which was what Whitman intended
although he seemed to deny it when he said that his best
disciple was the one who learnt how to destroy the master.
And that also is what all fit readers intend. They do not read
in order to become someone else. They read in order to become more fully and more distinctly themselves. They go forth
from themselves and after a while they return home having
gained something and lost something. Thus reading becomes
an experience, and although it may begin by prolongation
through the imagination of the author's experience, it ends
by becoming a part of the reader's consciousness, by a process
of absorption, in itself an experience which can in certain
circumstances be as impressive as that which originally inspired
the author. Far from being a question of subjection no great
book can be adequately appreciated unless it is read with
something of the quality that went to its making. We can't

---

[21] *The Ballad of the Sad Café* (Boston: Houghton Mifflin Company, 1951), pp. 24–
25. Reprinted by permission of the publisher.

all hope to be geniuses, nor is that necessary or desirable, any more than it is necessary or desirable that all readers should become writers: the end of reading is living, not reading or writing. Reading should tune our sensibilities to such a pitch that we are able to respond to the poet in the book and the poet in ourselves: a book is not read until the reader becomes its equal. (Holbrook Jackson) [22]

4

Even a moment's reflection will show that the spoken American language is backed by expressive features lacking in the written language: the rise or fall of the voice at the ends of phrases and sentences; the application of vocal loudness to this or that word or part of a word; the use of gesture; the meaningful rasp or liquidity, shouting or muting, drawling or clipping, whining or breaking, melody or whispering imparted to the quality of the voice. Written English, lacking clear indication of such features, must be so managed that it compensates for what it lacks. It must be more carefully organized than speech in order to overcome its communicative deficiencies as compared with speech. In speech, we safeguard meaning by the use of intonation, stress, gesture, and voice qualities. In writing, we must deal with our medium in such a way that the meaning cannot possibly be misunderstood. In the absence of an actual hearer capable of interrupting and demanding further explanation, a clear writer is always conscious of "a reader over his shoulder." All this despite the fact that writing, being permanent, as compared with speech, which is evanescent, allows not only reading but also rereading.

(Harold Whitehall) [23]

5

Calm is the morn without a sound,
   Calm as to suit a calmer grief,
   And only thro' the faded leaf
The chestnut pattering to the ground:

---

[22] "The Writer and Reader," from *The Reading of Books* (New York: Charles Scribner's Sons, 1947).

[23] "Writing and Speech" from *Structural Essentials of English*, copyright 1951, by Harold Whitehall, copyright 1954 © 1956, by Harcourt, Brace and Company, Inc., and reprinted with their permission.

Calm and deep peace on this high wold,
    And on these dews that drench the furze;
    And all the silvery gossamers
That twinkle into green and gold:

Calm and still light on yon great plain
    That sweeps with all its autumn bowers.
    And crowded farms and lessening towers,
To mingle with the bounding main:

Calm and deep peace in this wide air,
    These leaves that redden to the fall;
    And in my heart, if calm at all,
If any calm a calm despair:

Calm on the seas, and silver sleep,
    And waves that sway themselves in rest,
    And dead calm in that noble breast
Which heaves but with the heaving deep.

(Alfred, Lord Tennyson)

The words of Dylan Thomas, written about his experience with the English Festival of Spoken Poetry, provide a fitting synthesis not only for what we have tried to say regarding criteria for vocal effectiveness, but for the entire section on voice. Of evident vocal faults the poet wrote:

> Many readings were plagued with the more obvious sicknesses of reading-aloud: insistent sibilance, the, for want of a better phrase, "Old Vic" voice: an affected inflecting that strangles rhythm and truncheons meaning. There was the "dead voice": a way of speaking that pretends to emphasise the importance of flat understatement only because the ability to *give* isn't there. The smile, not the voice, beautiful: the supposition of an arch, nudging connivance between speaker and listener; the attitude of "*We* know, though the others don't." There was, though, rarely, the *acting* of the spoken, the taught, but never taut, gesture to illustrate an unillustratable, except by inflection, point or temper of a line, the starry-eyed horizon-searching, the mechanical handwork of simulated passion, like a soprano milking a goat.[24]

---

[24] "The English Festival of Spoken Poetry" in *Quite Early One Morning*, pp. 164–165. Copyright 1954 by New Directions. Reprinted by permission of New Directions.

The Interpreter's Use of His Voice   295

But of the effective readings, the poet wrote:

> They find the words of the poem . . . acquire a surprising pleasant strangeness when boomed, minced, Keened, crooned, Dyalled, or Wolfitted. Known words grow wings; print springs and shoots; the voice discovers the poet's ear; it's found that a poem on a page is only half a poem. And the speakers, realising the inadequacy of their hitherto silent interpretation, sometimes set about learning the business of reading aloud; which is to say, they set about learning the poems which they know by heart, by head and tongue. They put that noise on paper, which is a poem, into their chests and throats, and let it out: they find that good poets are better than they (the readers) thought they were, for crying out loud.[25]

Summary

Like other motor activities, accurate, easy speech requires practice and discernible goals. For best results in the interpretative situation, attention should be removed from technical details, but before meeting his audience the interpreter will, by means of recordings and critical listening, seek the attainment of correctness, clarity, appropriateness, and vividness in the use of his vocal mechanism. Beginning with the accurate formation of individual sounds, he will integrate these sounds in the flow of speech in such a way that the meaning is clear and the total effect pleasing. At all times he will work for careful distinctions and over-all variety, managing intonational and inflectional movement, the four degrees of stress, junctures, and blending in conformity with the conventional patterns of English or American-English.[26] If he successfully meets established criteria of correctness, clarity, appropriateness, and vividness, it is very likely that he will also meet that encompassing standard expressed in the words of Dylan Thomas, when "the voice discovers the poet's ear."

---

[25] "The English Festival of Spoken Poetry," in *Quite Early One Morning*, pp. 161–162.

[26] We have followed Kenyon in discussing stress, but find no disagreement between Kenyon and the authors of *Phonetics: Theory and Application to Speech Improvement*. In all matters pertaining to the integration of the elements (connected utterance), we have taken these authors, Carrell and Tiffany, as guides.

Part Four

The Interpreter and His Audience

This Polydore,

·   ·   ·   ·   ·   ·

When on my three-foot stool I sit and tell
The war-like feats I have done, his spirits fly out
Into my story; say, "Thus mine enemy fell,
And thus I set my foot on's neck;" even then
The princely blood flows in his cheek, he sweats,
Strains his young nerves, and puts himself in posture
That acts my words. The younger brother, Cadwal,

·   ·   ·   ·   ·   ·

Strikes life into my speech and shows much more
His own conceiving. ∾ WILLIAM SHAKESPEARE

IN THE OPENING CHAPTERS of this book we discussed some aspects of
the social nature of speech, and we called interpretation a writer-
reader-audience event. We have examined in some detail the contribution the writer makes and the skills the interpreter must develop
to fulfill his function of revealing and sharing the meanings of the
literature. Now let us take a look at the audience and its role in the
interpretation event.

The Audience Situation

What is an audience? It has been said that the word is a mere abstraction and that, in reality, there are only separate individuals. In one sense this is true. Yet an audience is more than just a number of people—a crowd of pedestrians at a street corner waiting for the traffic light to change is not an audience, but they might become one if an officer blew his whistle and began ordering them to move. Persons assembling in a theater are not an audience in the minutes when they are looking for their seats, but, once settled in them, as curtain time approaches they start to become an audience. The peculiar trait binding diverse individuals together as audience is a predisposition to perceive and discriminate in a certain way in response to a common stimulus. Indeed, a satisfactory definition of an audience is "two or more persons responding to a common stimulus." Or, put it this way, an audience situation exists when one human being is the center of attention of other human beings. In interpretation, the interpreter furnishes the "common stimulus" and is the center of attention.

Rhetoricians from ancient to modern times have stressed the importance of any speaker analyzing the needs and probable responses of his listeners. If the interpreter has some knowledge of audiences in general, he will be better able to adjust to any particular audience. Whether it be a classroom audience, a meeting of Rotarians or other service group, or persons gathered to hear an announced program of readings open to the public or to an invited number (such occasions today are often called "Reading Hours"), the members of the audience will be alike in some respects and different in others. Before facing the audience a speaker or interpreter should estimate the differences and the likenesses of the group—its general education, age and sex, and background interests and tastes.[1] Just as the individual silent reader brings whatever he knows and is to each reading experience, so the audience comes to the experience of oral interpretation with certain capacities and expectations. All these factors affect both choice of materials and delivery. A Katherine Mansfield story depicting the moment of crisis in a sensitive woman's life ("Bliss," for example) might be a discriminating choice for twenty or twenty-five young matrons gathered in a pleasant living-room, but it would put the

---

[1] See Austin J. Freeley, *Argumentation and Debate: Rational Decision Making* (San Francisco: Wadsworth Publishing Company, Inc., 1961), Chapter 18.

members of the real estate board to sleep. The irony and broad humor of "The Apostate" by George Milburn would probably be lost on a group of "joiners," who, on the other hand, might heartily enjoy a scene from *The Taming of the Shrew*.

The occasion itself affects listeners' responses. An audience of men and women gathered for a Valentine dinner will wish to laugh, not to suffer the awesome tension of the scene in which Othello smothers Desdemona, lines which might well be read to the same audience at some other time. Later in this book [2] we shall further discuss principles of programing. Now let us consider some of the general principles which operate when groups assemble.

The Individual and the Group

Psychologists tell us that persons in a group do not always respond as they might as individuals, that membership in a group affects all the psychological functions: perception, discrimination, judgment, thinking, and emotion.[3] In other words, the group exercises an influence upon the individual. People differ, of course, in their ability to resist external pressures: there are a few individuals who are so affected by association with a group that they are less alert, less aware than when they are alone; others seem to come to life, to think and feel keenly, to "ooze" awareness; most of us feel a heightening of responses in congenial company. A group seems to contain possibilities for contagious excitement. Not only does a speaker stimulate the audience and the audience the speaker, but members of the group stimulate one another. A maximum degree of this interstimulation results in what is called "polarization." An interpreter seeks to polarize the group. When he, or any other speaker, appears, some members of the audience will respond more quickly than others, some will have longer attention span, some will be more emotionally sensitive, some will empathize more readily.[4] Through social facilitation these persons will affect those around them, and responses of all in the group will be heightened as a result. Just seeing and hearing another laugh or weep helps to touch off the same response in the rest of us. (This is why opera singers sometimes arrange for a claque.) As a rule people

---

2 See Chapter 12.

3 Based on Muzafer Sherif and Carolyn W. Sherif, *An Outline of Social Psychology*, rev. ed. (New York: Harper & Brothers, 1956).

4 See the last section of this chapter for an explanation of empathy.

hesitate to show a response not shown by others in the group. An interpreter should look for sympathetic souls in his audience and establish full communication with them, in the hope and with the expectation that they will gradually "infect" the entire audience. There is belief that these ready responders are more apt to be sitting near the front or in the center of the group. Wherever they are, the interpreter wisely recognizes their presence.

Though he may face an indifferent audience, it is doubtful that an interpreter will find himself obliged to read to a hostile audience. There have been such, of course—the Romans waiting for Antony to speak, the Congressional Committee listening to the evasive answers of known labor racketeers, or the majority of the United Nations General Assembly facing Russia's Khrushchev. But, usually, audiences want the interpreter to succeed, to be effective, to command respect and attention, to direct thinking, to arouse feelings and emotions, and to stimulate them to an aesthetic experience. For all this to be done, it is necessary that attention be arrested and maintained.

Control of Attention

The psychologists' name for factors controlling attention is "factors of advantage." The factors are: change, strength, striking quality, and definiteness of form; they relate both to the literature being presented and to the interpreter's use of body and voice. In the last two chapters much of the discussion was really an application of these factors to the interpreter's skills. An interpreter's voice must be heard, but an unchanging level of loudness will become monotonous and destroy attention. Stimuli which are more intense will prevail over weaker ones; a speaker cannot compete with the thunder of a jet overhead. Unusual ideas and those combining the new and the familiar will challenge attention. Clarity begets understanding, confusion sends the hearer off into the world of his own daydreams. If the interpreter does his part, extraneous pressures or suggestions, internal factors such as drowsiness or worry—all such factors—will be insufficient to distract the audience, for the stimulus situation will be definite and strong. Up to a point an audience will try to "stay with" an interpreter, but, if he does not furnish clues of sufficient energy to stimulate imagination or if there seems to be no organization of ideas and all is a jumble, in frustration they will cease to listen.

Indicating the importance of attention, Vivas defines aesthetic experience as one "of rapt attention," stating furthermore that attention is aesthetic "when it is so controlled by the object that it does not fly away from it to meanings and values not present immanently in the object." [5] The implication for the interpreter, seeking to give the audience the aesthetic experience of the literature, is that during his presentation it is "a consummation devoutly to be wished" that the members of the audience think only about the thoughts and feelings encompassed by the literature. Thinking, we are told, is subvocal speech, that is, when we think, we talk to ourselves. As we listen to words spoken at an average, over-all rate of about 125 a minute, we are speaking to ourselves at a far higher rate. During this speaking to ourselves,

The brain deals with words at a lightning pace, but when we listen, we ask this brain to receive words at an extremely slow pace. It might seem logical to slow down our thinking when we listen to coincide with the 125-word-per-minute speech rate. But slowing down thought processes is a difficult thing to do—almost painful. Therefore, when we listen, we continue thinking at high speed while the spoken words arrive at low speed. In the act of listening the differential between thinking and speaking rates means that our brains work with hundreds of words in addition to those we hear, assembling thoughts other than those spoken to us. To put it another way, we can listen and still have spare time for thinking.[6]

An audience responding aesthetically will confine its "spare time" thinking to what is intended by the writer and, in turn, by the interpreter.

The Active Listener

To hear is not to *listen*. Hearing is a passive process; listening is *active* and requires energy and concentration. Although we spend nearly half our time in situations requiring listening, Nichols and Stevens found that we listen at about a 25 per cent level of efficiency. Perhaps our hearing has become dulled by the constant bombardment of sound: radios turned on from morning to night spouting endlessly repeated commercials, cars with loudspeakers blaring advertising as they crawl down the street, juke boxes and hi-fi sets operating at maximum intensity, and "soft music" piped into the bank or the dentist's

---

[5] Eliseo Vivas, *Creation and Discovery* (New York: Noonday Press, 1955), pp. 95–96.
[6] Ralph G. Nichols and Leonard A. Stevens, *Are You Listening?* (New York: McGraw-Hill Book Company, Inc., 1957), p. 79.

office making painless the payment on the mortgage or the grinding drill. In sheer self-defense we cease to listen. If, however, we carry this habit over to occasions requiring listening, such as Reading Hours, we do not accept our responsibility as members of an audience and, as students of interpretation, miss learning opportunities which could help us improve our understanding as silent readers and our own skills as interpreters.

A skilled speaker or interpreter is highly sensitive to the audience "feedback," modifying his behavior according to his perception of the audience's reactions. Indeed, by its reactions the audience can stimulate the interpreter to a high level of performance, or it can demoralize him to a point where he struggles to continue at all. Following an opening act of a play, actors may congratulate one another upon having a "good" audience, referring not at all to its size, or they may console one another because the audience is so "cold" and "dead." We all crave "good" listeners, and we all know how much they help us to talk. The "good" listener shows a readiness to listen and react to the speaker, so that the act of communication is a two-way process.

Here is the way "feedback" operates:

Nearly all of us have unconsciously developed a special set of senses that, in effect, measure the way people listen when we talk to them. In public speaking [or in interpretation] we call the process "circuit-response," and each speaker [or interpreter] attempts to derive positive benefit from this well-known phenomenon. It operates something like this:

As he speaks, the talker's words go out to the listener, and simultaneously the talker expects a reaction to bounce back from the listener. Sometimes the reaction returns in the form of words or even grunts . . . .

But these are the simple reactions. Most of the time the talker's words bring reactions that are only fleeting visual cues. The listener's face may brighten up just slightly to show he understands and approves. The listener looks away from the talker; something is wrong. He looks the talker straight in the eye; things are better. He smiles, nods his head or moves forward ever so slightly and the talker learns that his words are being received well. On the other hand, the listener may screw up his face, scowl, scratch his head, or loosen his collar, and the talker feels that his words are not having the right effect. There are hundreds of visual cues—some almost invisible to the human eye—that convey meaning from listener to speaker.

And then there's one important reaction that is neither visual or oral. It is silence, of which there are several brands. There's a cold chilling brand of silence. There's a demanding kind of silence . . . . And there's a warm, receptive quality in some forms of silence that connotes understanding and a desire to hear more. Or silence may be simply neutral, leaving the door open for the talker to proceed, but not giving him much encouragement.

From all such reactions a talker takes his bearings.[7]

There are those who say that the whole burden rests upon the performer and that, if he cannot maintain interest, the members of the audience are at liberty to yawn, slump, and daydream—or even to produce their own reading matter and pursue it. Recognizing fully the responsibility of the performer, we, nevertheless, maintain that a member of the interpretation audience is responsible to the interpreter. As a member of such an audience, you can help the interpreter by sitting up in your seat, looking at him, and allowing *all* your senses to serve as receptors. Listen for the *whole* idea of the story, poem, or essay, trying to grasp its basic pattern and seeking its total impact. In your "spare" thinking time there will be moments when you will think ahead of the words, others when you will think back over what has been spoken, and still more when you will "listen between the lines" and search for implications and connotations.

Among the listening faults listed by audiologists, here are some most applicable to the interpreter's audience:

1. Refusal to attend to selections deemed "uninteresting" before they are heard
2. Refusal to attend to difficult material
3. Continuous evaluation of delivery (listening for a pitch pattern or counting the gestures)
4. Easy surrender to distractions
5. Feigned attention

Perhaps the person wishing to become an active listener should be warned particularly about the first two faults listed. A student once read, to a university class, a poem by the New England poet Robert Frost. The poem, "After Apple-Picking," was well interpreted, and the reader, in her introduction, had related it to the experiences of her audience, most of whom she knew came from rural areas. Following the reading, a student, asked a question about the poem, answered, "I don't know; I didn't listen because I don't like poetry."

Suppose that in your silent reading you have found Robert Browning's "Saul" difficult to understand and that you therefore close your

---

[7] Nichols and Stevens, pp. 36–37.

ears when another reads it aloud in your presence; if the interpreter does even a fair job, it is probable that lines which before seemed obscure will become clear, provided you truly *listen*. You will find that habits of concentration can be strengthened by resolutely giving full attention to an interpreter. A listener who earnestly seeks to understand and appreciate the words spoken and who maintains his concentration will agree that enjoyment of literature is enhanced by listening to it and that interpretation *can* add dimension to written symbols. Appreciation, either on the part of the interpreter or the listener, is indeed an active process; its very essence is a *doing*.

The Interpreter in Relation to His Audience

As Aristotle observed long ago, an audience must accept a speaker as a person before it will accept what he has to say. Aristotle stated that audience acceptance was determined by the speaker's *ethos*, a term referring to the speaker's intelligence, moral standards, and good will toward others. From the very moment a speaker or interpreter appears in view, members of an audience begin making judgments of his *ethos*, probably giving him in those early minutes a full measure of attention. During the period of his introductory remarks and initial adjustment to the audience the wise interpreter will seek to gain its good will and establish *rapport*.

Empathy

Throughout the interpretation the matter of rapport will rest largely upon a psychological mechanism known as empathy, defined by the dictionary as the "imaginative projection of one's own consciousness into another being." Empathy involves motor mimicry. Motor response, we are told, plays a part in all perception. Sometimes there is only a remembered muscular response of which we are unaware; sometimes, visually perceiving actual motion, we sense the changes of tension within our bodies, as we imitatively assume postures and facial expressions of others. A speaker fidgets on the platform; we soon find ourselves twisting and turning in our seats. We feel "into" his movements, unconsciously copying them ourselves. Or, we sense in our bodies the height of a towering pine and its sway in the wind; we stretch with the player reaching to catch a forward pass and sag with him when the pass is intercepted. We vicariously swing on the trapeze with the circus performer and take the high dive with the exhibition diver.

Observe a group of men watching a televised prize fight and note their clenched fists and thrusting or dodging movements as they re-enact the fight, partially, if not completely. Perhaps you remember that, similarly, during the big scene in the movie of *Ben Hur*, you helped drive the chariot until you were exhausted and your arms sore, at the end of the race. The principle of empathy was the basis too of a bit of humorous business in *My Fair Lady*: Doolittle, finding himself in unaccustomed elegant surroundings, kept scratching himself here and there; soon Professor Higgins, to his dismay, was repeating the gesture in detail. The extent to which empathy operates for a silent reader is seen in an experience reported by I. A. Richards:

Reading Captain Slocum's account of the centipede which bit him on the head when alone in the middle of the Atlantic, the writer has been caused to leap right out of his chair by a leaf which fell upon his face from a tree. Only occasionally does some such incident show how extensive are the motor adjustments made in what appear to be the most unmuscular occupations.[8]

True, people differ in their degree of empathy and in empathic readiness. Yet this *feeling into* what we attend, or empathy, operates in both life and art, and nowhere probably more than in the relationships between speaker (debater, actor, or interpreter) and auditor. Moreover, we are told that aesthetic effect rests upon empathy. It enables us to interpret the expressive movements of another and leads to understanding and appreciation.

The role of empathy in interpretation is threefold. We have already spoken of the interpreter's need to externalize his responses to the literature, which is another way of saying that he must reveal his empathic responses to the thoughts and feelings in whatever he is reading. He must manifest them in body and voice. This is the first role of empathy. Next, the audience will feel into what the interpreter is doing; that is, they will "pick up" his empathy or, to an extent, copy his responses. And, last of all, a sensitive reader will respond to empathic cues given him by his audience. If the subject or the style of a

---

[8] I. A. Richards, *Principles of Literary Criticism* (New York: Harcourt, Brace and Company, Inc., 1924), p. 107.

presentation adversely affects a body of listeners, their composite re-action will strike the interpreter and may adversely affect the re-mainder of his presentation. If, on the other hand, the delight of one or more listeners influences those around them and the total response communicates pleasure to the interpreter, he is likely to be moved toward a better presentation than he dreamed himself capable of giving. When this happens, he says he has the audience "in his hand."

Control and Judgment

At the same time that the interpreter must arouse empathic re-sponses in his audience he must exercise control and judgment, al-lowing no response to go unheeded. He must be certain that he is at all times arousing the *intended* empathic response, one in harmony with the meanings of the literary object.

The interpreter will take his selection, his audience, and himself into serious consideration and see them in proper proportion. Clear vision of this kind is possible only to the person of mature outlook.

The mature interpreter will adequately prepare himself for meeting an audience; he will have control of his material and of himself. He will furthermore have what we call "friendly" feelings toward his audience. All who succeed with audiences must possess a vital quality made of a magic amalgam of warm feelings, quick intelligence, and adequate self-confidence. A friendly person is rarely described as timid, withdrawn, or hesitant. At the same time, he is never a show-off or ap-parent egotist. Friendliness seems to stem from a sense of one's own worth and to increase as one learns to adjust to the attitudes and actions of others. No matter how talented or learned you may be, you cannot suggest to an audience that they really are lucky to be sitting in front of you. Instead, you must suggest that you are all sitting down together to explore or enjoy a work of art. You must take great care not to underestimate your audience, just as earlier you took care to avoid underestimating yourself. True friendliness exists when there is a sense of mutual benefit. As an interpreter you will receive from your audience in proportion as you give to them.

Summary

In this chapter we have examined the audience situation, some general characteristics of audience behavior, and relationships between the oral interpreter and the listener. We have learned that both performer and listener play an active role and must be sensitive to each other. The interpretation event may be said to be truly successful when reciprocity is established among writer, reader, and audience.

We know that attitude and training can blunt or sharpen perception, that the ability to discriminate among experiences and therefore to appreciate true artistry rarely comes to the immature person. We know, too, that the audience which elects to turn out or to tune in for a reading of poetry, drama, or other literature has responded in advance to some element in the interpretation form. Since the interpreter cannot do as much concretely and overtly for his audience as can be done with theatrical effects in full production, he must assume a willing cooperation on the part of those who come to hear him. Yet he can in no way sidestep his responsibility. Clarity to satisfy the rational powers of his listeners and vitality and suggestion sufficient to stimulate feeling and imagination are of the utmost importance. Attention must be held, and appropriate, adequate empathy aroused.

 *II*

Criteria for Interpretation

The highest requisite of a good speaker, a good reader or a good actor, is the power to see what is not visible to the eyes, to realize in imagination every situation, to see the end from the beginning by the imagination, and to realize a unity of purpose in each successive idea. Every artist must be a "maker-see." ∿ SAMUEL S. CURRY

The artist's work is the making of the emotive symbol; this making involves varying degrees of craftmanship, or technique. ∿
SUSANNE K. LANGER

A thoroughly competent critic is one who has both intimate experience with the art he is judging and possession of reliable criteria of criticism. ∿ STEPHEN C. PEPPER

WE BEGAN OUR STUDY OF INTERPRETATION with a survey of the nature of the art, linking it to the great rhetorical and poetic traditions. Then, in detail, we examined the nature of the literary object, the means for its analysis, and the application of our knowledge to particular kinds of writing. Next we turned to the interpreter's media, body and voice, and the development of skills in their use. In the last chapter we learned something about audiences and speaker-listener relationships. We are now ready to bring together the many aspects of

311

this writer-reader-audience event and to ask what is the configuration of factors that make up a successful or effective interpretation performance? What are the standards to which the interpreter should aspire? What are the criteria by which one is to judge the interpreter's performance?

These questions can be answered by a knowledge of certain aesthetic principles, which will now be considered. We have seen that interpretation itself is an art and that it is the interpreter's obligation to provide the listener with the aesthetic experience of the literature read. The aesthetic effect of the interpreter's performance, then, is limited first, as we have observed throughout our discussion, by what is inherent in the literature itself and next by the interpreter's control of (1) himself, (2) the literary object, and (3) the audience. We have examined various types of literature. Now let us consider these three aspects of control.

The Interpreter's Control of Himself

When we say that an interpreter has control of himself, we mean that he evidences respect for himself, for his media, for the literary object, and for his own artistic integrity. He wins prestige for himself in the eyes of the audience, being neither arrogant nor obsequious, yet poised and confident. He must earn fair-minded hearing for the literature by first being accepted by the audience as a person. His entire behavior will indicate a wish to share meanings and feelings with his audience. There assuredly is no *one* right thing to *do*; we cannot give specific rules for platform deportment! We can, nevertheless, state that the norm requires erect carriage, a good balance between tension and relaxation, a feeling of ease and friendliness, and an attitude of approaching, not withdrawing from, the audience. In the introduction to the program, at least, there will be direct eye contact, the most telling clue to mental directness, a primary requisite. Occasionally speakers seem able to maintain physical but not mental directness; they never seem to talk *to* others, they see their audience but do not look *at* them. No doubt mental directness, existing with or without direct eye contact, is allied to the speaker's interest in his audience and his wish to communicate thoughts and feelings.

Self-control implies, too, a mastery of skills of body and voice, resulting in neither denial nor idolatry of the media, but in what has been called the "expressive exploitation" of media.[1] Consider again the diagram in the first chapter.[2] There we see that the literature is Created Object I, its interpretation before an audience becoming Created Object II. Through his skills the interpretative artist reveals his understanding and artistic response. Thus we might say he is the art-instrument. As such, he brings to the interpretation performance a heightened awareness, a readiness to respond, a high degree of concentration, and skills of expression equal to the demands of the literary object. His entire behavior demonstrates a sense of authority in the situation.

On the negative side, let us say that control of self eliminates distracting factors such as affectations, mannerisms of body or voice, and evidences of stage fright or other self-consciousness. Facing an audience, the successful interpreter focuses his attention upon the thoughts and feelings of the literature, not upon himself; he does not listen to the sound of his own voice or admire the grace of his gestures. We hasten to add, however, that there is a *paradox* here, because in a sense the performer, no less than the listener, serves as critic during the interpretation performance. The interpreter shares his critical reactions to the literature with his listeners, and at the same time he must be a critic of all he does, guiding his performance constantly to put the audience into possession of the intended aesthetic experience. These two aspects of performance were what the Italian actor Tommaso Salvini had in mind when he said: "An actor lives, weeps, laughs on the stage, but as he weeps and laughs he observes his own tears and mirth. It is a double existence, this balance between life and acting that makes for art." [3] Communication, as Stanislavski says, is achieved by the external form the actor uses, and this external form implies control. This is as true for the interpreter as for the actor.

The Interpreter's Control of the Literary Object

In his preparation, in his effort to find the form appropriate to the literature, or to control the material, the interpreter will necessarily attend to his techniques. Just as there are in performance Created Ob-

---

[1] See Theodore M. Greene, *The Arts and the Art of Criticism* (Princeton: Princeton University Press, 1940), p. 401.

[2] See p. 7.

[3] Quoted by Constantin Stanislavski, *Building a Character* (New York: Theatre Arts Books, 1949), p. 167.

ject II and the interpretative artist, there are similarly two ways of looking at the art object, the "audience standpoint" and the "studio standpoint." [4] Now, as we speak of the control of the literary object, we are adopting the "studio standpoint," searching for the elements of form in the art of interpretation and for guides in the interpreter's preparatory practice.

Need of Form [5]

There are those who say all should be left to chance, to the inspiration of the moment, and that the interpreter must only "be natural"—a word which through the centuries has had many different meanings. Because we align ourselves with those who call the interpreter an artist and his performance one of the speech arts, we believe that, although an appearance of spontaneity must be kept, there is need of form. This is *not* saying there must be *this* or *that* form; it is an assertion only that there must be form, the need of which is universally recognized by aestheticians considering any art—painting, architecture, ballet, sculpture, literature (or even cooking!). Life is chaotic, nonselective, and accidental; art is ordered, discriminating, and patterned. Just as there can be no separation between form and function or form and substance of the human hand, for example, so, in art, there can be no dividing of form and content, or form and subject. In an earlier chapter we stated that the style of the writer is inseparable from what he says; likewise, in artistic performance, the style of utterance is an organic part of the literature. Control of the literature implies initially that the interpreter understands, appreciates, and responds to his material and that he finds a form of utterance equivalent to the style of the writing.

Form and Technique [6]

An artist's technique is his manner of giving form to the art object. In a craft, control of technique is the end sought. Not so in art, where technique is a *means*, a way of handling material, a use of the media. Technique is best when it is least conspicuous, either by its

---

[4] See Susanne K. Langer, *Feeling and Form* (New York: Charles Scribner's Sons, 1953), p. 393.
[5] See p. 6 f.
[6] See diagram, p. 7.

absence or presence. Without it there is no clear, discernible form; with an excess of it there is empty exhibitionism. Eugene O'Neill, American playwright, is quoted as saying, "Actors generally get between me and the performance; I catch myself recognizing the technique all the time and what they are doing when they put over a point."[7] O'Neill's remark recognizes the primacy of the script, whether the performance be acting or interpretation.

To repeat, the form of the interpretation must be equivalent to the form of the literature, from which it must spring. There are many definitions of form: it is organization, fulfillment of expectations, an ordered complex, and unity in diversity. When the form is apprehended, a totality is apparent, a total impact felt. By the time an interpreter comes to the end of a lyric, a story, or any selection, thoughts and feelings have taken "shape." When anything is well done, we say it has shape or form: after an exciting concert, the singer was in "good form"; after a disappointing golf tournament, the "pro" of our choice was in "bad form" and "his game went to pieces." By his form of expression, the interpreter must *keep together* the experience made available by the writer. To achieve this unity, he will reveal antitheses, expressed or implied; elements of variety and contrast; transitions of time, place, thought, and character; situation-attitude relationships; turning points and crises; and climax. (A word of warning: do not rely primarily upon an increase of loudness for climactic effect. There are more effective means—greater inner intensity of emotion, heightened bodily tension, and contrast or change in pitch or in rate and rhythm.) Recognizing that there can be no foreground without background, the interpreter will emphasize and subordinate in relation to the significance of the words spoken and their importance to the whole. By vocal change he will *point* key lines and call special attention to items of foreshadowing, anticipations, and repetitions that serve as motifs. Important items will be given more time, the less important hastened. Some ideas, we know, call for quickening, others for retardation; some for crescendo, others for diminuendo. Perhaps the most mature of all techniques, skillful timing leads to a sense of progression and movement, carrying the listener along to the end. Sometimes this progression is inherent in the regularized movement of ideas; sometimes the movement is not regularized. In either case, dependent upon repetition and expectancy, it constitutes rhythm, an essential of form.

---

[7] Quoted by Henry Hewes, *The Saturday Review* (November 24, 1956).

Rhythmic patterns, moreover, relate to and control emotion. Remembering that form, rhythm, and feeling are inseparable, the interpreter will look for nuances and shadings inherent in the author's words and give them emotional differentiation. He will widen the range of feeling and sharpen all possible contrasts to avoid the "disorganized mush" which is the inevitable result when an interpreter has failed to find the gesture of which the word is the symbol. "I laughed" and "I despised" may occur within seconds of one another in the text, but they demand wide difference in expression of body and voice.

The interpreter, in short, will know for what effect he is working and will make *use* of all the devices, in fact, which the writer before him has employed. Inasmuch as literature and interpretation are temporal arts, the form will remain latent until the end of the performance, but, bit by bit, it will take shape, yielding clarity of meaning and vividness of feeling.

Illusion and Aesthetic Distance

During the reading an illusion will be created, inducing the listener to believe the words spoken and infecting him with a specific quality of feeling. The interpreter must *seem* to be convinced that "Earth has not anything to show more fair," as he reads Wordsworth's description of London in the early morning, though he himself may prefer the sight of traffic on the freeway at five in the afternoon; he must *seem* to know pain as he tells us about Pepé's gangrenous wound in "Flight." The expression, in body and voice, must be an effect equal to the thought and feelings symbolized by the writer's words, which serve as cause. This is another way of saying that the interpreter must empathize before he speaks. As Langer says, "Verbal utterance is the overt issue of a greater emotional, mental, and bodily response, and its preparation in feeling and awareness or in the mounting intensity of thought is implicit in the words spoken. Speech is like a quintessence of action." [8] The utterance is the end process, and the interpreter must create an *illusion* of the inward activity which issues in speech. Simple exposition has one dimension of inward activity, angry dialogue another. The dimension of the performance must be equal to that of the thoughts and feelings denoted and connoted by the words.

---

[8] Langer, p. 314.

Note that we have again used the word *illusion,* for the reason that throughout the interpretation performance both interpreter and audience ideally maintain aesthetic distance, or a degree of *disinterestedness.* According to this theory concentration in aesthetic contemplation is on the immediate activity, whereas in situations of interestedness the emphasis is on the culmination of the activity. For instance, swimming for one's health is an interested, motive-full activity, whereas skin diving for fun is a disinterested activity. Or again,

Imagine a fog at sea. For most people it is an experience of acute unpleasantness. Apart from the physical annoyance and remoter forms of discomfort such as delays, it is apt to produce feelings of peculiar anxiety . . . The listless movements of the ship and her warning calls soon tell upon the nerves of the passengers; and that special, expectant, tacit anxiety and nervousness, always associated with this experience make a fog the dreaded terror of the sea . . . for the expert seafarer no less than for the ignorant landsman.

Nevertheless, a fog at sea can be a source of intense relish and enjoyment. Abstract from the experience of the sea fog . . . its danger and practical unpleasantness . . . direct the attention to the features "objectively" constituting the phenomenon—the veil surrounding you with an opaqueness as of transparent milk, blurring the outlines of things and distorting shapes into weird grotesqueness . . . note the curious, creamy smoothness of the water, hypocritically denying as it were, any suggestion of danger; and above all, the strange solitude and remoteness from the world, as it can be found only on the highest mountain tops; and the experience may acquire in its uncanny mingling of repose and terror, a flavor of such concentrated poignancy and delight as to contrast sharply with the blind and distempered anxiety of its other aspects . . . . our practical interest snaps like a wire and we watch the consummation of impending catastrophe with the marveling unconcern of a mere spectator.[9]

In essence, what Bullough is telling us is that passengers on the *Titanic* suffered through an *interested* experience, but that spectators of a moving picture depicting that story may suffer though a *dis*interested one, as they relive the terrors of those on the ship. The passengers had no aesthetic distance—they were busy trying to save themselves. In aesthetic appreciation, on the other hand, "incitements to struggle for self-preservation" are absent.

---

9 Edward Bullough, " 'Psychical Distance' as a Factor in Art and an Aesthetic Principle," *A Modern Book of Aesthetics,* edited by Melvin M. Rader, 3rd ed. (New York: Holt, Rinehart and Winston, Inc., Copyright 1960), p. 395.

For clarity, let us look at other examples. We may *enjoy* the almost unbearable tension of the scene in which Othello smothers Desdemona. Yet, if we did not know at the same time that we are experiencing an illusion, as decent human beings we would leap onto the stage to save the poor actress from death. We may appreciate the design and rhythm of the Laocoön statue—the figures of a man and his boys being crushed by a serpent. If we were to stumble upon such a scene in life, however, we would be impelled to come to their aid. (An amusing cartoon in *The New Yorker* showed an artist sketching just such a scene; the caption was: "Don't stand there sketching, man. Go get help!" The artist was maintaining a high degree of aesthetic distance!) One more illustration: an interpreter wept copiously as she read, from *Victoria Regina*, the scene following Albert's death. The listeners forgot all about Victoria in their concern for the poor girl whose nose got red and whose voice was choked. The reader was "underdistancing," which destroys aesthetic distance as effectively as does "overdistancing," the more common fault, especially of the beginning interpreter. Interpretation is not just voicing words. There must be feeling tone, there must be illusion. Yet the interpreter should never give an illusion so strong as to make himself and others forget the experience is one of art, not life. A *balance of empathy and aesthetic distance characterizes an artistic interpretation performance.*

Sense of Performance

Much of what we have said so far about control of self and of the literary object adds up to the interpreter's having a sense of performance. This very word *performance* has significance. It means the act of furnishing forth, of carrying out or into full execution, and of doing so in a set or formal manner, or with skill, or with a special technique. It demands that an interpreter be free from his book, glancing at it quickly and unobtrusively. It includes having a sense of the medium used, a sensitivity to it, and skill in its control. It calls for a high expenditure of energy and a convincing vitality. (George Bernard Shaw once said that no matter how artists might differ one from another all would share one common quality, vitality or a sense of aliveness.) A sense of performance leads to control of the audience, which is the third type of control we have said the interpreter must have in order to project an intended aesthetic response.

The Interpreter's Control of Audience

Interpretation cannot be mere private musing. It takes place before others, and good manners demand that the interpreter be aware of his audience and relate himself to them. Unless he gets and holds attention, of course, there can be no sharing of the literary object. This need of sharing brings up the whole matter of audience contact, which is not quite the same in interpretation as it is in effective public speaking or in the proscenium theater. That there must be rapport between audience and interpreter we have stated several times, but here too there is a paradox, because, although the interpreter is always reading *for* his audience, he does not always read *to* them. In Chapters 4 to 7, we found that, though some kinds of lines require direct eye contact, others seem too private for that, or that the interpreter should direct them to an imaginary and specified or defined listener. Some selections present an *open*, others a *closed* situation, and, as we have seen, reader-audience relationship is not the same in a lyric as in a story, or in a story as in a drama. Moreover, this relationship does not necessarily remain the same throughout any one reading, but it ebbs and flows as the attitude changes from a subjective or private to an objective or public one.

But whether the attitude be subjective or objective the interpreter must maintain a sense of "out-thereness." [10] The interpreter who has such a sense is said to *project*; without it, no matter how easily he may be heard—for projection is more than a matter of loudness—he is said *not* to project. In its roots, to project means to throw forward. The interpreter who projects gives such dimension to thoughts and feelings that they can be shared with everyone in the audience. He has a lively sense of communication, an awareness of how his listeners are responding, and an ability to adjust to their needs and desires. In a sense he thinks and feels for all who listen to him.

From the "audience standpoint," what are the tests of performance? We have already said that audiences gather with certain expectations. In the interpretation event, perhaps more than anything else the listener expects and wishes to be "moved," not to be "left cold." He does *not* want to remain indifferent or to hope the reading will soon end so that he can escape. He expects to be "bothered," to be "moved" by the words of the writer, to "care" about the subject matter, to

---

[10] See p. 257.

share the experience of the literature. He is ready to be stimulated in an appropriate manner, and, if the interpreter does not so stimulate him, the listener feels cheated or disappointed, failing to find the "aesthetic emotion" anticipated.

Saying that perception of good art always calls forth the aesthetic emotion, Langer defines the emotion as "a pervasive feeling of exhilaration" which gives us *forms of imagination* and *forms of feeling, inseparably.*" [11] When we find a performance of music, ballet, theater, or interpretation fully satisfying, indeed, we often use the word "exciting" as we speak of it. Just as we may have forgotten the munching of peanuts behind us, an aching back, a half-finished letter on the desk at home, or an appointment at the dentist's for tomorrow, so do we feel that the performance has carried us out of ourselves to the imaginative world of the poem, story, or play and that for the time being the only reality is what the writer is offering us. On the other hand, we do not want our feelings stirred over trifles. We do not want the interpreter to be like the Chekhovian character who is stirred by what is trivial and left untouched by what should move him, nor do we want him to be "passion's slave." Restraint is necessary, lest the listener be offended or embarrassed. He subconsciously, at least, must be assured that the interpreter has not only reserves of voice and bodily energy and expressiveness, but also reserves of emotion, that the inner intensity of the speaker could well produce utterance of even greater dimension, and that something has been left to imagination. On this point Roy Campbell spoke amusingly:

> They praise the firm restraint with which you write.
> I'm with you there of course.
> You use the snaffle and the curb all right,
> But where's the bloody horse? [12]

The interpreter's concentration will in turn control the concentration of the audience, so that the listeners forget both themselves and the reader and respond to the literary object. If appropriateness characterizes all that the reader does, the audience will accept the performance, "stay with" him, and be able to retain an image of the whole.

---

[11] Langer, p. 393 and p. 397.

[12] "On Some South American Novelists" in *Selected Poems* by Roy Campbell (Chicago: Henry Regnery Company, 1955), p. 198. Reprinted by permission of Henry Regnery Company.

The interpreter will seem to do everything needed or desired. At the end of the performance there will be a feeling of completion and satisfaction; feeling will have grown and led to a point of climax. The cognitive elements are indispensable in an aesthetic experience, but the affective ones bring us to the essence of the work of art.

To condense the matter of evaluating an interpretation performance, the listener who takes the active role of critic may well ask:

What response did the interpreter arouse? Was it appropriate to the literature? Can the listener retain an image of the whole?

What did the interpreter *do* to project meaning and to stir feelings? What did he do which hindered this? What could he have done to make thought clearer and feeling more vivid?

Did he control himself, his material, and his audience?

And when we come to the end of these questions there still seems to be an x quality, an indefinable something which, when the interpretation has truly yielded aesthetic pleasure, we cannot label, for it is indeed true that the total effect is greater than the sum of the parts. Perhaps this is where talent enters the picture. An artist's talent, according to Langer, is "essentially the native ability to handle such ideas as one has, to achieve desired effects. It seems to be closely linked with body-feeling, sensitivity, muscular control, verbal or tonal memory, as well as the one great mental requirement, aesthetic responsiveness . . . And what is known as 'average talent' for art can be developed to a considerable extent by giving it exercise." [13]

Also, each interpreter has his own style, the "particular individualized manner of execution that permeates any highly integrated volitional activity," [14] and it relates to all the coexistent, complex factors of personality. Just as the pianist or violinist gives us something that is not in the score, so the interpreter projects the literary object through his own prism or "personal idiom." (Chopin said that Liszt found values in Chopin's compositions, of which he, the composer, had not been aware.) The particular relationships of mind, emotional capacity, physique, voice, attitudes, and sensitivity of the individual yield, in some happy cases, memorable and pleasurable results.

---

[13] Langer, p. 407.

[14] Gordon W. Allport, *Personality, A Psychological Interpretation* (New York: Henry Holt and Company, Inc., 1937), p. 490.

Conclusion

In the first chapter of this book we indicated that to be artistic, the act of interpretation must result in a recognizable and memorable form and yield pleasure to the observer or listener. In the present chapter we have been exploring the ramifications of that idea.

Although we have found few absolutes for our criteria of excellence in the art of interpretation, we believe the generic aesthetic traits of unity in variety, theme, thematic variation, emphasis, and evolution according to a rhythmic pattern exist here as in other arts.[15] Like other performers, the interpreter will exhibit strength and vitality, ease, precision, and clear purpose—integrating sound, meaning, and feeling. He will arouse a pleasurable, intended response from his hearers, bringing them to the full aesthetic experience of the literary object.

In conclusion, let us say that, although it is true great art is precisely that which never was nor will be taught, the art of interpretation lies closer within the reach of the ordinary man than does any other art. The very fact that it is an art of language gives it a universality in range of a man's potentialities and in audience appeal which none but the speech arts approximate. From it, both interpreter and listener can find that moment "during which all the powers and processes of mind and body are functioning harmoniously, and which leaves us in a state of heightened vitality physically, and exaltation, spiritually." [16] This is the service, indeed, of *all* art, and to such a standard must the interpreter consecrate his powers.

---

[15] See Eliseo Vivas, *Creation and Discovery* (New York: Noonday Press, 1955), p. 97.

[16] Max Schoen, *Art and Beauty* (New York: The Macmillan Company, 1932), p. 154.

Programing

There can be no interpretation without the collaboration of the audience, and that collaboration it is the business of the artist to secure. ∽ PAUL M. PEARSON

IN THIS CHAPTER we shall look at some of the more public aspects of interpretation. In recent years there has arisen an increased demand for the interpreter's services at school, club, church, civic, and other gatherings. The appearances of the Drama Quartette, which triumphantly toured the country reading Shaw's "Don Juan in Hell," [1] quickened general interest in hearing literature interpreted by persons with superior skill in the art. Since then other professional groups have presented similar programs. As we have already indicated, however, interpretation is not a new art. Writers of early Greece and Rome, in their attempt to reach their public, depended upon oral presentation of their works; through the centuries storytellers have occupied high positions among many peoples; and in late nineteenth-century America, with the growth of the Chautauqua circuit, readers of power and skill delighted audiences and received handsome remuneration for their efforts. Styles have changed in interpretation as in public speaking or other arts, but the art itself has remained popular. (The Interpretation Interest Group is the largest of those in the

---

[1] The third act of *Man and Superman*, often omitted when the play is produced.

323

Speech Association of America.) At present there is wide interest on the part of both those who read to others and those who make up the audiences. In short, there seems to be general recognition that literature comes to its full life only when it is well spoken.

Let us suppose that, as an interpreter, you have achieved sufficient skills in analysis and in your control of self, literary object, and audience to present programs for various groups, on various occasions, either as a solo interpreter or as a member of a group. We shall now examine some of the general principles of programing which will guide you as a solo interpreter in selection and arrangement of materials.

Programs

Selection of Literature

It is beyond the scope of this book to treat literary criticism except as it pertains to the analysis of the literary object. We urge the interpreter to read widely, to acquaint himself with the best of the old and the new, and to remember that the development of taste and judgment in any art is a lifetime proposition. We urge that the interpreter learn the principles upon which writing is to be judged and limit himself to writings of high standard. Even so, he faces problems of selection.

Suppose you find Thurber's "The Night the Bed Fell on Father" utterly hilarious, Poe's "Annabel Lee" moving, and Hemingway's "The Killers" exciting. Should you put them together for a program? This is the kind of question any interpreter faces when he has been asked to appear before a group. The answer is seldom found in lumping together, hit-and-miss, three or four favorite selections.

Like any speaker, the interpreter must first consider the nature of the audience and the occasion. One interpreter at a memorial service read the last act of Thornton Wilder's *Our Town*, and for the particular audience this proved a good choice, whereas Evelyn Waugh's *The Loved One*, which also concerns death, would have been a miserable choice. An interpreter's program must meet the audience's expectations, tastes, education, and general cultural patterns and suit the reason for which the audience has assembled. The general age level and the preponderance or men or women are also factors to be taken into account. The more homogeneous the audience the simpler is the matter of choice of literature. A group of college seniors who have been studying contemporary poetry should respond favorably to a program of such poetry, but an assembly of high school freshmen might not. Scenes from *Volpone* by Ben Jonson may delight an audience which would be bored by *No Time for Sergeants,* and vice versa. Language of the kind in *The Home of the Brave,* acceptable to a group of veterans, would probably alienate a missionary society. In some cases, serious, difficult material may be appropriate for both audience and occasion; in others, nonsense verses. The formality or informality of the situation is likewise a factor. Special occasions like Christmas, Thanksgiving, or other holidays call for particular kinds of material.

Having analyzed the audience and occasion, the interpreter chooses from literature characterized by universality, emotional and imaginative appeal, variety and contrast, progression and climax. He may, of course, solve his programing problem by deciding to use a single essay, lyric, narrative, or drama. He may limit himself to selections by some one author. If, however, he chooses to use several selections by different authors, he will need to find a way of combining them into a unified whole; he will wisely choose a central idea to which he can relate the selections. He may arrive at this by choosing one selection suitable for the particular audience and occasion and then looking for others which can be used with it to make a balanced, unified program, *or* he may choose a theme and then look for selections. In either case, the program must fit a specified time limit; have a beginning, middle, and end; build to a climax; and create a unified effect.[2]

General Principles of Arrangement

Although for certain audiences or on particular occasions it might be wise to depart from the observations we are about to make, we can say that the opening selection of a miscellaneous program should be relatively short, fairly light in tone, and open, rather than closed, in situation. It should have wide appeal and employ a structure relatively easy to comprehend, being neither the most humorous nor the most emotional part of the program. It takes a few minutes to "polarize" the audience, to prepare them for their best listening, and to

---

[2] See p. 328 f. for sample programs.

lead them to their readiest empathy. Essay or narrative will probably, in most cases, serve better than lyric or drama, and the subject matter should be within the realm of experience of most persons in the audience.

The interpreter will place toward the end of the program that which he most wants his listeners to remember. It is desirable that this number be broadest in comedy or strongest in emotional appeal, building to a higher climax than what precedes it, although there are times when it is advisable to follow the selection of strongest emotion by a briefer, more relaxed one which serves much the same purpose as the scene of resolution which Shakespeare uses at the end of his plays. In other words, the emotion may be too strong to leave the audience there; the listener may need a few moments of letdown after the peak of emotion, moments to catch his breath and return to the world of reality. Frost's "Home Burial," for example, might well be the climax of a program, but it would be a poor closing number.

Between the first and last number the interpreter will place selections which develop his central idea, and so carry the program forward, and which contribute to variety and contrast. It is prudent to let the selections vary in length, structure, attitude, and emotion, and to avoid placing together those too much alike in the cognitive and the affective elements or in style. One number may, of course, lead into another, and too wide a jump from one emotion to another is not easily accomplished. Yet, within the program as a whole, there are, ideally, sharp contrasts.

Short poems or excerpts are usually better grouped together, for the program, like the interpreter's performance, must have shape or form. A selection too short to stand alone—a sonnet, for example—will be lost, outbalanced by the other numbers, unless it is part of a larger unit within the whole. In his recordings "The Ages of Man" and "One Man in His Time," John Gielgud admirably succeeds in combining a number of short selections and achieving unity.

If the selections are all the work of one author, they will need to be arranged in some sort of developmental order. Sometimes a chronological arrangement makes good programing; sometimes a topical grouping is better. Whatever the arrangement, it is wise to choose representative selections, endeavoring to introduce the listeners to many facets of the author's works. Again, special attention must be given to the climactic order within the groups as well as within the whole program.

We have mentioned a sense of progression in relation to both the literary object and the interpreter's performance. Likewise, a program should yield this sense of "going somewhere," of one thing leading to another, and of "coming full circle" at the end. The audience should leave with a sense of satisfaction and completion, feeling that the journey taken with the interpreter has reached its objective and been worthwhile.

Introductions

The introduction to a program serves to relate the interpreter to the audience and the audience to the literature. A bald statement such as, "I am going to read 'The Catbird Seat' by Thurber," is hardly an adequate introduction. No better is one that merely adds the author's birth and death dates to an announcement of title and author. Contrasted with such laconic introductions are those going on and on until all audience interest is lost and those giving a full paraphrase of the selection to follow. Time should not be wasted in the introduction, but enough information to orient the audience to interpreter and literary object is essential.

Sometimes it is wise to refer to the occasion which has brought the audience together, to a recent event known to all, or to some kind of common bond between interpreter and audience. Sometimes it is a good idea to tell briefly why one has chosen a certain theme, author, or selection. Whatever is said should arouse curiosity and eagerness to listen to the literature, pointing the direction the program will take and probably hinting at the response sought.

Here is an introduction to a miscellaneous, hour-long program presented to an adult audience of men and women:

My theme tonight is "Women." You all remember, I know, the nursery rhyme we used to chant, "What are little girls made of? Sugar and spice and all things nice." You remember too the Biblical story of the creation of Eve. More than 2000 years ago a Greek satirist, Simonides, set down his ideas about what women are made of; he wrote: . . .

Then the interpreter read a few sentences from the humorous essay by Simonides.

Do not conclude from this sample introduction that a funny story should always be included. There is nothing much worse than dragging in such a story, willy-nilly. On the other hand, when the story is appropriate for the occasion and pertinent to what follows, it may be a good way to start the process of "polarization."

Here is an example of an introduction that alienated a classroom audience of college men and women:

I am going to read the final scene from *Death of a Salesman* by Arthur Miller. You may have heard this scene called sentimental. People who call it that or people who say that this play is not high tragedy are pseudo-critics and pseudo-intellectuals. I have no patience with such intellectual snobbery or superficiality. The play is definitely tragedy, and there is no sentimentality in it.

The interpreter here assumed that everyone in his audience held his view, but, unfortunately, there were some who felt he was labeling *them* "pseudo-intellectuals." Even those who agreed with him about the play were uncomfortably aware that he had offended some of his listeners. Interpreters should not be so lacking in tact.

Some additional *don'ts* for introductions are:

1. Do not apologize for your selection or for anything else. ("I couldn't find a story I really liked, but this one will have to do.")
2. Do not antagonize the audience by talking down to them or by giving them information it is reasonable to suppose they know. ("I am going to read a scene from *Abe Lincoln in Illinois*. Lincoln is a famous American who was President during the Civil War.")
3. Do not throw out false leads. ("Amy Lowell was a famous poet. She smoked black cigars. I shall now read 'Lilacs.'")
4. Do not read your opening remarks with your nose buried in the text. (It is preferable to speak extemporaneously rather than to read an introduction.)

And the chief *do* is to establish rapport with your audience, remembering that the introduction serves as a bridge between interpreter and audience and between audience and literature.

Transitions

When the program is composed of more than one number, the interpreter will need to make smooth transitions in moving from one selection to the next. Here again he should be brief and to the point, but often a minimum of two or three sentences will be necessary to lead from one selection to another. Sometimes a word or phrase from a preceding selection can be related to the next one. Sometimes points of similarity can be mentioned, sometimes aspects of contrast. An interpreter, for example, who finished an essay about Grandma and her garden from Bertha Damon's *Grandma Called It Carnal*, said:

Grandma's love of flowers is perhaps typical of the New Englander, for about almost any country doorstep are clusters of lilacs. To Amy Lowell lilacs are a symbol of New England, as we see in her poem entitled "Lilacs."

Following this poem the same interpreter said:

Many other New England writers share Amy Lowell's feeling of pride and her sense of identity with her native region. Robert Tristram Coffin once said that the greatest luck that could come to anyone was to be born in Maine. From his *Maine Ballads* I have chosen three to read for you. The first . . .

Not only do the transitional remarks prepare the listener for the next selection, but they are also moments of slight relaxation, and the interpreter should take advantage of them as such. The more intense the emotion in any particular selection, the more necessary it will be to give the audience time between numbers, a few moments for them to reflect on what has just been experienced, to shift weight, or to indulge in a cough which has been suppressed. The skillful interpreter will be sensitive to the audience's empathy at this time, just as he is during the actual reading, and he will adjust to their needs, pausing as is necessary.

Sample Programs

As we have said, a program should yield a unified total effect. Central ideas or themes around which the program can be arranged are almost infinite in number. Here is a list to which you can add:

Americana	Marriage
Animals	Remembrances of Childhood
Battle of the Sexes	Scenes and Characters of New
Children	England (of the South; of
Cities	the Northwest; of the
Death	Pacific; and so on)
Husbands and Wives	Southern Writers
Jealousy	War
Kings and Queens	Woman Looks at Man
Man Looks at Woman	Women

Below are a number of sample programs, which will suggest still other possibilities of selection and arrangement.

I

The Winter Poetry of Robert Frost

1. a) The Onset
   b) The Runaway
2. a) Dust of Snow
   b) A Patch of Old Snow
   c) Looking for a Sunset Bird in Winter
3. An Old Man's Winter Night
4. Snow
5. a) Good Hours
   b) Stopping by Woods on a Snowy Evening
6. Good Bye and Keep Cold

II

Man Looks at Woman

1. a) She Was a Phantom of Delight ....William Wordsworth
   b) She Walks in Beauty ....Lord Byron
   c) Romeo and Juliet (II.ii.1–25) ....William Shakespeare
   d) Song ....John Donne
2. The Catbird Seat ....James Thurber

III

The Other Side of Love in the Spring

1. The Unicorn in the Garden .... James Thurber
2. a) Barbara Allen .... Anonymous
   b) La Belle Dame sans Merci .... John Keats
   c) Neutral Tones .... Thomas Hardy
3. Scenes from *The Father* .... August Strindberg

IV

Scenes and Characters of New England

1. "Cowslips" from *Grandma Called It Carnal* .... Bertha Damon
2. a) Lilacs .... Amy Lowell
   b) Selections from *Maine Ballads*........ Robert P. Tristram Coffin
   c) Mr. Flood's Party .... Edwin Arlington Robinson
3. A Servant to Servants .... Robert Frost
4. Excerpts from *Our Town* .... Thornton Wilder

Readers' Theater

A book published in London in 1806 stated:

Another species of dramatic reading has of late years been practised in private companies assembled for that purpose. It differs from that just mentioned [one person reading a play] by limiting each individual to the reading of the part of a single character. In this entertainment, as on the stage, the characters of the drama are distributed among the readers according to their supposed talents; and each being furnished with a separate book, either the whole play, or certain select scenes from one or more, are read by the performers sitting around a table, whilst others of the company serve as the audience. The reading is performed by each in his best manner, the part allotted to each is often nearly committed to memory, and such gestures are used as can be conveniently executed in a sitting position posture. Higher efforts are here required in order to keep the auditors alive to the interest of the scene, thus divided and stript of all that aids delusion, and mutilated of its complete action. On these occasions . . . sometimes dresses are assumed or modified the more nearly to approach theatrical exhibition . . .[3]

---

[3] Gilbert Austin, *Chironomia* (London, 1806), pp. 203–204.

In the early part of the present century a similar form of presentation was called Library Playreading, and today it is occasionally called that, but more often the term Readers' Theater is heard. The form employs both dramatic and nondramatic literature and has no completely uniform methods, but its effectiveness when handled by persons of taste and skill is seldom disputed. It is amazing how quickly audiences accept the conventions of the form and how their imaginations respond to fill in details of setting, costume, lights, and action. Many listeners find it a more satisfactory form than that of a full-scale dramatic production.

Selection of Literature

A wide range of literature has been successfully used by Readers' Theater groups, including these titles: [4]

Essay, Lyric, Narrative

A Christmas Carol .... Charles Dickens
Brother to Dragons .... Robert Penn Warren
Canterbury Tales .... Geoffrey Chaucer
Dear Liar: the Letters of GBS and Mrs. Patrick Campbell
John Brown's Body .... Stephen Vincent Benét
I Knock at the Door .... Sean O'Casey
The Adventures of Alice in
    Wonderland .... Lewis Carroll
The Aspern Papers .... Henry James
The Beast in the Jungle .... Henry James
The Bridge of San Luis Rey .... Thornton Wilder
The Devil and Daniel Webster .. Stephen Vincent Benét
The Open Boat .... Stephen Crane
The Ring and the Book .... Robert Browning
The Short Happy Life of
    Francis Macomber .... Ernest Hemingway
Segregation .... Robert Penn Warren
Tristram .... Edwin Arlington Robinson

---

[4] When the presentation is part of an educational program, without charge for admission, permissions are generally granted gratis.

Antigone ....Sophocles
Blood Wedding ....Federico Garcia-Lorca
Blithe Spirit ....Noel Coward
Hedda Gabler ....Henrik Ibsen
John Gabriel Borkman ....Henrik Ibsen
King Lear ....William Shakespeare
Phèdre ....Jean Racine
The Circle ....Somerset Maugham
The Great God Brown ....Eugene O'Neill
The Glass Menagerie ....Tennessee Williams
The Importance of Being Earnest .....Oscar Wilde
The Other House ....Henry James
The Silver Cord ....Sidney Howard
The Way of the World ....William Congreve
Troilus and Cressida ....William Shakespeare
Under Milk Wood ....Dylan Thomas

An examination of these titles will reveal that farce does not lend itself easily to this form of interpretation. Selections emphasizing ideas, characters, and mental and emotional conflict between them, rather than situation, will be good choices.

Techniques

Obviously some of the titles listed require a large cast, others a small one. For some it would be feasible to have several parts read by one person, and some require a narrator to keep the central thread of the material clear and to give unity to the whole. In all cases, a director is needed to keep the attitude, idea, and style unified.

All that has been said in earlier chapters regarding the techniques of the individual interpreter, both in analysis and in performance, applies to Readers' Theater. In addition, there are some conventions and principles which can be stated.

Scripts are always used, reading stands may or may not be used. Interpreters may be seated in a semicircle of chairs and read from their seats; they may be seated upstage, coming forward to read at stands placed in a row or slightly curved line downstage, returning to their chairs when they are no longer in the scene. They may be seated on high stools before individual reading stands, or they may get to their feet for parts of the reading.

Even when seated, the interpreter can suggest entrances and exits by slight shifts of body weight or slight turns. When "on scene" he must listen actively to all lines read and respond in facial expression and body tension. Indeed, this listening technique is one of the chief requisites of the form; without it the performance falls apart. Some directors prefer that all eyes be upon the speaker, whose eyes are never —or almost never—turned to those on stage. Others want both listeners and speakers to look *out* at all times. When not "on scene" the interpreter, it is generally agreed, should closely follow the lines of the text, keeping his eyes on the script and remaining as motionless as possible, in order to do nothing to call attention away from the lines as they are spoken.

One of the difficulties for the interpreter not experienced in this form is to keep a sense of characters talking to each other and yet not to bring the scene "on stage," for the convention of the fourth wall does not obtain in Readers' Theater. Whether dialogue is being read by one interpreter or by several, the scene is kept in the realm of the audience. Lines of dialogue are addressed to a character visualized in the distance, but the angle of address can be changed slightly as one person or another is spoken to. (This is a point of difference between solo interpretation and group presentation. In the former, the interpreter is usually advised to adhere to one angle for any given character.)[5] Throughout the performance the individual interpreters must maintain a sense of location or environment, imagining vividly the place of the action and realizing the movement of others within the scene.

When the material is not limited to dialogue alone, parts of it may be addressed directly to the audience: exposition, description, and nondramatized narration. Sometimes a narrator handles all such material, sometimes not. For example, in arranging a short story, it may be effective to assign all description, interior speech, and dialogue of one character to one interpreter, letting a narrator read those parts not specifically limited to one character or another. In a long presentation two narrators may be used, as is indicated in the script of *Under Milk Wood* by Dylan Thomas.

As the dialogue moves from one speaker to another, cues must, of course, be properly handled. This is one of the reasons that all persons in the group should follow the text at all times. A speaker entering a

---

[5] See Chapter 7.

scene must fit his entire manner to what has just preceded. He must understand what motivation brings him into the scene and, later, what takes him out of it. He will adjust to the level of loudness, for example, set by the other interpreters, departing from that level only for purposive contrast, and he will keep up the pace of the scene, working with the others to build climax, but sacrificing none of the values of the material. The basic rhythm of the literature must be sensed by the entire group, and each interpreter must fit himself to it.

Problems of characterization are the same as for the solo interpreter. The physical, mental, and emotional make-up of the character must be imagined fully, his motivations understood, and his purposes analyzed. Full action will not be depicted, but revelation of attitude is important. The body and voice must manifest the meaning and feeling of all words spoken, and specific actions are to be suggested.[6] There are times when it may seem appropriate for an interpreter to move from one reading stand to another, following the entrance or exit of one or more participants, and sometimes, in a symbolic fashion, one area of the forestage is reserved for certain characters or certain threads of the plot of story or drama. Movement to indicate transitions may need to be larger than in the solo interpretation performance.

Whatever is done in Readers' Theater, nevertheless, as in the solo performance, should grow out of the demands of the literature. This principle holds not only for the reading of the text but also for whatever is done in the way of staging and lights. The nightmarish quality of *The Adventures of Alice in Wonderland* was, in one production, artistically brought into focus by the use of platforms and pencil lighting, devices which should not be used indiscriminately. Without being obtrusive, the type of chair or stool used can suggest a particular environment, as can the clothing worn by the interpreters. Color, line, and texture of dress or suit can contribute to the over-all effect. Formal evening attire sets one tone, informal dress another. Sometimes a degree of uniformity in dress is wise—in the performance of *Alice* mentioned before, it seemed proper to have all but Alice in plain black street clothes with no ornamentation of any kind and Alice in a very simple blue and white gingham. In a performance of *Mary Stuart* it proved most effective to have Mary in a modified period dress of brilliant red velveteen. In any case, it is suggested that only modifications of modern dress are suitable, and lighting should be for

---

6 See Chapter 8.

mood, not for realistic or representative effect. (A basic consideration for lights is that the readers be able to see their scripts and that their faces be seen by the audience.)

Generally speaking, the interpreter does well to adhere to texts where properties are unnecessary. Unless used with great care and taste, they will only call attention to themselves, pull the scene "on stage," and seem an anachronism. Seldom, if ever, are they needed. If the interpreters fully accept the medium of Readers' Theater, imagining details of setting, lights, costume, and action, the audience will do the same and will reject "imaginary gardens with real toads in them," [7] which the use of properties may become.

Sound effects likewise are generally unsuitable. In *Hedda Gabler*, for instance, there is no need to produce the "off-stage" pistol shot at the end of the play, any more than there is need earlier to have a real stove into which Hedda thrusts a real manuscript. The lines of dialogue make explicit the action which, suggested by the interpreter, is completed in both interpreter's and listener's imagination.

The ultimate challenge in Readers' Theater is to create a unified whole and not to leave the audience feeling that five or six people have been in front of them, holding scripts and reading, but bearing no relation to one another. The "star" system is totally out of place, and each interpreter at all times must contribute to the total effect sought.

Summary

An interpreter faces problems in choosing and arranging materials to be presented for certain audiences on certain occasions. After he has analyzed both audience and occasion, he will follow general principles, explained in this chapter, in selecting and arranging the literature. He will remember that certain kinds of material are better for the opening of a program, others for the close. Also, he will endeavor to plan a program having variety and contrast, progression and climax, and unity.

Introductions and transitions should be brief, pertinent, and tactful. A number of sample themes and programs have been included to illustrate principles of arrangement.

---

[7] See p. 146.

In the second half of the chapter the form of interpretation called Readers' Theater has been described. Titles of material suitable for this form of presentation cover a wide range in structure, content, and style. Techniques of presentation vary according to the demands of the literature, just as in solo work, and all of the techniques explained earlier in this book apply to the individual interpreter's participation in the group form. In addition, there are certain aspects of performance demanding special attention in Readers' Theater, which, we repeat, must yield a total, unified impact.

Bibliography

This is a selected bibliography and does not include titles to which reference has been made earlier.

GENERAL

Bacon, Wallace A., and Robert S. Breen. *Literature as Experience*. New York: McGraw-Hill Book Company, Inc., 1959.

Boleslavski, Richard. *Acting: The First Six Lessons*. New York: Theatre Arts Books, 1933, 1949.

Butcher, Samuel Henry. *Aristotle's Theory of Poetry and Fine Art, with a critical text and translation of the Poetics*. With a prefatory essay, Aristotelian Literary Criticism, by John Gassner. 4th ed. New York: Dover Publications, 1951.

Cobin, Martin. *Theory and Technique of Interpretation*. Englewood Cliffs, N.J.: Prentice-Hall, Inc., 1959.

Cowley, Malcolm, ed. *Writers at Work: The Paris Review Interviews*. New York: The Viking Press, Inc., 1958.

Cunningham, Cornelius Carman. *Literature as a Fine Art*. New York: The Ronald Press Company, 1941.

Dolman, John, Jr. *The Art of Reading Aloud*. New York: Harper & Brothers, 1956.

Duncan, Hugh Dalziel. *Language and Literature in Society*. Chicago: The University of Chicago Press, 1953.

Geiger, Don. *Oral Interpretation and Literary Study*. South San Francisco, California: Pieter Van Vloten, 1958.

Lee, Charlotte I. *Oral Interpretation*, 2nd ed. Boston: Houghton Mifflin Company, 1959.

Lowrey, Sara, and Gertrude E. Johnson. *Interpretative Reading*, rev. ed. New York: Appleton-Century-Crofts, Inc., 1953.

McGaw, Charles. *Acting is Believing*. New York: Rinehart & Company, Inc., 1955.

Selden, Samuel. *The Stage in Action*. New York: F. S. Crofts & Company, 1941.

Seldes, Gilbert. *The Great Audience*. New York: The Viking Press, Inc., 1950.

————— *The Public Arts*. New York: Simon & Schuster, Inc., 1956.

Seyler, Athene, and Stephen Haggard. *The Craft of Comedy*, 2nd ed. New York: Theatre Arts Books, 1957.

Sherif, Muzafer, and Carolyn W. Sherif. *Groups in Harmony and Tension; An Integration of Studies on Intergroup Relations*. New York: Harper & Brothers, 1953.

Smith, Joseph F., and James R. Linn. *Skill in Reading Aloud*. New York: Harper & Brothers, 1960.

Woolbert, Charles H., and Severina E. Nelson. *The Art of Interpretative Speech*, 4th ed. New York: Appleton-Century-Crofts, Inc., 1954.

LITERARY CRITICISM AND AESTHETICS

Beebe, Maurice, ed. *Literary Symbolism: An Introduction to the Interpretation of Literature*. San Francisco: Wadsworth Publishing Company, Inc., 1960.

Brooks, Cleanth. *Modern Poetry and the Tradition*. Chapel Hill: The University of North Carolina Press, 1939.

————— and Robert B. Heilman, eds. *Understanding Drama*. New York: Henry Holt & Company, Inc., 1945.

————— and Robert Penn Warren, eds. *Understanding Fiction*. New York: Appleton-Century-Crofts, Inc., 1943.

————————— *Understanding Poetry*, rev. ed. New York: Henry Holt & Company, Inc., 1950.

Cooper, Charles W. *Preface to Drama*. New York: The Ronald Press Company, 1955.

Crane, Ronald S., ed. *Critics and Criticism, Ancient and Modern*. Chicago: The University of Chicago Press, 1952.

Day-Lewis, Cecil. *The Poetic Image*. New York: Oxford University Press, 1947.

Dewey, John. *Art as Experience*. New York: Minton, Balch & Company, 1934.

Eliot, T. S. *Selected Essays, 1917–1932*. New York: Harcourt, Brace and Company, Inc., 1932.

Housman, Alfred Edward. *The Name and Nature of Poetry*. New York: The Macmillan Company, 1933.

Hyman, Stanley Edgar. *The Armed Vision: A Study in the Methods of Modern Literary Criticism*. New York: Alfred A. Knopf, Inc., 1948; Vintage ed., abridged, 1955.

James, Henry. *The Art of the Novel: Critical Prefaces*. New York: Charles Scribner's Sons, 1934.

Kerr, Walter. *How Not to Write a Play*. New York: Simon & Schuster, 1955.

Kitto, Humphrey Davy Findley. *Form and Meaning in Drama*. London: Methuen & Company, Ltd., 1956.

Langer, Susanne K. *Problems of Art*. New York: Charles Scribner's Sons, 1957.

Lubbock, Percy. *The Craft of Fiction*. London: Jonathan Cape, Ltd., 1926; paperback ed., New York: The Viking Press, 1957.

Lucas, F. L. *Greek Drama for Everyman*. New York: The Macmillan Company, 1954.

——————— *Tragedy: Serious Drama in Relation to Aristotle's Poetics*, rev. ed. New York: The Macmillan Company, 1958.

Main, C. F., and Peter J. Seng. *Poems: The Wadsworth Handbook and Anthology*. San Francisco: Wadsworth Publishing Company, Inc., 1961.

O'Connor, William V., ed. *Forms of Modern Fiction*. Minneapolis: University of Minnesota Press, 1948.

Prall, D. W. *Aesthetic Analysis*. New York: Thomas Y. Crowell Company, 1936.

Richards, Ivor Armstrong. *How to Read a Page*. New York: W. W. Norton & Company, Inc., 1942.

——————— *Practical Criticism*. New York: Harcourt, Brace and Company, Inc., 1929.

Schramm, Wilbur Lang. *Approaches to a Science of English Verse.* Iowa City, Iowa: State University of Iowa Press, 1935.

Stallman, Robert Wooster, ed. *Critiques and Essays in Criticism 1920–1948.* New York: The Ronald Press Company, 1949.

Stauffer, Donald A. *The Nature of Poetry.* New York: W. W. Norton & Company, 1946.

Tate, Allen, ed. *The Language of Poetry.* Princeton, N.J.: Princeton University Press, 1942.

Vivas, Eliseo, and Murray Krieger, eds. *Problems of Aesthetics.* New York: Rinehart & Company, Inc., 1953.

West, Ray B., ed. *Essays in Modern Literary Criticism.* New York: Rinehart & Company, Inc., 1952.

INDICES

Baird, A. Craig, ed. *American Public Addresses, 1740–1952.* New York: McGraw-Hill Book Company, Inc., 1956.

————— *Representative American Speeches.* New York: The H. W. Wilson Company (annually, 1938–present).

Bruncken, Herbert, ed. *Subject Index to Poetry; A Guide for Adult Readers.* Chicago: American Library Association, 1940.

Cook, Dorothy E., and Isabel S. Monro, comps. *Short Story Index: An Index to 60,000 Stories in 4320 Collections.* New York: The H. W. Wilson Company, 1953.

Granger, Edith. *Granger's Index to Poetry,* 4th ed. New York: Columbia University Press, 1953.

Hastings, Henry C., comp. *Spoken Poetry on Records and Tapes; An Index of Currently Available Recordings.* Chicago: American Library Association, 1957.

Ottemiller, John Henry. *Index to Plays in Collections; An Author and Title Index to Plays Appearing in Collections Published Between 1900 and 1950,* 2nd ed. New York: The Scarecrow Press, Inc., 1951.

Paperbound Books in Print: An Index to 4500 Inexpensive Reprints and Original Editions with Selective Subject Guide. New York: R. R. Bowker Company (semiannually).

Sutton, Roberta Briggs, comp. *Speech Index: An Index to 64 Collections of World Famous Orations and Speeches for Various Occasions.* New York: The H. W. Wilson Company, 1935.

342   *Bibliography*

———— *Speech Index 1935–1955*. New York: The Scarecrow Press, Inc., 1956.

West, Dorothy H., and Dorothy M. Peake, comps. *Play Index: 1949–1952*. New York: The H. W. Wilson Company, 1953.

Index of Topics

345

Analysis, literary object, 65–66
Analysis, model, 79–87
Anapestic foot, 56
Angles of address, *see* Address, angles of
Appreciation, an active process, 306
Appropriateness, 47, 281, 289
  examples, 324
  to given audience, 17
  to given occasion, 15
  tests of vocal, 290
  see also Preparation, drama
Aristotle, 14, 52
Art, 7–11
  defined, 7–9, 322
  form implied, 7
  organization of experience, 7
  originality, 8
  pleasurable response, 8, 11
    interpreter's treatment, 201
    situation, theme, 8
Assonance, 123, 127, 134
Attention, controlling factors, 302
Attitude of speaker, physical, 220
Audience:
  control of attention, 302–303
  defined, 300
  determining needs, 300–301
  effect on interpreter, 10
  factor in programing, 17, 324
  "feedback," 304–305
  individual and group, 301–302
  interpreter's rapport with, 306–308
  limitations, 17
  listening vs. hearing, 303, 304
    listening faults, 305
  role in interpretation event, 299–302
  speech vs. essay, 69–70
  see also Empathy
Auditory appeal, 122
Austin, Gilbert, 331
Author, *see* Writer

B

Balance, 84
Ballad, metrical design, 58
Baum, Paull Franklin, 56
Behavior tendencies:
  approach, withdrawal, 250–251
Bibliography, general, 339–343
Blackmur, R. P., 45
Blair, Dr. Hugh, 270
Blending, 272
  equated with closed juncture, 278–279
Bodily expression:
  as a whole, 251–252
  degree of movement, 257
  expansion, contraction, 251–252
  face, 253–254
    reflecting sensory responses, 254
  factor in stage presence, 252
  hands, 253
  head, 253
  interaction with voice, 246–247
  necessity for control, 254
  parts, 252–255
  physical nerve center, 251–252
  posture, 251–252
  practice materials, 260–266
  relation, parts to whole, 256
  relation to vocal expression, 245–247, 267–268
  shifts in weight, 252
  tension, relaxation, 257
  see also Body
Body:
  basic behavior tendencies, 250
  criteria for effectiveness, 257–259
  management and control, 10, 220, 251
  response related to emotion, 249–250
    no set patterns, 251
  see also Action, Bodily expression
Boyer, Charles, 4

Introduction to play:
  establishing the mood, 203
  methods, 203, 223
  proportion to the whole, 203
Irony, 39, 44, 60, 129, 134

J

Judgment, criteria for, 10
Juncture, 54, 273, 278–281
  as closed, 278–279
  as open, 278–279
  defined, 278
  exercises, 279, 280–281
  loudness, 273
  pitch, 273
  related to blending, 278–279
  related to pause, 278

K

Kazner, Kurt, 4
Key lines:
  clue to theme, 40
  significance of, 40
  use of repetition, 40
Kinesthetic appeal, 42–43, 122, 172

L

Langer, Susanne K., 314, 316, 320, 321
Language:
  as action, 59, 247
  affective element, 25, 27, 321
    tone of speaker, pervasive feeling, 38
  a-rhythmic form, 56
  cognitive element, 25, 27, 321
    what, who, to whom, where, when, 38
  concreteness, 41–42, 82–83, 98, 109
  connotation, 43
  figures of speech, 43–46
  imagery, 41–42, 82–83, 98, 108

"interrelated configurational features," 273
  tempo, variations of, 60
  voicing of, 4
    as educational medium, 4
  word arrangement, 41, 53
Language patterns, 279–280
Listening, 270, 271, 303–306
  see also Audience
Literary content:
  close reading demanded, 26
  subject to interpreter's perception, 26
Literature:
  source of knowledge, 5
  source of self-knowledge, 5
Literature for interpretation:
  choice of, 14, 15, 324, 329
  see also Selections for interpretation
Liveliness, vividness, energy, 291
Loudness, 273
  see also Stress
Lyric:
  bibliography, 23–24, 339–343
  characteristics, 21, 29, 119–120
  dialogue in, 129
  emotional quality, 133
  levels of meaning, 121, 125, 129
  open to closed situation, 19–20
    see also Situation
  poetic mode (chart), 16
  questions for interpreter, 132
  test for situational aspects, 134
  see also Selections for interpretation
Lyric, short, problems of presentation, 133

M

Masculine rhyme, 135
Massey, Raymond, 4
Material for interpretation:
  appropriateness, 15–18

Rhyme, 59, 123, 131, 135
  feminine, 135
  masculine, 135
Rhythm, 53–60
  a-rhythmic form, 56
  defined, 53–54
  in drama, 217
    important ingredients, 217
  in English prosody, 56
  metrical aspects, 56
  patterns of, 54
  in prose, 55, 85–86
    illustrations, 86
  repetition as base, 85–86, 122, 123, 126
  variety as basis of reading, 60
  in verse, 56
    revealed in entire structure, 58
  see also Meter
Rhythmic patterns, for emotion, 316
Richards, I. A., 54, 307
Rondeau, 58

S

Scansion, example, 126
Scene:
  in drama, 225
  in narrative, 166, 170, 175
    degree of closure, 166
Scenes or units, tabulated, 216–217
Schoen, Max, 322
Selections for interpretation:
  drama, 225–242
  lyric, 135–146
  narrative, 176–199
  speech, essay, 111–117
Sense pattern to inner form, 125
Sensory appeal, 41–42
  see also Auditory, Kinesthetic, Visual
Sentence:
  basic elements, 51
  structure, 49–50, 83, 84
  variations, 52

Sentence, periodic, 52, 84
Setting:
  influence on mood and action, 167, 212
  time and place:
    in drama, 225
    narrative, 174
  traditional part of narrative, 147
Sherif, Carolyn W., 301
Sherif, Muzafer, 301
Shift (or step), defined, 275
Simile, 44, 64, 83
Situation:
  adaptation to modes, 21
  closed situation:
    defined, 18, 22, 32
    in dramatic dialogue, 38
    examples, 19, 34, 128
    indirect communication, 19
    modes of literature, 20
    in narrative scene, 166
    primary importance in drama, 211
  determining type, 20
  effects on interpreter's style, 21
  motivation, 19
  open situation:
    defined, 19, 22
    direct communication, 19
    examples, 19, 29, 71
    modes of literature, 20
  test, open or closed, 20
  variations, open to closed, 20, 32, 120, 319
    chart, 120
    within essay, 109
    lyric, 19–20
    within speech, 88–89
Situational components, 27–37
Sonnet, levels of meaning, 62
Speaker, physical attitude of, 220
Speech:
  bibliography, 23, 339–343
  characteristics, 21, 70

Index of Topics 353

Index of Selections

Index of Selections 357